Yoga in the Modern Wor.

Today yoga is a thoroughly globalized phenomenon. Yoga has taken the world by storm and is even seeing renewed popularity in India. Both in India and abroad, adults, children and teenagers are practicing yoga in diverse settings; gyms, schools, home, work, yoga studios and temples. The yoga diaspora began well over a hundred years ago and we continue to see new manifestations and uses of yoga in the modern world.

As the first of its kind this collection draws together cutting edge scholarship in the field, focusing on the theory and practice of yoga in contemporary times. Offering a range of perspectives on yoga's contemporary manifestations, it maps the movement, development and consolidation of yoga in global settings. The collection features some of the most well-known authors within the field and newer voices. The contributions span a number of disciplines in the humanities, including anthropology, philosophy, studies in religion and Asian studies, offering a range of entry points to the issues involved in the study of the subject. As such, it will be of use to those involved in academic scholarship, as well as to the growing number of yoga practitioners who seek a deeper account of the origin and significance of the techniques and traditions they are engaging with. It will also—and perhaps most of all—speak to the growing numbers of 'scholar-practitioners' who straddle these two realms.

Mark Singleton teaches at St. John's College, Santa Fe, USA. He works on the history of ideas within transnational modern yoga, and he is a contributor to the *Encyclopedia of Hinduism* (Routledge 2008).

Jean Byrne is affiliated to the University of Queensland, Australia. She lectures in Eastern Philosophy and runs The Yoga Space in Perth, Australia.

Routledge Hindu Studies Series

Series Editor: Gavin Flood

University of Stirling

Former Series Editor: Francis X. Clooney, SJ

Harvard University

The Routledge Hindu Studies Series, in association with the Oxford Centre for Hindu Studies, intends the publication of constructive Hindu theological, philosophical and ethical projects aimed at bringing Hindu traditions into dialogue with contemporary trends in scholarship and contemporary society. The series invites original, high-quality, research-level work on religion, culture and society of Hindus living in India and abroad. Proposals for annotated translations of important primary sources and studies in the history of the Hindu religious traditions will also be considered.

Epistemologies and The Limitations of Philosophical Inquiry
Doctrine in Mādhva Vedānta
Deepak Sarma

A Hindu Critique of Buddhist Epistemology
Kumārila on Perception: The 'Determination of Perception' Chapter of Kumārila Bhaṭṭa's *Ślokavārttika* – Translation and Commentary
John Taber

Śaṃkara's Advaita Vedanta
A Way of Teaching
Jacqueline Hirst

Attending KṚṢṆA's Image
Caitanya Vaiṣṇava Mūrti-sevā as Devotional Truth
Kenneth Russell Valpey

Advaita Vedānta and Vaiṣṇavism
The Philosophy of Madhusūdana Sarasvatī
Sanjukta Gupta

Classical Sāṃkhya and Yoga
An Indian Metaphysics of Experience
Mikel Burley

Self-Surrender (prapatti) to God in Śrīvaiṣṇavism
Tamil Cats or Sanskrit Monkeys?
Srilata Raman

The Caitanya Vaiṣṇava Vedānta of Jīva Gosvāmī
When Knowledge Meets Devotion
Ravi M. Gupta

Gender and Narrative in the *Mahābhārata*
Edited by Simon Brodbeck and Brian Black

Yoga in the Modern World

Contemporary Perspectives

Edited by Mark Singleton and Jean Byrne

Routledge
Taylor & Francis Group
LONDON AND NEW YORK

First published 2008
by Routledge
2 Park Square, Milton Park, Abingdon, Oxon OX14 4RN

Simultaneously published in the USA and Canada
by Routledge
270 Madison Ave, New York, NY 10016

Routledge is an imprint of the Taylor & Francis Group, an informa business

Transferred to Digital Printing 2009

Typeset in Gentium Basic by
HWA Text and Data Management, London

British Library Cataloguing in Publication Data
A catalogue record for this book is available from the British Library

Library of Congress Cataloging-in-Publication Data
Yoga in the modern world: contemproary perspectives / edited by Mark Singleton and Jean Byrne
p. cm. – (Routledge Hindu studies series)
1. Yoga. I. Singleton, Mark 1976– II. Byrne, Jean, 1972–
B132.Y6Y535 2008
181′.45–dc22 2007051681

ISBN10: 0-415-45258-9 (hbk)
ISBN10: 0-415-57086-7 (pbk)
ISBN10: 0-203-89499-5 (ebk)

ISBN13: 978-0-415-45258-8 (hbk)
ISBN13: 978-0-415-57086-2 (pbk)
ISBN13: 978-0-203-89499-6 (ebk)

In memory of Primoz Pecenko

Contents

About the editors and contributors

Editors

Mark Singleton works on the history of ideas within transnational modern yoga. His recent publications include a special yoga issue of *Asian Medicine, Tradition and Modernity* (ed., 2007) and various entries on modern yoga for the Routledge-Curzon *Encyclopedia of Hinduism* (2008). A major study of the contexts of postural yoga in the modern age is forthcoming. He teaches at St. John's College, Santa Fe, New Mexico.

Jean Byrne conducts research on the intersection of feminist philosophy and nonduality through the University of Queensland. She has lectured in Buddhist philosophy at The University of Queensland and Bond University and now runs *The Yoga Space* in Perth, Australia. She is also an authorized Ashtanga Yoga teacher.

Contributors

Joseph S. Alter teaches anthropology at the University of Pittsburgh. His research is in the field of medical anthropology, and his most recent publications are *Yoga in Modern India: the Body Between Science and Philosophy* (Princeton University Press, 2004) and *Asian Medicine and Globalization* (University of Pennsylvania Press, 2005). He is currently working on a book on nature cure and modernity in contemporary India.

Mikel Burley teaches in the Department of Philosophy and the Department of Theology and Religious Studies at the University of Leeds. His publications include *Classical Sāṃkhya and Yoga: An Indian Metaphysics of Experience* (Routledge, 2007), *Haṭha-Yoga: Its Context, Theory and Practice* (Motilal Banarsidass, 2000), and several journal articles on both Indian and Western philosophy. He is also a qualified Yoga instructor with the Devon School of Yoga.

Kenneth Liberman is Professor of Sociology at the University of Oregon, where he also teaches courses on yoga. He was Fulbright Professor at the University of Mysore and has lived for three years in Tibetan monastic universities. His books include *Dialectical Practice in Tibetan Philosophical Culture* (Rowman & Littlefield, 2004), *Husserl's Criticism of Reason* (Lexington Books, 2007), and *Understanding Interaction in Central Australia* (Routledge, 1985).

Elizabeth De Michelis holds the Gordon Milburn Junior Research Fellowship at the Theology Faculty and Oriel College, University of Oxford, United Kingdom. She is currently researching the ancient and modern history of yoga and meditation in Hindu, Buddhist, and contemporary transnational contexts. She is especially interested in problems of knowledge transmission and authority validation, philosophy and texts, East-West dialogue and exchanges, and Indic-inspired aspects of Western esotericism.

Klas Nevrin is a Ph.D. candidate in the Department for History of Religions, Stockholm University (Sweden). His research interests include modern yoga and contemporary improvisational musical performance. He is currently involved with the philosophical and methodological elaboration of a performance-studies approach, informed by recent work on embodiment, emotion, aesthetics, ritual, and hermeneutical phenomenology. He is also a professional improvising pianist.

Stuart Ray Sarbacker, Senior Lecturer in Religion at Northwestern University, specializes in the history of religions with a focus on South Asia. His work is centered on the theory and practice of yoga and tantra in the traditions of Hinduism, Buddhism, and Jainism, especially in the Indo-Tibetan region.

Benjamin Richard Smith is a research fellow at the Centre for Aboriginal Economic Policy Research, The Australian National University. His research interests include aboriginal Australia, modern postural yoga, and the anthropology of photography. His recent publications include "Body, Mind and Spirit? Towards An Analysis of the Practice of Yoga," *Body & Society* 13 (2).

Sarah Strauss is Associate Professor in the Department of Anthropology at the University of Wyoming. She has conducted ethnographic research in India, Switzerland, and the United States on topics related to health and the environment. Recent books include *Positioning Yoga* (Berg Publishers, Oxford, 2004) and *Weather, Climate, Culture* (Berg Publishers, Oxford, 2003; coedited with Benjamin S. Orlove).

Prefatory Note

The idea for this book was conceived over a spicy masala dosa in Mysore, South India in the summer of 2005, while both editors were conducting fieldwork on the transnational practices of yoga. As we reflected on the considerable influx of non-Indian yoga "pilgrims" to this relatively small city—where international students converge to study yoga, chanting, Āyurveda, and Sanskrit with resident teachers—we became acutely aware that though there are millions of people throughout the world practicing this thing called "yoga," there is still a real lack of critical material exploring its actual, contemporary manifestations. The book stores of Mysore (and beyond) overflow with titles on yoga, but virtually none of them offered the kinds of critical reflection that could help us to understand the phenomenon we had observed in that city and in our own home countries. At the time of writing this preface three years later, it still remains difficult to find in-depth, scholarly research on the practices and belief frameworks that constitute yoga in the world today. In the course of our discussion that day in Mysore, we saw the need for a collection that would at once present a variety of possible approaches to the study of yoga in the modern age and be exemplary of the best scholarship in the field to date. This book is partially the result of that conversation.

The collection includes contributions from a number of research disciplines, including history, studies in religion, and anthropology. This diversity reflects the range of methodologies and perspectives that are being brought to bear on contemporary yoga by today's scholars and points to the enormous and varied potential for further research. The unifying principle of this volume is therefore thematic rather than methodological or hermeneutical, and it is hoped that the various approaches represented here will function as windows onto the multifacted, ever-evolving architecture of contemporary yoga.

As a result of this variety of approaches, the collection will appeal to those across the humanities and social sciences who have an interest in yoga, East-West dialogue, Indian religions, and philosophy. Both students and researchers will find the papers engaging and accessible, with contributions from some of the most established authors in the field, along with emerging voices. We hope that practitioners of yoga will also find this collection useful for gaining a deeper understanding of the practices and traditions in which they situate themselves.

Acknowledgements

I thank Dr. Elizabeth De Michelis for her continued support and generosity in my academic study of yoga. Thanks to the team of the former Dharam Hinduja Institute of Indic Research at Cambridge University (Elizabeth De Michelis, Dagmar Wujastyk, and Rajashree Dhanaraj) and to Professor Julius Lipner in Cambridge's Divinity Faculty for his overseeing of my work during my time at Cambridge. Thanks also to the participants in the Modern Yoga Graduate Workshop held at Cambridge University in 2005, at which several of the contributors to the present volume presented working papers. I am also grateful to Suzanne Newcombe (who was unfortunately unable to contribute) and to Klas Nevrin for their helpful comments on the project.

—M.S.

I thank Dr. Tamara Ditrich and Dr. Michelle Boulous Walker for their unwavering support of my research and the University of Queensland Graduate School for the scholarship that enabled me to undertake research in India. Thanks to my yoga teachers, Sri K. Pattabhi Jois and Sharath Rangaswamy: I am eternally grateful for their teachings. My work was made possible by numerous family babysitters who helped me find the time to edit this collection. Mostly, my greatest appreciation is for my husband, Rob, and son, Jamie (born during this project), for reminding me what is important in life.

—J.B.

Introduction

Mark Singleton and Jean Byrne

The Yoga Boom

Yoga today is a thoroughly globalized phenomenon. A profusion of yoga classes and workshops can be found in virtually every city in the Western world and (increasingly) throughout the Middle East, Asia, South and Central America and Australasia. In gyms and health clubs, elementary schools and colleges, drafty church halls, the boardrooms of multinational corporations, or dedicated yoga studios and ashrams, yoga has taken the world by storm. It is even seeing renewed popularity among the growing urban middle classes of India, albeit in innovative guises.

Though the international yoga diaspora began well more than a century ago, it is really only since the mid-1990s that it has taken on the global proportions that make it such a visible—and profitable—enterprise today. Precise practitioner statistics are hard to come by and are often unreliable, but it is estimated that in 2004 there were more than 2.5 million practitioners of yoga in Britain alone, a truly exponential increase from previous years.[1] In the United States, indications of growth are even more startling. A 1994 Roper poll commissioned for the world's most popular yoga magazine, *Yoga Journal*, estimated that more than 6 million Americans (approximately three and one-third percent of the population) were practicing yoga—1.86 million of them regularly. Almost 17 million more—or about one in ten Americans—were "interested in yoga" but had not yet tried it (Cushman 1994: 47–8). Ten years later, another national poll estimated that 15 million Americans were practicing yoga regularly (Carter 2004), while the proportion "interested in yoga" had also risen substantially. *Yoga Journal* estimated in 2003 that approximately 25.5 million Americans (twelve percent) of the population were "very interested" in yoga. A further 35.3 million people (sixteen percent) intended to try yoga within the next year, and 109.7 million (more than half the population) had at least a "casual interest" in yoga (Arnold 2003: 10). Even if we approach these statistics with caution, it is clear that yoga is booming in America and worldwide.

This increase of interest in yoga has gone hand in hand with the emergence of a multi-billion dollar yoga industry.[2] Yoga, along with the commodities and merchandising associated with it, has become hot property in the twenty-first century. Notorious legal battles have even been fought over exactly who owns the techniques and methods of yoga, with particular styles, sequences, or elements being patented, copyrighted, and franchised by individuals, companies, and government.[3] Images of yoga are used to sell any number of products, from yoghurt to mobile phones to SUVs. Such instances have even prompted some to consider contemporary yoga, alongside other modern forms of quasi-religious belief and practice, as one more commodity fetish of late-capitalism.[4]

However, what exactly do we mean when we talk of "yoga" in these contexts? Is yoga in the modern world a single, cohesive entity subject to statistical analysis, copyrighting, and counter-copyrighting? Or rather is the profusion of styles and agendas evidence that there is no homogenous, contained entity that we can categorically identify as "modern" or "contemporary" yoga? If so, the statistics and lawsuits may be far less conceptually straightforward than those who carry them out suppose. How in this profusion of methods and goals are we to discover what we mean by yoga? And what precisely are we seeking through an examination of "yoga in the modern world"?

Examining Contemporary Yoga(s)

This collection takes as its organizing focus the theory and practice of yoga in modern and postmodern times and draws together for the first time cutting-edge scholarship on what one of our contributors terms "the production of yoga in a transnational world." By offering a range of perspectives on yoga's contemporary manifestations, it aims to map the movement, development, and consolidation of yoga in global settings in the modern era. This volume features both some of the most well-known authors within this field of inquiry and newer voices and offers a range of entry points to the issues involved in the study of the subject. As such, it will be of immediate use and relevance to those involved in academic study across a range of disciplines (in particular the humanities and social sciences) and to the growing number of yoga practitioners who seek a deeper, more critical account of the origin and significance of the techniques and traditions with which they are engaging. It will also—and perhaps most of all—speak to the growing numbers of "scholar-practitioners" who move between these realms and to those for whom such dichotomies are neither helpful nor relevant.

The collection is original insofar as it groups together for the first time varied and rigorous reflections on popular, transnational yoga by a group of academic scholars, some of whom also consider themselves practitioners of yoga. The contributors are professional researchers trained in philosophical, historical, and anthropological methods and (often) in the primary languages of the Indian yoga traditions. As a result, this collection offers a depth of analysis and a range of historical insight that can often be lacking in the presentation of yoga by practitioners and the popular media. It provides an important resource for all those wishing to think through the implications and history of yoga as practiced today.

The scholarly (i.e., university-based) study of contemporary yoga's popular forms is a recent undertaking, and indeed several of the authors represented here (notably Elizabeth De Michelis, Joseph Alter, and Sarah Strauss) were instrumental in first bringing it into the academic purview as a legitimate focus of inquiry. That contemporary, transnational yoga has remained below the academic radar for so long is initially surprising, given its immense popularity. There are several reasons for this relatively tardy appearance, the most significant of which may be the long-standing, mutual prejudice between those who *study* yoga professionally (as students, researchers, and teachers in university settings) and those who *do* it. Indeed, from the beginnings of the international transmission of yoga in the last quarter of the nineteenth century, Western academic writers have tended to denigrate (or, more often, simply ignore) practical, contemporary expressions of yoga in favor of the purely philosophical and theoretical.

The renowned "Orientalist" scholar of Indian religions, Max Müller, encapsulates this attitude when he declares that yoga in modern times has descended into "its purely practical and most degenerate form" (Müller 1899: xx). Like a number of other scholars at this time, he laments the transition from "rational beginnings to irrational exaggerations," which leads "from intellectual to practical Yoga" (Müller 1899: 458). A parting of the ways between practice and academic research is also evident in the work of Mircea Eliade, perhaps the greatest European scholar of yoga of the twentieth century. Though a sometime practitioner himself, Eliade kept this aspect of his life largely hidden (except in his fiction), discouraged his reading public from engaging with yoga on a practical basis, and was suspicious of the popular, practical forms of his day.[5]

Conversely, teachers and practitioners of yoga in modern times have often been in the habit of expressing their distaste for academia, which they may view as elitist, disembodied, and irrelevant to the real task at hand (i.e., *doing yoga*). In one common variant of this attitude, "bookish knowledge" is seen to be antithetical to the purely experiential work of self-realization through yoga.[6] Practitioners may also sometimes feel that critical academic examination of a teacher or school is antagonistic to a proper attitude of respect and reverence[7] or may simply be reluctant to subject to analytical scrutiny what is for them a deeply personal, sacralized aspect of their lives.[8]

However, are the two approaches incommensurable, as partisans from both sides would have us believe? Is an academic approach to contemporary yoga necessarily either antagonistic or irrelevant to its practice? And is the contemporary practice of yoga worthy of the censure and suspicion with which it has often been greeted by "serious"scholarship? In fact, is it really necessary or desirable at all to perpetuate such polarities between academic and nonacademic, intellectual and experiential approaches to yoga? And what do we really mean by stating such divisions? It might be more accurate, fruitful, and beneficial to the pursuit of our inquiry, indeed, to recognize the porosity of such categories, insofar as "intellectual" inquiry commonly relies on experiential knowledge, and the practical pursuit of yoga often calls for sustained intellectual engagement.

We should also consider the extent to which supposedly "objective" theoretical and scholastic knowledge on the one hand and direct experiential knowledge on the other are both exploited (in different contexts) to construct one's authority and status as a "scholar"or as a "practitioner." In other words, we need to be sensitive to the degree to which parties from both "sides"may have a personal or collective interest in maintaining such dichotomies. Finally, we should recognize that academia is not a monolithic entity but the site of enormously varied perspectives, methodologies, agendas, and engagements. To confine the academic within the realm of the purely intellectual (in contradistinction to the experiential) is to ignore the range of possibilities open to academic inquirers. It is hoped that the variety of perspectives on contemporary yoga in this book go some way to demonstrating such possibilities.

The Anxiety of Authenticity

The fault most commonly found with contemporary yoga, by both scholars and "informed" practitioners, is that it is *inauthentic* with regard to the Indian traditions it claims to transmit. In this view, many of yoga's manifestations in the (post-) modern, transnational world are simply *phony*, insofar as they speciously claim affiliation with a more or less ill-defined "tradition" of yoga, while simultaneously masking their modern accretions and innovations. Though certain markedly modern variants, such as Yogalates, Yogaerobics, or Hot Naked Yoga, blazon their trademarked hybridity for all to see, others explicitly project the impression that they partake of a pristine and unchanging, millennia-old lineage of yoga theory and practice. If there is one thing that recent studies on contemporary yoga have made more than clear, however, it is that in its dissemination in the Western world, yoga has undergone radical transformation in response to the differing world views, logical predispositions, and aspirations of modern audiences. Such new kinds of "export yoga,"[9] it also seems evident, were the result of a reframing of practices and belief frameworks within India itself over the last century-and-a-half, in response to encounters with modernity and the West. Modern, popular yogas in and out of India bear the clear traces of this dialectic exchange.

To what extent, then, must scholarship based on this evidence also imply a judgment about the authenticity of the practices and beliefs it scrutinizes? Some—though not all—of the contributors to this volume posit a degree of dislocation between the so-called emic[10] claims of practitioners and teachers and the historically determined innovations and transformations evident in contemporary yoga. Among these, a common methodological approach is to contrast modern manifestations of yoga against the Indian tradition and to thereby assess whether such practitioner claims are substantiated or not. It is hardly surprising—especially if the perceived tradition is taken as the gold-standard of "true" yoga—that contemporary forms departing from this criterion may sometimes be judged negatively in terms of their authenticity. In the most extreme conclusions produced by this approach, the incense-burning, mantra-chanting, "stretch-and-relax" Western yogi is doomed to inhabit an empty, second-order world of simulacra and pastiche, remaining forever in thrall to the narcissistic imperatives of postmodern culture and terminally disconnected from the core Indian traditions. Though such a vision may partially resume the judgmental modus operandi of earlier Western scholarship, one might reasonably argue that it is not only acceptable but imperative to interrogate the auto-validating claims of popular yoga based on this divergence from the traditions they claim to be following. If certain kinds of "yoga" in the contemporary world possess a highly tenuous, often merely nominal, relationship with Indian yoga traditions, then is not one basic purpose of modern yoga studies to bring this dislocation into sharp relief? Following this line of reasoning, indeed, critical scholarship is the only way to distinguish "tradition" (itself a highly problematic, multivalent category) from popular innovation.

In considering such opinions, however, and given that the majority of scholars working on *modern* manifestations of yoga are from "the West," it also seems imperative to take into account postcolonialism's contributions to our understanding of the politics of knowledge and our aims and responsibilities as inquirers into Indian culture and tradition. Though there is no space to go into the matter in any depth here, these questions are further complicated by the multifarious, transnational, and transcultural nature of our object of inquiry: yoga in the modern world.[11] What ethical and cultural responsibilities do scholars have as they negotiate Western and Indian contexts of contemporary yoga? And to what extent are the widely divergent lexical uses of the word *yoga*, and the authority of "the tradition," exploited rhetorically by scholars (and indeed practitioners) to further their own professional or personal ends? The very breadth of the word's semantic field should give us pause to examine the agendas which attach to the term *yoga* in all its plurality, both in popular and scholastic discourses. Indeed, it might be helpful to think more generally of *yogas*, with a multiplicity of definitions and interpretations, rather than of a single yoga that we would seek to define and circumscribe.

Equally vital as a counterbalance to the gold-standard approach is a recognition of the plurality and mutability of (chronologically) premodern forms of yoga themselves. That is to say, "the Indian tradition" has itself been subject to often radical historical forces, adaptations, mutations, and fragmentation, just like contemporary yoga. To consider yoga in the modern period as primarily *divergence from* is to oversimplify the vectors of continuity and rupture within Indian yoga traditions themselves and to project an impression that they exist somehow outside of history. Such polarization of traditional and contemporary yoga (and their connotations of "real" and "less real"), therefore, fails both to recognize the heterogeneous, manifold, and changing nature of the former and to do justice to the real continuities that obtain in the latter.

Furthermore, do we not have an obligation to consider yoga's modern manifestations in and of themselves, rather than solely in negative contrast to real Indian yoga traditions? Geoffrey Samuel has recently argued that "[m]odern yoga has become a significant part of contemporary western practices of bodily cultivation, and it should be judged in its own terms, not in terms of its closeness to some presumably more authentic Indian practice" (Samuel 2007: 178). In other words, the unmistakably syncretic, (post-)modern and transnational phenomena that are termed "yoga"today should not be dismissed or condemned simply on account of their dislocation from the perceived tradition. Also important to consider is the fact that the concern for authenticity among scholars is often shared (in similar good faith, if in a different modality) by many yoga practitioners themselves. Often at the forefront of such practitioners' minds is not only the authenticity of the practices they engage in but their own authenticity with regard to themselves and their place and purpose in the world. Though it is by no means the case for all modern practitioners, it seems clear that for many, yoga is seen as the privileged site of an authenticity otherwise unavailable or deficient in their daily experience and is felt to provide, as one of our contributors puts it, a more "authentic" way of being. Of course, though good faith with regard to oneself and the world can never on its own be a gauge of historical and philosophical fidelity, and though the category of authenticity raises its own prickly ontological problems,[12] its consideration does nonetheless bring a vital ethical dimension to the study of modern yoga. As one contribution to this volume makes clear, and as the methodological approach of another implies, to dismiss practitioners' testimony merely on the grounds of divergence from tradition can be to ignore vital aspects of the very experience of modern yoga.

Putting the Modern in "Modern Yoga"

The unifying focus of this collection is the manifestation of yoga in modern, transnational contexts. However, can we really refer to an entity called *modern yoga* and assume that we are talking about a discrete and identifiable category of beliefs and practices, standing in contrast to traditional yoga? One previously mentioned consequence of this approach may be that expressions of yoga in recent times are viewed predominantly in terms of rupture and innovation rather than continuity. Another is that historical detail, inconsistency, and variation can find themselves subsumed by typology. In other words, typology can take precedence over historical detail when it exceeds its provisional, heuristic mandate and becomes received opinion. To some extent, this has already been the fate of the term *Modern Yoga* and its subdivisions. These conceptual entities, which did not exist prior to Elizabeth De Michelis's pioneering work on the topic (De Michelis 2004), have already become the predominant nomenclature among scholars of contemporary, transnational yoga. Though they have proven invaluable in delineating a field of inquiry, they should perhaps be used with prudence by students coming to the topic for the first time and should be recognized as provisional and workable constructs (as intended by their deviser) providing one entry point to the study of yogas of the recent past.

Another problem that arises in this context is how to understand the term *modern*. Does it refer uniquely to a chronological moment in history (say, from the late eighteenth century onward) or, in a more restricted sense, to the complex of socioeconomic, religious, political, and psychological circumstances often, and problematically, labeled *modernity*? Modernity does not simply, as David Smith points out, mean the modern age, but "the theorization of modern times, the quasi-theological sociological reductionism which is a reified caricature of modern times" and which includes as key features "rationalization, the autonomous individual, capitalism and the nation-state" (Smith 2003: iii). Though there is insufficient space to enter into the vexed and on-going debate about modernity's (and postmodernity's)[13] defining characteristics, it is important to note the polyvalences of the terms themselves, especially as they relate to yoga. To what extent is modern yoga a participant in, and product of, the forces of modernity? How are we to situate the practices and belief frameworks of transnational yoga in the twentieth and twenty-first centuries in relation to the intellectual, religious, scientific, and cultural histories of post-Enlightenment, industrialized Europe—or for that matter to "modern' India"? For instance, how (if at all) has the ostensibly prevailing ethos of secularized individualism—with its concomitant associations of self-development and personal potential—interacted with and altered the structural universe of Indian yogas? And if such features can correctly be identified as characteristically modern, how are we to understand the current "postmodern condition" of "Western" society, with its purported dislocations of identity, distrust of "grand narratives" (Lyotard 1979), and penchant for eclecticism and pastiche (Baudrillard 1981) in relation to the practices of yoga? Many of the contributors to this volume have, here and elsewhere, given careful and lengthy consideration to these issues,[14] but it seems to us that the history of yoga in its dialogic relation to modernity and postmodernity (and their semantic first-cousins modernism and postmodernism) still remains to be written.

Overview of the Collection

The collection is divided into three sections. The first, entitled Mapping the Terrain of Modern Yoga Studies, opens with Elizabeth De Michelis's introduction to modern yoga's history, forms, and scholarship. Following this is Joseph Alter's exploration of the methodological and ethical problems inherent in the study of modern yoga, via the example of yoga camps (*shivir*) in contemporary India. Finally in this section, Sarah Strauss examines the life and work of Swami Sivananda and the Divine Life Society, considering the adaptations and transformations undergone by yoga during the course of its contemporary, transnational passages.

The second section, Posturing for Authenticity, engages with questions of legitimization and historicization in modern yoga. Mark Singleton traces the ways in which Patañjali's *Yogasūtras* became the primary authority for modern yoga and suggests that the notion of a "Classical Yoga" is to some degree itself a product of early modern scholarship. In a similar vein, though radically different in approach, Ken Liberman explores the reflexivity inherent in notions of "authenticity" in modern yoga practice and posits some key characteristics that determine the legitimacy of modern yoga forms.

The final section, Spirituality, Sexuality, and Authority: Understanding the Experience of Modern Yoga Practice, presents a range of perspectives on the experience of modern yoga. Klas Nevrin opens with an analysis of the discursive environment in which modern yoga is practiced. Ben Smith's contribution explores the tensions of discipline, authority, and achievement in the increasingly popular practice of Ashtanga Vinyasa Yoga. Stuart Sarbacker reflects on the array of desired outcomes within modern yoga schools and the historical antecedents of these goals in terms of the "numinous"and "cessative." Lastly, Mikel Burley examines the role of sexuality and sensuality in both modern and pre-modern yoga.

Chapter Summaries

Part 1: Mapping the Terrain of Modern Yoga Studies

Chapter 1

Elizabeth De Michelis's study—Modern Yoga: History and Forms—provides a much-needed overview of the academic field of modern yoga and will be a useful starting point for those new to topic. Drawing to some extent on her earlier work in *A History of Modern Yoga, Patañjali and Western Esotericism* (2004), De Michelis presents a brief history of yoga and its academic study. Starting with the premodern era, she demonstrates that the precise beginnings of what we now call "yoga" are ambiguous. She then traces various strands of yoga's complex history from premodern to modern times, examining the complex acculturation processes through which yoga engages in ongoing dialogue with a range of religious traditions and interpreters.

De Michelis argues that the "canonization"of modern yoga was precipitated by the publication of Swami Vivekananda's *Rāja Yoga* in 1896. According to her, *Rāja Yoga* is a watershed in the intercultural exchange between East and West, in which Western occultism, (neo-)Hinduism, and both Eastern and Western physical cultures blend to provide the foundations for what she considers a properly *modern* yoga. The most prominent mode of modern yoga practice today is Modern Postural Yoga, which includes some of the most popular contemporary transnational styles, such as Sivananda, Ashtanga, and Iyengar yoga. This mode of practice, which first gained real prominence during the 1920s, has a strong focus on the practice of *āsana* (posture). De Michelis's analysis of yoga's history and acculturation in transnational contexts provides an invaluable optic with which to view the confusing terrain of yoga's contemporary manifestations. As a thorough background to the concept and study of modern yoga, it also functions as a prelude to the other chapters in the book.

Chapter 2

Though the burgeoning popularity of modern postural yoga in the West is undeniable, it is also increasingly evident that in India, in a very public way, practices claiming to derive from *haṭha* yoga are seeing a fervent renewal. Joseph Alter's contribution, Yoga Shivir: Methodological and Ethical Problems in the Study of Modern Yoga, is an examination of the "yoga camps" (*shivir*) now commonly held throughout India for a wide range of social groups, including prisoners, women, and school children. These *shivir* are generally large, free, public gatherings where students learn yoga techniques and listen to lectures promoting "Hindu" cultural values.

Reporting on his extensive fieldwork in northern India, Alter gives us an insight into the complexities of yoga *shivir*. His analysis of the spectacle of *shivir* highlights the way in which yoga, nationalism, and politics intersect in the practice of modern yoga in India (as such, this chapter reprises themes examined at great length in his other writing). While highlighting the importance of critical historicization, Alter also foregrounds the aspect of "performativity" in public yoga such as *shivir* and considers its consequences for claims to legitimacy and authenticity by yoga practitioners and sectarian groups. A sensitivity to the performative aspects of modern yoga, he argues, avoids the kinds of emic/etic, practitioner/scholar binaries mentioned earlier in this introduction. That is to say, the concept of performativity can provide a way out of the impasse of historical or philosophical inaccuracies often inherent in "emic" truth statements about the nature of yoga: Rather than dismissing such statements on grounds of fallaciousness, or accepting all such statements in an attitude of radical relativism, performativity allows us to focus instead on how and why such claims are made.

Chapter 3

Along with De Michelis and Alter, Sarah Strauss was among the first academic scholars to engage with modern yoga as a distinct field of inquiry. We have chosen to reprint here her insufficiently known 2002 article—Adapt, Adjust, Accommodate: The Production of Yoga in a Transnational World—in the hope that this will bring it to a wider audience. This chapter examines the way in which nationalist discourses figure in Swami Sivananada's promotion and production of yoga. Strauss demonstrates how transnational and global forces impact on the way we understand modern yoga, not just in India but throughout the world.

Part 2: Posturing for Authenticity

Chapter 4

Mark Singleton's chapter, The Classical Reveries of Modern Yoga: Patañjali and Constructive Orientalism, examines the construction of "authenticity"and the "classical" in contemporary yoga theory and practice. Focusing on the centrality of the *Yogasūtras* in the discourses of modern yoga practitioners and teachers, his chapter highlights the tenacity of links drawn between the text attributed to Patañjali and contemporary yoga practice. The vision of the *Yogasūtras* as the "classical" text of yoga practice is in many ways a modern phenomenon. With reference to modern Indian music and dance, he argues that Patañjali has been co-opted by modern yoga practitioners seeking to authenticate their own practices.

Chapter 5

In a more provocative vein, Ken Liberman's The Reflexivity of the Authenticity of Yoga draws on personal experience of yoga and Tibetan Buddhism to interrogate the authenticity of contemporary yoga practice. Liberman argues that in modern times, yoga and *bhoga* (sensual enjoyment) are not easily distinguishable. He questions the belief of many modern practitioners that there was once an original and pure yoga that now serves as the basis for the contemporary practice of yoga. This, he argues, is a "just-so story" that belies the true syncretism of contemporary practice. Taking inspiration from phenomenology, Derridean theory, and his own encounters with yoga and *Vajrayāna* Buddhism, Liberman's syncretic approach draws together diverse strands of philosophical thought to determine the indispensable and authentic features of yoga practice.

Part 3: Spirituality, Sexuality, and Authority: Understanding the Experience of Contemporary Yoga Practice

Chapter 6

The final section of the book explores the experiential dimension of modern yoga practice. Klas Nevrin's chapter, Empowerment, Sacralization, Purification: "Spiritual" Experience in Modern Postural Yoga, draws on research conducted among practitioners of yoga forms in the lineage of the great twentieth-century teacher Tirumalai Krishnamacharya (including Iyengar Yoga, Ashtanga Vinyasa Yoga, and Viniyoga). Nevrin aruges that there is a close and complex relationship between the body, the environment in which yoga is performed, and the practitioner's total experience of a yoga practice. This confluence of factors means that modern yoga is practiced and interpreted in a variety of particular discursive frameworks, even though their effect on people's embodied experience is generally unacknowledged by the practitioners themselves. Yet it is precisely the social and existential empowerment resulting from the practice of yoga that Nevrin believes to be central to the vast popularity of yoga in the modern world.

Chapter 7

Following Nevrin's analysis of modern practitioners in the Krishnamacharya lineage, Benjamin Smith's chapter—With Heat Even Iron Will Bend—is a unique "scholar-practitioner" look at the practice of Ashtanga Yoga in the tradition of Pattabhi Jois, one of Krishnamacharya's main students. Intertwining theory and personal experience, Smith explores the relationship between discipline and authority in one example of modern, transnational yoga. In the contemporary practice of Ashtanga Yoga, he finds remnants of the traditional Indian guru-student relationship, marked by the discipline expected of the student and the authority ascribed to the guru. Moreover, he argues that the way in which the traditional concept of *tapas* ("heat," "ascesis") figures in Jois's teaching is central to understanding the practice of Ashtanga (Vinyasa) Yoga in contemporary times.

Chapter 8

Moving from this analysis of a singular tradition to a comparative examination of various schools of yoga, Stuart Sarbacker's chapter, The Numinous and Cessative in Modern Yoga, examines the goals and teleology of contemporary yoga practice in comparison to forms within the Indian tradition. Building on his previous work on the yoga tradition (Sarbacker 2005), Sarbacker argues that though there may be seemingly substantial differences in the stated goals in modern yogas, this is by no means a new phenomenon. Discourses invoked and adopted by particular schools and sectarian groups often revolve around claims to the historical continuity of their practices and goals—a continuity that is then negatively contrasted with other schools and sectarian groups that are thought to lack comparable historical antecedents. For Sarbacker, such judgments fail to acknowledge the variations in desired outcomes in traditional Indian ascetic practice (*tapas*). These variations, Sarbacker claims, can generally be categorized as either "cessative" or "numinous" in teleological orientation. The former focus on liberation from pain and suffering, and the latter on the attainment or realization of divinity. Sarbacker's chapter illustrates the way in which the teleology of a particular school of yoga becomes a discursive framework in which the community or organization functions.

Chapter 9

The book's final chapter—Mikel Burley's From Fusion to Confusion: A Consideration of Sex and Sexuality in Traditional and Contemporary Yoga—considers the tensions between asceticism and eroticism in contemporary yoga. Burley's survey highlights the often contradictory attitudes towards sex and sexuality in both modern and premodern yoga. He first considers premodern attitudes toward sex and sexuality in *haṭha* yoga and then explores the tensions in modern yoga between imperatives of sexual restraint and the contemporary commercialization and eroticization of the yogic body. This eroticization, combined with a naïve or superficial understanding of Indian traditions, argues

Burley, leaves modern yoga practitioners confused yet free to navigate their own relationship with yoga, sex, and sexuality.

Notes

1 Statistics from the consumer research company TGI as reported in the London *Times* (Carter 2004). The article also notes that an increasing number of yoga practitioners are men. For further information on practitioner numbers in Britain, see De Michelis (1995) and Newcombe (2007).

2 A 260-page market report study based on yoga and tai chi line items by the Sporting Goods Manufacturer's Association of America in 2000 put the number of yoga and tai chi practitioners (combined) at a more modest 10 million (SGMA 2000). This statistic (and the report itself) reflects the purely commercial interests created by the "yoga boom."

3 On Bikram Choudhury's move to franchise his yoga technique, see Fish (2006); see Srivastava (2005) for a report on the Indian government's countermeasures to Bikram's strategy.

4 Carrette and King (2005). See also Kitiarsa 2007 and De Michelis and Liberman in this volume.

5 Eliade 1963: 125–6. See also Strauss, this volume. See De Michelis (2004: 9–12) for a consideration of the kind of "myopia" which prevented scholars of Asian religion such as Eliade and Raymond Schwab from taking modern yoga seriously.

6 See Bharati 1976: 175 and passim for an examination of the filtering of anti-scholastic trends among transnational Indian gurus into the yoga-practicing American counter-culture of the 1960s and 70s.

7 Author fieldwork data. Note also that American Indological scholarship more generally has recently come under fire for "invading the sacred" domain of Indian culture and religion (see Ramaswamy et al, 2007).

8 See Newcombe 2007. Newcombe points out that this does not reflect a more generalized anti-intellectualism among yoga practitioners in Britain, who tend to have higher educational levels than the rest of the population.

9 The phrase is adapted from Narayan's analysis of nineteenth- and twentieth-century Indian "export gurus" (Narayan 1993).

10 An "emic" account employs language that is meaningful for, and to some extent specific to, the particular belief framework of the subject/practitioner. This is in contrast to "etic" accounts, which describe behaviour or practice in terms other than those of the belief group in question and which may therefore be regarded as more "neutral" or objective than emic "belief statements." The terms were coined by the linguist Kenneth Pike (Pike 1967) and have since become important categories within anthropology.

11 On this topic, see in particular King (1999) and Vishwanathan (2003). See Smith (2003b) for a controversial counterpoint to the views and methods of King and Vishwanathan.

12 Note that Charles Taylor considers that the impulse toward authenticity characteristic of (post)modernity "should be taken seriously as a moral ideal" (Taylor 1991: 22). However, Corey Anton has built on this work to suggest that understandings of authenticity in modern settings can often be self-defeating and paradoxical (Anton 2001). See also Nevrin (this volume).

13 Smith wryly characterizes "post-modernity" as relating to "what it is like to be a well-to-do resident of a metropolis at any point in the history of civilization" (2003a: iii). However, there is of course an enormous, and still growing, body of literature dedicated to identifying the specific features of post-modernity. Landmark studies in this area include Lyotard (1979), Baudrillard (1981), Hassan (1987) and Harvey (1989).

14 See for example Alter (2004), Burley (this volume), Liberman (this volume), Strauss (2005) and this volume, Singleton (2005) and this volume.

Bibliography

Alter, J. (2004) *Yoga in Modern India: The Body Between Science and Philosophy*, Princeton: Princeton University Press.

Anton, C. (2001) *Selfhood and Authenticity*, Albany: SUNY Press.

Arnold, K. (2003) We're Listening, *Yoga Journal*, 174 (May/June): 10.

Baudrillard, J. (1981) *Simulacres et simulations*, Paris: Galilée.

Bharati, A. (1976) *The Light at the Center, Context and Pretext of Modern Mysticism*, Santa Barbara: Ross-Erikson.

Carrette, J. and R. King (2005) *Selling Spirituality, The Silent Takeover of Religion*, London and New York: Routledge.

Carter, M. (2004) New Poses for Macho Men, The Times Body & Soul Supplement (Saturday 22, May), Available HTTP: <http://www.newsint-archive.co.uk> (accessed 15 October 2007).

Cushman, A. (1994) Guess Who's Coming to Yoga? *Yoga Journal*, 118 (September/October): 47–8.

De Michelis, E. (1995) The role of the Hindu Renaissance and New Age ideas in the Development of Modern Haṭha Yoga. [unpublished paper]

——(2004) *A History of Modern Yoga, Patañjali and Western Esotericism*, London: Continuum.

Eliade, M. (1963) Yoga and Modern Philosophy, *Journal of General Education*, 15: 124–37.

Fish, A. (2006) The Commodification and Exchange of Knowledge in the Case of Transnational Commercial Yoga, *International Journal of Cultural Property*, 13: 189–206.

Harvey, D. (1989) *The Condition of Postmodernity*, Oxford: Blackwell.

Hassan, I.H. (1987) *The Postmodern Turn: Essays in Postmodern Theory and Culture*, Columbus, OH: Ohio State University Press.

Hasselle-Newcombe (2002) Yoga in Contemporary Britain: A Preliminary Sociological Exploration [M.A. dissertation], London: Department of Sociology, London School of Economics and Political Science.

King, R. (1999) *Orientalism and Religion: Post-Colonial Theory, India and the Mystic East*, London: Routledge.

Kitiarsa, P (ed.) (2007) *Religious Commodifications in Asia: Marketing Gods*, Routledge Studies in Asian Religion and Philosophy. London: Routledge.

Lyotard, J.F. (1979) *La condition postmoderne: rapport sur le savoir*, Paris: Editions de Minuit.

Narayan, K. (1993) Refractions of the Field at Home: American Representations of Hindu Holy Men in the 19th and 20th Centuries, *Cultural Anthropology*, 8 (4): 476–509.

Newcombe, S. (2007) Stretching for Health and Well-Being: Yoga and Women in Britain, 1960–1980, *Asian Medicine, Tradition and Modernity (Special Yoga Issue)* 3: 37-63.

Pike, Kenneth Lee (1967) *Language in relation to a unified theory of structure of human behavior*, 2nd ed. The Hague: Mouton.

Ramaswamy, K., A. de Nicolas, A. Banerji, (eds) (2007) *Invading the Sacred: An Analysis of Hinduism Studies in America*, Delhi: Rupa & Co.

Samuel, G. (2007) Endpiece, *Asian Medicine, Tradition and Modernity (Special Yoga Issue)* 3: 177–88.

Sarbacker, S. (2005) *Samādhi, The Numinous and Cessative in Indo-Tibetan Yoga*, Albany: State University of New York Press.

Singleton, M (2005) Salvation Through Relaxation: Proprioceptive Therapy and its Relationship to Yoga, *Journal of Contemporary Religion* 20 (3) 289–304.

SGMA (Sporting Goods Manufacturer's Association of America) (2000) *Yoga/Tai Chi Participation Report*. [The report can be accessed, for a fee, at www.sgma.com].

Smith, D. (2003a) *Hinduism and Modernity*, Religion in the Modern World Series, Oxford: Blackwell.

——(2003b) Orientalism and Hinduism, in G. Flood (ed), *The Blackwell Companion to Hinduism*, Oxford: Blackwell, 45–63.

Srivastava, S. (2005) What happens when spirit meets wallet? It's patently obvious, *Asia Times Online* (July 2), Available HTTP: <http://www.atimes.com/atimes/South_Asia/GG02Df02.html> (accessed 14 October 2007).

Strauss, S. (2005) *Positioning Yoga: Balancing Acts Across Cultures*, Oxford: Berg.

Taylor, C. (1991) *The Ethics of Authenticity*, Cambridge, MA: Harvard University Press.

Viswanathan (2003) Colonialism and the Construction of Hinduism, in G. Flood (ed), *The Blackwell Companion to Hinduism*, Oxford: Blackwell, 23–44.

Part I

Mapping the Terrain of Modern Yoga Studies

1 Modern Yoga

History and Forms

Elizabeth De Michelis

Nowadays, Modern Yoga can be found all over the world, especially in developed countries and cosmopolitan milieus. It is unobtrusively but visibly expanding: New classes are taught, yoga studios are opened, and distinctive yoga styles are developed every day. There is still, however, widespread ignorance as to its history, characteristics, and internal dynamics, though this is being progressively redressed, as the present book and other publications demonstrate.

This chapter provides an introduction to the topic: The first section proposes a model of premodern yoga[1] that may be used to understand the historico-cultural foundations and components of this family of disciplines; the second section provides a definition and brief history of Modern Yoga; the third discusses types of Modern Yoga; the fourth explores key differences between modern and premodern forms of yoga under four headings (differences between Eastern and non-Eastern thought; privatization of religion; commodification; medicalization); and the fifth and last section highlights a couple of research approaches that could be especially relevant and potentially revealing for further modern yoga studies.

The Construction of Yoga: Cultural and Historical Background

The precise historical origins of yoga, itself a very diverse array of theories and practices, are not known. As Gerald Larson, one of today's foremost experts on Sāṃkhya-Yoga philosophy, explains, "Yoga is as old or older than recorded history, its origins for the most part lost in the antiquity of Central, Western, and South Asia" (2000: xiii). Certainly a great part of what is known as yoga owes much to the Sanskritic cultural mould[2] and to an ongoing dialogue between what would be described today as the three great religious traditions: Hinduism, Jainism, and Buddhism.[3] And further, when we reflect that yoga as a fairly systematized discipline has been in existence for at least 2,500 years,[4] it will become apparent that many of the variations of this discipline must have been created through interaction with yet other world views and practices,[5] adaptation to different times and geographical locations, and elaboration by different individuals.[6]

If the ways of yoga are so rich, diverse, and long-lasting, how can we orient ourselves through the maze of earlier forms to establish conceptual foundations that will sustain a discussion of Modern Yoga? How can one navigate through the complex panorama of pre-modern forms of yoga without getting thoroughly confused? A heuristic tool for this purpose is offered below: A simplified framework or model representing yoga as a building, with cornerstones positioned according to architectural principles and supporting the actual fabric of the building. The reader should, however, always bear in mind that this is a theoretical device, useful only for general orientation in the field, and that any specific study or research project would call for much more in-depth contextualization and analysis.

In this model, the first three cornerstones are found in yoga as represented in the *Bhagavad Gītā*. This text is especially important and representative because it is ancient,[7] uniquely influential up to our day, and catholic in scope.[8] We should indeed notice that the message of the *Bhagavad Gītā* is largely expressed in terms of variations of yoga discipline, a fact that in and of itself reveals not only the importance but the pervasiveness of forms of yoga in Indic religious and speculative traditions. It is not possible to go into detail here; suffice it to say that this text describes early forms of yoga as being of three fundamental types: *karmayoga*, the yoga of (primarily ritual) action; *jñānayoga*, the yoga of knowledge (understood as metaphysical "gnosis"); and *bhaktiyoga*, the yoga of devotion (toward the deity and often—especially in the case of tantra, see next paragraph—also toward teacher and lineage).[9]

Tantra yoga is our fourth corner stone. Though probably as ancient as the other three forms of yoga, at least in its prototypical forms[10] tantric yoga, as part of the wider flourishing of tantra, seemingly started to become widespread from the sixth century CE.[11] This is a complex subject[12] but, in a nutshell, we can say that tantric forms of yoga aim at bringing about the (actual or imagined,[13] but in all cases purposive and transformative) assimilation of practitioner and what we may call metaphysical entities: deities, cosmic powers, perfected transcendent qualities, and the like.[14] Tantric yoga is further characterized by its engagement with (at times extreme) psycho-physical states,[15] including distinctive explorations of liminality such as the moment of orgasm and the time of death.[16]

Virtually all forms of yoga can be analyzed with reference to these four components. Indeed, if the best one-word translation of yoga is "discipline,"[17] the four qualifiers—*karma*, *jñāna*, *bhakti* and *tantra*—can be understood as yoga's cardinal directions or as conceptual filters through which the discipline is actually interpreted and applied. Different mixtures and emphases of these will produce different types of yoga, which may eventually emerge with specific appellations or just blend in as part of the wider orthopractical profile of a given religious school or denomination.

The common substratum of all pre-modern styles of yoga and meditative practice, acting as the theoretical architectural principles in our metaphorical scheme, is their reliance on the Indic *karma/saṃsāra/mokṣa* philosophical complex. This seminal set of beliefs, shared by all Dharmic religions,[18] postulates that human beings "undergo continuing reincarnations (*saṃsāra*), that a person's current incarnation and experiences are, at least in part, the fruit of past actions (*karma*), and that release or liberation (*mokṣa*) from this ongoing cycle is possible and desirable" (Milner 1993: 298).[19] Simply put, yoga is the discipline whereby one attains, or gets progressively closer to, *mokṣa* (or *nirvāṇa*).[20]

And last, to the edifice itself, the fabric of the building: These are the individual, institutional, and social complexes that support and nurture, among many other things, the cultivation, shaping, and transmission of yoga and related practices. Regarding the former two activities, as Hardy explains in his introduction to *The Religions of Asia*, forms of centralized authority and meaning-definition are "simply absent in the East" (1990: 9).[21] This does not mean that there are no sources of authority and no extensive institutional structures. There are, indeed, plenty of each: priests and *sādhus*[22] of many different kinds, *gurus* and their followers, the lineages these "religious professionals"[23] embody, and the texts they revere and propagate. There are pilgrimage centers and circuits, sacred places and wayside shrines; there are temples, monasteries, hermitages, and households where these practices are kept alive, but overall these structures are far more fluid and polycentric in their operations, whether theoretical or performative, than non-Asian observers may expect.[24] As for the passing on of yogic types of knowledge, the emphasis, in a way ideally, but very often also in practice, is on live transmission "from one [person] to another,"[25] which further contributes to keeping the whole structure decentralized.[26]

Thus we have the building of premodern yoga: It has four cornerstones grounding and undergirding the overall structure, and shared theoretical principles. These latter are, however, applied in different ways by different groups, thus resulting in a kind of "house of many mansions" as the visible outcome—a house within which, moreover, individual practitioners and scholars may travel widely, even across confessional divides, whether to relocate or just to gather and share knowledge. We need to find out as much as we can about premodern yoga to be able to see lines of continuity or discontinuity between these older practices and the more recently emerged forms of Modern Yoga, to which we now turn.

Definition and Brief History of Modern Yoga

This section provides a working definition of Modern Yoga and a simple historical outline; much more on these topics will be found in the texts cited below and in sources mentioned therein and throughout the rest of this book.

The expression *Modern Yoga* is used here to signify those disciplines and schools that are, to a greater or lesser extent, rooted in South Asian cultural contexts[27] and more specifically draw inspiration from certain philosophies, teachings, and practices of Hinduism.[28] These teachings and practices, by virtue of export, syncretic assimilation, and subsequent acculturation processes, have by now become an integral part of (primarily) urban cultures worldwide[29] and are usually represented, disseminated, and discussed primarily (though not exclusively) by way of the English language.[30]

As for the history of Modern Yoga, a short chronology of main historical phases is set out below for the reader's convenience. In brief, however, it can be stated that, while drawing on ancient models, theories, and techniques, early forms of Modern Yoga were largely born of symbiotic relations between Indian nationalism, Western occultism, neo-Vedāntic philosophy and, in the case of Modern Postural Yoga,[31] systems of modern physical culture.

Also worth noting is that a "material versus spiritual" discourse popular around the turn of the twentieth century clearly reveals how, at the popular level, Westerners were looking for alternative forms of belief and spiritual practice, while South Asians appropriated these practices as ways to counterbalance the Western powers' sociopolitical, economic, and ideological colonization of the subcontinent with a South Asian "spiritual" colonization of the West. Modern yoga turned out to be one of the most powerful, enduring, and influential religio-cultural products in this context.[32]

MODERN YOGA HISTORY: KEY POINTS

ca 1750. onward: Antiquarian, encyclopedic, economic and socio-political (read colonial) concerns give rise to modern Western interest in the Orient.[33] This interest is mainly highbrow, academic, and intellectual. South Asian partners in dialogue are traditional scholars and a newly formed intelligentsia that collaborates with foreign authorities in the urban centers of power.

1830s: Breakup of dialogue between foreign authorities and indigenous intellectuals in the aftermath of the "Anglicization" debate.[34] The South Asian intelligentsia finds keen alternative partners in dialogue in Western esotericists. Their ideological elaborations will prove seminal and influential with regard to socio-political and religious movements in the fast modernizing subcontinent.[35]

ca 1850: Around the middle of the century, we witness the first signs of an important shift: Oriental religions begin to be considered as possible forms of practice in places other than Asia, as opposed to being regarded as "neutral" objects of study.[36]

1893–1896: These trends reach a high point with the coming together of representatives of modernizing South Asian religions and Western esotericism at the 1893 Chicago Parliament of Religions and in the ensuing ideological syntheses. One of the direct results of this venture was the meteoric success of Swami Vivekananda, who virtually overnight became a popular icon of "spirituality"in Asia, America, and Europe. In 1896, he published *Rāja Yoga*, a seminal text in the development of modern yoga.

End nineteenth-begin twentieth century: Emerging New Age religion (see Hanegraaff 1996: 521–2) and fast-modernizing Asian religions begin an ongoing, influential and highly productive dialogue, which continues to the present time. The early forms of modern yoga established at the beginning of the twentieth century continue to grow and develop: distinctive types of Modern Yoga (see below) start to emerge.

1915–1949: In Europe and elsewhere, the two World Wars somewhat slow down the spread of Modern Yoga and related ideas. Culturally and intellectually, however, they create powerful backlashes that will open up spaces for a more widespread diffusion of these disciplines and related philosophies. In Asia, the newly independent Indian nation starts promoting the cultivation of native arts and sciences, including (modernized forms of) yoga.

1950s and 1960s: Though still regarded as a somewhat marginal and eccentric pursuit, the practice of Modern Yoga achieves widespread popularity. New forms of yoga ("denominational"; see below) emerge as one of the key phenomena of the 1960s counterculture.

1990s to date: After a slight dip in popularity in the 1980s, Modern Yoga is enthusiastically taken up by a new generation of practitioners. This promotes even wider popularization, and speeds up the ongoing process of acculturation.

Types of Modern Yoga[37]

Over a century down the line from the elaboration of the earliest forms of fully fledged Modern Yoga, we can find yoga enthusiasts in most developed, cosmopolitan milieus, and we see many kinds of yoga being advertised and adopted by the public. How might we make sense of this at times bewildering variety? If analyzed on the basis of the specific practices emphasized and how these are used both within the schools and in terms of wider social dynamics, we will be able to distinguish five key types.

The early Modern ***Psychosomatic*** Yoga of Vivekananda, enshrined in his 1896 *Rāja-Yoga*.[38] The bedrock of this type is each school's interpretation of Patañjali's *aṣṭāṅgayoga*,[39] to which other elements from (neo-)Hindu or Western esoteric traditions (or both) are added.

The ***neo-Hindu*** style of Modern Yoga. The key ideological themes of this yoga were already present in South Asian culture toward the end of the nineteenth century and came to full flower from the 1920s. This type of yoga is especially receptive to influences from the martial and gymnastic traditions of both indigenous and Western origins. It often encompasses irenic or more confrontational notions of Hindu revivalism, nationalism, or supremacy (or both).[40]

Postural and ***Meditational*** forms of Modern Yoga include elements of the two former forms and started to develop from the 1920s onward. All in all, however, Modern Postural Yoga schools put a much stronger emphasis on postural practice and have contributed the most to developing and codifying relatively advanced and sophisticated canons of postural theory and practice (Sjoman 1999, Singleton 2007a). Their religio-philosophical teachings, however, are relatively unfocussed and usually polyvalent and therefore mostly compatible with transnational trends tending toward secularization or acculturation (or both; De Michelis 2004, Part II). By and large, when people talk about "yoga"in everyday English, this is the type of practice that is intended.[41]

The situation is more complex with regard to Meditational Yoga, which also started to develop from the 1920s.[42] At the level of practice, and often of entry, these schools focus primarily on their own specific set of meditational practice(s). Socio-philosophically, they tend to be rather self-contained, as opposed to being part of a wider, transnational yoga or "spiritual" community, as psychosomatic or postural schools tend to be, or are closely embedded in, modern forms of Hinduism as neo-Hindu yoga schools. They are often headed by charismatic founders or leaders (or both) whose authority pervades the institution, sometimes in capillary fashion. Their teachings may develop toward idiosyncratic forms of belief, which in turn stimulate the creation of specific practices or of specific interpretations of practice. These developmental trajectories often bring them progressively closer to ***Denominational*** forms of yoga:[43] groups that promote their own forms of (usually meditational) yoga but seemingly as a means to propagate, affirm, or reinforce very distinctive and sometimes controversial[44] world views, belief systems, and lifestyles rather than to connect with wider societal, ideological, or religious webs of meaning. It should be noted that denominational schools of modern yoga, differently from the others, only started to appear from the 1950s onward and became really noticeable on the religious scene from the 1960s, as many Indian charismatic teachers were enthusiastically adopted (and materially supported) by the then emerging counterculture.[45]

The socio-cultural dynamics of modern yoga types would benefit from further research. The above typology could be improved, enriched, and possibly used as a foil to interpret other religious phenomena. Some ideas for further research, within which the above typology could be used, are set out in the last section of this chapter. Before we get to that, however, we will discuss some of the main differences between modern and premodern forms of yoga.

Key Differences Between Modern and pre-Modern Forms of Yoga

As seen in the previous section, there are many types of Modern Yoga and, within each type, we will find a range of schools of thought and practice that also differ from each other. Thus, it is impossible to discuss differences between pre-modern South Asian styles (themselves quite diverse) and modern ones as if they all applied in the same way and across the board. However, it is possible to provide some basic tools for discussion by highlighting key areas of difference between the two. These are very likely to be of relevance in any comparative or analytical discussion of Modern Yoga. These differences are listed below under four headings.

Differences Between Eastern and Non-Eastern Thought

Existing research (Sjoman 1999; De Michelis 2004; Alter 2004 and 2005; Nevrin 2005; Singleton 2007a) demonstrates that the religio-philosophical underpinnings of Modern Yoga are often composed, from Vivekananda onward, of somewhat unstable intellectual mixtures: syncretic rather than synthetic in Pye's sense of the words.[46] The syncretic elements of modern yoga's theorization derive primarily from four intellectual traditions: Dharmic religions, Abrahamic religions,[47] modern empirical science, and modern esotericism.[48]

The situation is quite different, however, when we consider premodern forms of yoga, which are fully rooted in the conceptual universe of Dharmic religions. Though, of course, they themselves are always changing and evolving, these traditions will be found to be more synthetically stable, simply because the practical and theoretical implications of their axiomatic ideas, such as the concept of *dharma* itself, and the *karma/saṃsāra/mokṣa* philosophical complex discussed above,[49] have been cultivated, rationalized, and recorded for at least two-and-a-half millennia in systematic, uninterrupted, cumulative and, broadly speaking, logically coherent fashion.

Differences emerge more strikingly when the internal logic of the ideas and theories expressed in any one context is brought back to its axiomatic implications. To give just one centrally important example: The internal logic of Dharmic traditions implies that a *saṃsāric* mode of being is an inescapably limited state, which will thus be understood (though not—and this is important—in judgmental fashion) to be inherently reduced. The converse applies to many Modern Yoga and other modern esoteric interpretations of *saṃsāra*-inspired reincarnationist ideas, which will often be understood by followers to be part of an "ameliorative worldview" (Dawson 2006, par. 18), informed by post-Enlightenment ideas of progress, and by "a very Western and modernist notion of self and identity which is individualistic and reflexive" (Hamilton 2002: 247).

Privatization of Religion

Another element of divergence between premodern and modern forms of yoga is that the latter have undergone, generally speaking, noticeable processes of "secularization." The long-standing and variegated debate on secularization can offer interesting insights when applied to modern yoga studies. With roots going back to the nineteenth century and beyond,[50] secularization theories have been thoroughly criticized over the last couple of decades, with sociologist Peter Berger, formerly one of its more prominent advocates, now regarding secularization as his career's "big mistake" (1998: 782). The debate is far from closed, however, and new light has been cast on it by, among others, Inglehart and Norris (2004), who proposed specific updates and redefinitions of secularization theory on the basis of worldwide statistical data.

Of the discussions opened up in this context, the one on the privatization of religion is arguably the most directly relevant to Modern Yoga studies. Simply put, the evidence here is that in many secularized milieus, religious authority is appropriated by the individual, as opposed to being defined by birth and by socio-institutional conventions. Here, in Luckmann's words,

> [t]he "autonomous" consumer selects...certain religious themes from the available assortment and builds them into a somewhat precarious private system of "ultimate" significance. Individual religiosity is thus no longer a replica or approximation of an "official" model (1990: 134).

Other authors have observed the same or related phenomena and described them in terms of "subjectivization, believing without belonging," or as choosing to be "spiritual but not religious."[51] It is in the area of privatized religion that modern yoga is most often situated.[52]

The case of pre-modern practitioners of yogic and related practices is quite different. They would have been (and still are) immersed in the premodern Dharmic conceptual universe, with theories and practices shaped by socio-religious categories, institutions, teachings, lineages, and cultural conventions that would have been much more prescriptive or, at least, much more historically, geographically, and culturally cohesive. This does not mean that syncretism would not be possible. In this case, however, the scope and variation of syncretic possibilities would be much more closely bound, socio-culturally restricted, and chronologically slow to develop. Individuals, in other words, would be unlikely to have as free a hand as Modern Yoga practitioners with regard to shaping their beliefs and practices.

Commodification

The commodification of yoga in its modern forms is unprecedented. This is not to say that premodern styles of yoga and related disciplines were never entangled in matters of wealth and power.[53] Rather, what is referred to here are the forms of commodification characteristic of global capitalism and postmodern consumer societies. The proliferation of "yoga goods" and media; the growth of commercially run yoga activities such as yoga studios and retreats; the registration (carried out or attempted) of yoga patents, trade marks, and copyrights:[54] All of these are, of course, unprecedented phenomena that did not and could not have happened in the same way in premodern contexts.

A whole range of issues could be usefully examined here. To mention a few: the role played by specific media in the expansion and formulation of Modern Yoga in the twentieth century and beyond;[55] the exploitation, corporate or otherwise, of contemporary spirituality;[56] or the ambivalence created in Modern Postural Yoga practice by internal ideological tensions between a drive toward acquisitiveness and introspective, renunciatory attitudes.[57]

Medicalization

Therapy, especially in the field of mind-body medicine, along with well-being and fitness issues, have all been important contexts within which yoga has become a visible player. On the one hand, there are studies within the "hard" scientific domain: Here we find, perhaps unsurprisingly given yoga's focus on human beings as psychosomatic entities, that almost all of the work takes place in the health sciences, including areas of (bio)medical research, clinical applications, and sports-fitness disciplines.[58] On the other hand, yoga is also portrayed by most Modern Yoga schools as "therapeutic" in a more general and, as it were, existential sense (i.e., as a "holistic" tool that teaches how to live a better life and cope with difficulties). In all of the above instances, yoga has to struggle, as Alter points out, with a history of "magic, alchemy and sex" (2005: 119). "This 'other' history," writes Alter, "both undermines and authorizes the idea of yoga as medicine" and, the author goes on to argue, it is this "tension between pragmatic rationalism and esoteric magic which makes yoga powerful" (ibid.). Finally, the themes occupying a continuum between esoteric "relaxationism"[59] and more orthodox medical attempts at "neutralising stress"[60] complete the panorama of the ways in which modern yoga has been medicalized. Eminently psychosomatic in scope, they also act as "bridges" between the strictly biomedical, the psychological, and the more holistic aspects of the contemporary therapeutic explorations of yoga.

The fact that therapeutic issues in the widest sense of the word are so central to forms of yoga both ancient and modern should not come as a surprise: After all, this discipline is ultimately concerned with what we could call "metaphysical health."[61] From the beginning, its *raison d'être* is the dispelling of the (postulated) malaise of *avidyā*, the foundational "ignorance" or "nescience" intrinsic to the human condition.[62] However, from those times onward, the ways in which yoga practitioners and theorists have approached issues of health, healing, and therapy (whether psychosomatic or metaphysical) have been significantly shaped by changing needs, circumstances, and conditions. Still, there is little doubt that the modern medical domain, both orthodox and alternative, has proved to be the most successful context within which globalized forms of Modern Yoga have progressed toward acculturation in most developed societies. Thus, the wider medicalization of yoga, and issues related to it, are likely to be one of the crucial analytical filters through which the study of the modern manifestations of this discipline can fruitfully progress.

Other Areas and Directions of Study

A review of humanities and social sciences scholarship was published in 2007 and will not be reproduced here.[63] However, two important considerations regarding possible further areas of research should briefly be mentioned in conclusion. One relates to the so-called Easternization debate, the other to the need for interdisciplinary work, with special reference to indological studies.

The Easternization debate was initiated by sociologist Colin Campbell with a conference paper presented in 1997 and published in 1999. Here he argued that we are witnessing "a major paradigm shift in religious orientations, from the transcendentalism of western religion to an Eastern, immanent concept of the divine" (33). Ten years down the line, he has published a book on the same topic (Campbell 2007). Unfortunately, it has not been possible to look at this publication before completing the present manuscript, but some preliminary remarks can nevertheless be made. Interim reviews responding to the 1999 paper, and one unpublished review of the 2007 book (Altglas), reflect the present author's early impression that Campbell, though accurate in his field observations and in some of his theorizing, may be confusing, at least to some extent, "Eastern"with "[W]estern esoteric."[64] Despite the possible limitations of Campbell's thesis, important elements of Modern Yoga and related modern meditative disciplines could be fruitfully brought to light and examined in the context of this discussion. The existing debate can be used to ask important questions as to what may be peculiarly Eastern, what Western, and what syncretic (or indeed synthetic) in Modern Yoga, and these are crucial discriminations to make—not only vis-à-vis Modern Yoga phenomena but with regard to modern and contemporary forms of globalized religiosity as a whole. Conceptual clarity and discriminating historical awareness could in fact potentially play a major role in neutralizing contemporary trends toward socio-political strife and widespread confusion about religious belief and practice.

The next point links with the previous one to the extent that the above discussion, though still very worthwhile, would be missing a crucial discussant if the Indological voice were to be absent. So far, there has not been enough sustained, primary engagement with Modern Yoga phenomena on the part of language-trained, text-based, Indological scholars.[65] Anthropologists, sociologists, and historians are key voices, visibly active in the academic arena and followed by a budding generation of younger professionals. However, they are doomed to fail in certain areas if the necessary Indological scholarship is not brought to bear on this type of research. Conversely, an engagement with Modern Yoga issues may help free Indology from the "ivory tower" label that, however undeservedly, is at times applied to this discipline. Carried out in the right measure, to suitable standards, and with appropriate interlocutors, such a dialogue could prove of virtually immediate use and benefit to both academic institutions and modern yoga milieus alike. Perhaps both camps should think of promoting such engagement, in both word and deed, whenever the occasion arises.

Notes

1 For the purposes of this paper, "pre-modern" is used negatively to signify all that is *not* Modern Yoga (i.e., not influenced by Western intellectual traditions and cultural forms; for a definition of Modern Yoga see next section). Broadly speaking, this would mean any pre-1750 forms of yoga and any such which may have been cultivated up to our day, provided they have not been (or not substantially) affected by Western influences. Pre-modern forms are in fact far from extinct; thus, the appellation will be used as a *qualitative*, not chronological, qualifier. Some insight into premodern forms may be gained by looking for example at work by Ghurye and Chapekar (1964); van der Veer (1989); Gross (1992); Sawyer (1993); and Mallinson (2005). Other useful sources are the many ethno-photographic volumes on the topic, such as Hartsuiker (1993). Generally speaking, however, with regard to the permeability of all traditions and cultures, the reader should bear in mind that the schematizations presented here are ideal-typical, abstract, heuristic devices and should be applied only carefully and in discriminating fashion to real-life situations.

2 Whether the original (prehistoric and early historic) roots of Sanskritic (vedic) culture were indigenous to South Asia or the result of migration has become a contentious and heavily politicized issue; see Bryant (2001) about the context and content of both academic and politico-ideological debates. For a much more condensed view of the debate, essentially reaching the same conclusions, see Mukherjee (1998: 80), who states: "To the pure academics the question is still an open one." It is very difficult to know how much and how exactly these two strands, Sanskritic and "other," may have interacted. Though there are no complete answers to this problem so far, and may never be, the topic is of great importance as it touches the very roots, both practical and theoretical, of all yogic and meditative schools, ancient and modern. One way to gain some understanding of this stimulating debate is to look at work by Bronkhorst (1993); Bronkhorst and Deshpande (1999); and Olivelle (1993 and 1995), amongst others. Here various "vedic," "non-vedic," and other possible sources of Indic asceticism and meditative practice are discussed and problematized, the latest addition to the debate being Bronkhorst's (2007) formulation of a "Greater Magadha" cultural influence as a crucial, though so far largely unexplored, contributor to the development of early Indic culture.

3 Also sometimes called "Dharmic" religions (along with Sikhism) owing to the central role that the concept of *dharma* plays in all of them. As Hardy puts it, according to these traditions

> [w]ithin the world can be found a rhythm, a structure or pattern (e.g. ... the *Dharma*) which is decisive for man's own destiny and fulfilment. Religion spells out how to harmonize one's individual being with this universal rhythm. ... Wherever we find the belief in such a cosmic rhythm, it goes along with the assumption that "ordinary" man has not yet achieved his harmonisation with it (1990: 5–6).

4 We know from Buddhist sources that the Buddha practiced yoga with recognized masters before he decided to try other approaches and, eventually, attaining enlightenment. As his life's dates are around the fifth century BCE (precise dates

vary depending on authority), yoga as a specifically named discipline must be at least 2,500 years old.

5 See, for example, the thesis put forward by Eliade (1973, Ch. 8), but disputed by Filliozat (1991: 378–9), that the roots of yoga are to be found, at least in part, in shamanic practices. Sarbacker (2005, Ch. 3) also reviews these topics. Exchanges between Islam (primarily Sufism) and yoga will not be discussed here, but on this see Ernst (2003 and 2005).

6 Leaving aside the possibility of revelatory or visionary events, we should not forget that any type of knowledge transmission ultimately takes place through individuals (whether in person, through texts or other forms of encoding). This is true across the board, but such dynamics have been emphasized and have played specific roles in the transmission of yogic instruction, as shown by the importance given to teacher-pupil (*guru-śiṣya*) interaction. Concerning this, see also the discussion of *paramparā* in note 25 below.

7 Ca. 200 BCE is "a likely date" of composition according to van Buitenen (1981: 6).

8 "Its importance ... is demonstrated by its uniquely pan-Hindu influence," and its relevance is "suprascholastic or suprasectarian" (van Buitenen 1981: 6). "It is this universal acceptance of the revelatory relevance of the *Gītā* that makes it so unique" (ibid.).

9 For condensed and expanded textbook overviews of the three yogas, see Klostermaier (1989: 145–288); for a more Indological overview, see van Buitenen's introduction to his translation of the text (1981: 1–29, especially 14–29).

10 About the vedic roots of *Tantra*, see Hartzell (1997, Ch. 2) and White (1996).

11 See Hartzell (1997: 256 and Ch. 3).

12 There is a growing literature on various aspects of tantra, and the reader can refer to it for a fuller treatment of this topic. Good places to start are Padoux (1981 and 2002) and Hartzell (1997).

13 Depending on variations across different sets of practice, and related aims. For an overview of the principles and dynamics involved see Flood (2006).

14 For a range of examples across Dharmic religions, see White (2000).

15 Such as the ones brought about by ascetic and (if applicable) shamanic-type practices, by specific yogic techniques, and by the use of entheogens (i.e., psychoactive plants used in religious contexts).

16 About sexual yoga, see Hartzell (1997, Ch. 9).

17 'In short, the word *yoga* can designate any discipline that makes us capable of some mastery. In fact, that is the actual meaning of the word, which signifies "bring under a yoke, adjustment, adaptation" Filliozat (1991: 377). "Discipline" should be understood here not only as "effort" but in the more general sense of "training" and of systematization, transmission, and ordered application of knowledge.

18 Each of which, however, fits them in their own religio-philosophical models in different ways. About the appellation "Dharmic," see note 3.

19 This author offers an interesting discussion of the topic from a sociological point of view. For a textbook treatment, see Klostermaier (1989, Ch. 14). For a more in-depth analysis of *karma*-related problems in a range of Indic *darśanas* (lit. points of "view;" i.e., philosophical schools), see Bronkhorst (2000).

20 And different styles of yoga will define such progression in different ways, whether theoretical, practical, or both.

21 Those new to the study of Indic traditions will benefit greatly from reading this brief text (pp. 1–9), which highlights some of the misunderstandings most often found amongst Westerners, and some of the seminal ideas characteristic of Asian thought.

22 That is good men, holymen, saints, sages (from the adjective meaning "straight, right").

23 For a comprehensive textbook treatment of the Hindu "professional religious," see Klostermaier (1989, Ch. 22).

24 See Julius Lipner (1994) who, with reference to Hinduism, writes,

> The Great Banyan [of the Calcutta botanical gardens] is not a bad symbol of Hinduism. Like the tree, Hinduism is an ancient collection of roots and branches, many indistinguishable one from the other, microcosmically polycentric, macrocosmically one, sharing the same regenerative life-sap, with a temporal foliage which covers most of recorded human history. But unlike the botanical model, the Hindu banyan is not uniform to look at. Rather, it is a network of variety, one distinctive arboreal complex shading into another, the whole forming a marvellous unity-in-diversity (5–6).

See also David Smith:

> [In Hinduism there] was no overall authority, no Inquisition, no Synod to rule and regulate what men thought; practice was regulated, behaviour was governed by caste councils. Social life was, relatively speaking, orderly and stable; intellectual life was a free for all (2005: 58).

25 This is the meaning of *paramparā*, a key concept in Indic traditions, which implies both the passing on of teachings and knowledge in a general way (which may include instruction by example, by acting as a role model, and by quality of "presence"), and more specific transmissions within lineages (usually by way of *dīkṣā*, initiation). It highlights the crucial importance of personalized, "live," embodied (as opposed to more dogmatic or textual) forms of transmission. For an examination of the *guru*'s role in different traditions, Indic and otherwise, see Rigopoulos (2004); about the tantric *guru*, see Padoux (2005); for a well-informed and highly entertaining account of one of the more popular ways in which these dynamics operate, see Narayan (1992); for an internal, monastic Advaitic view, see Sarasvati (1991). As a more practical example of both *paramparā* transmission dynamics and of the more 'fluid' structures of Hindu religious institutions, see Sundareśan (2000).

26 To understand more about the way such networks are organized and how they work, see the sources mentioned in notes 1 and 25.

27 How far this is the case varies from school to school, and on levels of assimilation into local cultures, and of syncretism with non-South Asian philosophies and ideas.

28 As indicated above, Jainism and Buddhism are very important with regard to the overall history of yoga, and in some cases also to its modern context, but though occasionally elements from these and other religions may be found in specific yoga styles, it may safely be said that most of what is called "yoga" in everyday English stems broadly from a Hindu background (or Neo-Hindu and New Age to be more precise; see De Michelis 2004). And though Sikhism has a voice in the modern yoga world (see Feuerstein 2001: 333–7, and the 3HO organization: http://www.3ho.org), neither this tradition nor Jainism or Buddhism are treated in this chapter.

29 The implication is that, generally speaking, these cultures are technologically developed, cosmopolitan, and culturally postmodern. For geographical data and related discussions see Hoyez (2005).

30 Though European, Asian, South American, and other languages are also used, there are very often strong links with English-speaking cultures by way of personal interactions, books, teachings, travels, yoga and retreat centres, and the like on the parts of leaders, pioneers, and key representatives. This is also related to the fact that English usage has been and still is very prominent in South Asia.

31 The one most often associated with the word *yoga* in contemporary English—see typology in the next section.

32 This is a topic that could be fruitfully discussed in relation to the Easternization thesis (see concluding section about the latter).

33 A good account of the Indian situation is provided by Kopf (1969). Regarding the Western, and more specifically continental European, side of things see Schwab (1984).

34 For a good account see Jones (1997: 25-30).

35 See, for example, Jones (1997) about the role played by the Brahmo Samaj and the Arya Samaj in modern Indian history. Farquhar (1915), a more contemporary account, gives a good impression of the period's religious ferment. For the role of Western esotericism, see De Michelis (2004).

36 The attitudes and affirmations of Thoreau are exemplary in this context. In 1849 he wrote: "... I would fain practice the yoga faithfully....To some extent, and at rare intervals, even I am a yogi" (Thoreau 1968, vol. 6: 175).

37 The typological discussion presented here is a revised and updated version of the ones published in De Michelis (2004: 188 and 2007). Work on this topic is ongoing.

38 Later examples: Swami Sivananda of Rishikesh and his many pupils who established yoga-promoting organizations worldwide (see Strauss 2000); the Himalayan Institute of Swami Rama; Kripalu Yoga.

39 "The yoga of the eight limbs;" see *Yogasūtras* II.28 to III.8, comprising *yama* (restraints), *niyama* (observances), *āsana* (yogic posture), *prāṇāyāma* (regulation of breath/energy), *pratyāhāra* (sense withdrawal), *dhāraṇā* (concentration), *dhyāna* (meditation), and *samādhi* (meditative absorption).

40 See Alter (2004). Singleton (2007a: 86–93 and passim) traces the early developments of these schools. Contemporary examples are the Baratiya Yog Sansthan discussed by Alter (1997) and, most likely, the contemporary "yoga phenomenon" of Swami Ramdev, see www.divyayoga.com (informed guess—no independent data found on this movement so far). The Santa Cruz (Mumbai) Yoga Institute and the Kaivalyadhama Institute at Lonavla (Maharashtra) should probably be classified as combinations of these first two types (i.e., psychosomatic and neo-Hindu).

41 Influential and widely know postural schools are those established by some of Tirumalai Krishnamacharya's (1888–1989) pupils: B.K.S. Iyengar's Iyengar Yoga, Pattabhi Jois' Ashtanga Yoga, and the yoga taught by T.K.V. Desikachar (formerly Viniyoga), though the latter could also be seen to be veering toward the psychosomatic mode. Examples of other schools influential in the postural domain, which is expanding very rapidly at the moment, are the more postural aspects of Swami Vishnudevananda's Sivananda Yoga (in other ways this organization may be seen as representing modern psychosomatic yoga tendencies) and Bikram's Yoga.

42 Perhaps the most famous early example is the Self Realization Fellowship of Swami Yogananda. A later example are the Brahma Kumaris, see Walliss (2002).

43 The TM (Transcendental Meditation) movement of Maharishi Mahesh Yogi is a likely example of this dynamic (see Forsthoefel and Humes 2005, Ch. 3). Another example is ISKCON which, after a number of scandals and much soul-searching, has now been working for years toward attaining a more socially integrated (neo-)Hindu profile (for a variety of perspectives, see Bryant and Ekstrand 2004). In this context, it is interesting to note the recent creation of a new type of "ISKCON postural yoga," Atma Yoga (see www.yogamandir.com).

44 See for example Rajneesh/Osho, Sahaja Yoga (Coney 1999), and earlier forms of ISKCON.

45 Such as early forms of Transcendental Meditation (TM) and Shri Chinmoy's meditation school. About the general happenings of the time see for example Roszak (1969) and Cox (1977). Interesting reports and updates on several denominational schools will be found in Forsthoefel and Humes (2005).

46 Pye (1993), adopts the term *syncretism* and divests it of all judgemental connotations to "facilitate the analysis of dynamic religious processes." He then defines it as containing "multiple possibilities in coherent tension." Synthesis, on the other

hand, implies that "out of multiple possibilities, a new conclusion has been reached" (ibid.: 5–6).

47 Abrahamic religions and cultures are the ones defined by Judaism, Christianity, and Islam.

48 Modern esotericism, especially in the form of New Age and neo-Hindu speculations and theorizations. About the former see Hanegraaf (1996); about the latter see Bharati (1970) and Halbfass (1988, Ch. 13 and *passim*); about both as found in Modern Yoga, see Baier (1998); Ceccomori (2001); De Michelis (2004); Newcombe (2005); and Singleton (2007a).

49 For more on such axioms ("fundamental facts that are regarded as so totally self-evident that they are not reflected upon and usually carried along as unconsciously made assumptions"; Hardy 1990: 4) see ibid.: 1–9.

50 For overviews, see Dobbelaere (1998) and Inglehart and Norris (2004, Ch. 1).

51 Respectively, Heelas and Woodhead (2005: 9–10) and Davies (1994, *passim*), discussing the British situation, and Fuller (2001), discussing the American situation.

52 Even when modern yoga is somehow anchored to mainstream traditions—and there are many cases of this as any Google search on "yoga + [name of religion]" will show—it is likely to retain strong elements of privatized religiosity.

53 See, for example, Flügel and Houtman (forthcoming) for both past and contemporary perspectives and White (1996) about the role played by *siddhas* in relation to secular and magical powers. About related themes in contemporary Hinduism and neo-Hinduism, see McKean (1996), along_with Fuller (1997).

54 See Fish, who writes about "transnational commercial yoga" (2006: 189) and discusses the case of Bikram Yoga in this context.

55 Singleton, for example, looks at how "the rapid expansion of print technology and the cheap, ready availability of photography" was key to the creation of modern postural yoga (2007a: 187ff).

56 As Carrette and King (2005) suggest.

57 See Smith (2007).

58 There is no space to review these here, but a discussion of this topic, including more on mind-body medicine, will be found in De Michelis (2007: 10–16).

59 About relaxationism, see Singleton (2005, and 2007a, Ch. 5, Part 2).

60 See De Michelis (2007: 10–16).

61 Alter (1999) writes about "metaphysical fitness" in a discussion that is, methodologically, closely related to the present one, though focusing primarily on Āyurveda.

62 See, for example, occurrences of this term in Michaël (1980).

63 See De Michelis (2007: 8–10). Other articles in this collection, edited by Mark Singleton (2007b), will also be useful in this context.

64 See Hamilton (2002) and Dawson (2006) for stimulating and enriching critiques of Campbell's thesis.

65 There has been more of a rapprochement in North America: Academic and nonacademic examples of publications of this kind are Rosen (2005), and the magazine *Nāmarūpa*.

Bibliography

Alter, J. S. (1997) A Therapy to Live By: Public Health, the Self and Nationalism in the Practice of a North Indian Yoga Society, *Medical Anthropology*, 17: 309–35.

——(1999) Heaps of health, metaphysical fitness: Ayurveda and the ontology of good health in medical anthropology, *Current Anthropology*, 40, Supplement: S43–65.

——(2004) *Yoga in Modern India: The Body between Science and Philosophy*, Princeton: Princeton University Press.

——(2005) Modern Medical Yoga: Struggling with a History of Magic, Alchemy and Sex, *Asian Medicine, Tradition and Modernity*, 1: 119–46.

Altglas, V. (2008) Review of Colin Campell, *The Easternisation of the West* (2007), *Journal of Contemporary Religion*, 23: 1 94–8.

Baier, K. (1998) *Yoga auf dem Weg nach Westen*, Wurzburg: Konigshausen and Neumann.

Berger, P. (1998) Protestantism and the quest for certainty, *The Christian Century*, August 26–September 2: 782–96.

Bharati, S.A. (1970) The Hindu renaissance and its apologetic patterns, *Journal of Asian Studies*, 29: 267–88.

Bronkhorst, J. (1993) *The Two Sources of Indian asceticism*, Bern: P. Lang.

——(2000) *Karma and Teleology: A Problem and its Solutions in Indian Philosophy*, Tokyo: International Institute for Buddhist Studies.

——(2007) *Greater Magadha: Studies in the culture of early India*, Boston: Brill.

Bronkhorst, J., and M.M. Deshpande (eds) (1999) *Aryan and Non-Arian in South Asia: Evidence, Interpretation, and Ideology*, Cambridge, MA: Department of Sanskrit and Indian Studies, Harvard University.

Bryant, E. (2001) *The Quest for the Origins of Vedic Culture*, Oxford: Oxford University Press.

Bryant, E.F. and M.L. Ekstrand, (eds) (2004) *The Hare Krishna Movement: The Postcharismatic Fate of a Religious Transplant*, New York: Columbia University Press.

Campbell, C. (1999) The Easternization of the West, in Wilson, B. and Cresswell, J. (eds) *New Religious Movements: Challenge and Response*, London: Routledge, 35–48.

——(2007) *The Easternization of the West: A Thematic Account of Cultural Change in theModern Era*, Boulder, CO: Paradigm Publishers.

Carrette, J. and R. King (2005) *Selling Spirituality: The Silent Takeover of Religion*, London: Routledge.

Ceccomori, S. (2001) *Cent Ans de Yoga en France*, Paris: Edidit.

Coney, J. (1999) *Sahaja Yoga: Socializing Processes in a South Asian New Religious Movement*, New Delhi: Oxford University Press.

Cox, H. (1977) *Turning East : Why Americans Look to the Orient for Spirituality—And whatthat Search can Mean to the West*, New York: Simon and Schuster.

Davies, G. (1994) *Religion in Britain since 1945: Believing Without Belonging*, Oxford: Blackwell.

Dawson, A. (2006) East is East, except when it's West: The Easternisation Thesis and Western Habitus, *Journal of Religion and Society* 8, Available HTTP:<http://moses.creighton.edu/JRS/.> (accessed 3 August 2007).

De Michelis, E. (2004) *A History of Modern Yoga: Patañjali and Western Esotericism*, London: Continuum.

——(2007) A Preliminary Survey of Modern Yoga Studies, *Asian Medicine, Tradition and Modernity*, 3: 1–19.

Dobbelaere, K. (1998) Secularization, in Swatos, W. H. J. (Ed.), *Encyclopedia of Religion and Society*, Walnut Creek, CA: AltaMira Press.

Eliade, M. (1973) *Yoga: Immortality and Freedom*, Princeton, New Jersey: Princeton University Press.

Ernst, C.W. (2003) The Islamization of yoga in the Amrtakunda translations, *Journal of the Royal Asiatic Society*, 3: 199–226.

——(2005) Situating sufism and yoga, *Journal of the Royal Asiatic Society*, 3: 15–43.

Farquhar, J.N. (1915 [1913]) *Modern religious movements in India*, London: The Macmillan Company.
Feuerstein, G. (2001) *The Yoga Tradition: Its History, Literature, Philosophy and Practice*, Prescott, AZ: Hohm Press.
Filliozat, J. (1991) *Religion, Philosophy, Yoga: A Selection of Articles*, Delhi: Motilal Banarasidass Publishers.
Fish, A. (2006) The Commodification and Exchange of Knowledge in the Case of Transnational Commercial Yoga, *International Journal of Cultural Property*, 13: 189–206.
Flood, G.D. (2006) *The Tantric Body: The Secret Tradition of Hindu Religion*, London: I.B. Tauris.
Flügel, P., and G. Houtman (eds) (forthcoming, 2009) *Asceticism and Power in South and Southeast Asia*, London: Routledge.
Forsthoefel, T.A., and C.A. Humes (eds) (2005) *Gurus in America*, Albany: State University of New York Press.
Fuchs, C. (1990) *Yoga im Deutschland: Rezeption-Organisation-Typologie*, Stuttgart: Kohlhammer Verlag.
Fuller, C.J. (1997) Review of *Divine Enterprise: Gurus and the Hindu Nationalist Movement* by Lise McKean, *The Journal of the Royal Anthropological Institute*, 3: 804–805.
Fuller, R.C. (2001) *Spiritual but not Religious, Understanding Unchurched America*, Oxford: Oxford University Press.
Gross, R.L. (1992) *The Sadhus of India: A Study of Indian Asceticism*, Jaipur: Rawat Publications.
Ghurye, G.S., and L.N. Chapekar (1964) *Indian Sadhus*, Bombay: Popular Prakashan.
Halbfass, W. (1988) *India and Europe: An Essay in Understanding*, Albany: State University of New York Press.
Hamilton, M. (2002) The Easternisation Thesis: Critical Reflections, *Religion*, 32: 243–58.
Hanegraaff, W.J. (1996) *New Age Religion and Western Culture: Esotericism in the Mirror of Secular Thought*, Leiden: Brill.
Hardy, F. (ed) (1990) *The Religions of Asia*, London: Routledge.
Hartsuiker, D. (1993) *Sādhus, Holy Men of India*, London: Thames and Hudson.
Hartzell, J.F. (1997) Tantric Yoga: A Study of the Vedic Precursors, Historical Evolution, Literatures, Cultures, Doctrines, and Practices of the 11th Century Kashmiri Saivite and Buddhist Unexcelled Tantric Yogas [unpublished thesis], New York: Columbia University.
Heelas, P., and L. Woodhead (2005) *The Spiritual Revolution: Why Religion is Giving Way to Spirituality*, Oxford: Blackwell.
Hoyez, A.-C. (2005) L'Espace-Monde du Yoga [unpublished thesis], Université de Rouen.
Inglehart, R., and P. Norris (2004) *Sacred and Secular: Religion and Politics Worldwide*, New York: Cambridge University Press.
Jones, K.W. (1997) *Socio-Religious Reform Movements in British India*, Cambridge: Cambridge University Press.
Kakar, S. (1983) *Shamans, Mystics, and Doctors: A Psychological Inquiry into India and its Healing Traditions*, Boston: Beacon Press.
Klostermaier, K.K. (1989) *A Survey of Hinduism*, Albany: State University of New York Press.
Kopf, D. (1969) *British Orientalism and the Bengal Renaissance: The Dynamics of Indian Modernization, 1773-1835*, Berkeley: University of California Press.

Larson, G.J. (2000) Foreword, in D.R. Brooks, S. Durgananda, P.E. Muller-Ortega, et al. (eds) *Meditation Revolution: A Historyand Theology of the Siddha Yoga Lineage*, pp. xiii–xv, New Delhi and Delhi: Muktabodha Indological Research Institute and Motilal Banarsidass.
Lipner, J.J. (1994) *The Hindus: Their Religious Beliefs and Practices*, London: Routledge.
Luckmann, T. (1990) Shrinking transcendence, expanding religion? *Sociological Analysis*, 51: 127–38.
Mallinson, J. (2005) Rāmānandī thyāgīs and haṭha yoga, *Journal of Vaishnava Studies*, 14 (1): 107–21.
McKean, L. (1996) *Divine enterprise: Gurus and the Hindu Nationalist Movement*, Chicago: University of Chicago Press.
Michaël, T. (1980) *Introduction aux voies de yoga*, Paris: Editions du Rocher.
Milner, M.J. (1993) Hindu eschatology and the Indian caste system: an example of structural reversal, *The Journal of Asian Studies*, 52: 298–319.
Mukherjee, B.N. (1998) The unsolved Aryan problem, *Indologica Taurinensia*, 23– 70–80.
Narayan, K. (1992) *Storytellers, Saints and Scoundrels: Folk Narrative in Hindu Religious Teaching*, Delhi: Motilal Banarsidass.
Nevrin, K. (2005) Krishnamacharya's Viniyoga: Modern Yoga and Śrī Vaishnavism, *Journal of Vaishnava Studies*, 14: 65–93.
Newcombe, S. (2005) Spirituality and "Mystical Religion" in Contemporary Society: A Case Study of British Practitioners of the Iyengar Method of Yoga, *Journal of Contemporary Religion*, 20: 305–21.
Olivelle, P. (1993) *The Āśrama System: The History and Hermeneutics of a Religious Institution*, New York: Oxford University Press.
—(1995) Review of *The Two Sources of Indian Asceticism* by Johannes Bronkhorst, *Journal of the American Oriental Society*, 115 (1): 162–4.
—(1998) *The Early Upaniṣads: Annotated Text and Translation*, New York: Oxford University Press.
Padoux, A. (1981) A Survey of Tantric Hinduism for the Historian of Religions, *History of Religions (Chicago)*, 20: 345–60.
—(2002) Corps et cosmos: l'image du corps du yogin tantrique, in V. Bouiller, and G. Tarabout, (eds) *Images du Corps dans le Monde Hindou*, Paris: CNRS Editions.
—(2005) The tantric guru, in G.D. Flood (ed) *The Blackwell Companion to Hinduism*, Oxford: Blackwell.
Pye, M.E. (1993) Syncretism vs synthesis, [paper given at the 1992 annual conference of the British Association for the Study of Religions], Winchester: Occasional Paper published by the British Association for the Study of Religions.
Rigopoulos, A. (ed) (2004) *Guru. The Spiritual Master in Eastern and Western Traditions: Authority and Charisma*, Venezia: Cafoscarina.
Rosen, S. (ed) (2005) Yoga and Vaishnavism [thematic journal issue], *Journal of Vaishnava Studies*, 14 (1).
Roszak, T. (1969) *The making of a Counter Culture: Reflections on the Technocratic Society and its Youthful Opposition*, Garden City, NY: Doubleday.
Sarasvati, P.C. (1991) *The Guru Tradition*, Bombay: Bharatiya Vidya Bhavan.
Sarbacker, S.R. (2005) *Samādhi: The Numinous and the Cessative in Indo-Tibetan Yoga*, Albany: State University of New York Press.
Sawyer, D.W. (1993) The monastic structure of Banarsi Dandi Sadhus, In B.R. Hertel and C.A. Humes (eds) *Living Banaras: Hindu Religion in Cultural Context*, Albany: State University of New York Press.

Schwab, R. (1984) *The Oriental Renaissance : Europe's Rediscovery of India and the East, 1680-1880,* New York: Columbia University Press.

Singleton, M. (2005) Salvation Through Relaxation: Proprioceptive Therapy in Relation to Yoga, *Journal of Contemporary Religion,* 20: 289–304.

—(2007a) The Body at the Centre: Contexts of Postural Yoga in the Modern Age [unpublished thesis], University of Cambridge.

—(ed) (2007b) Special Yoga Issue, *Asian Medicine: Tradition and Modernity,* 3, 1.

Sjoman, N.E. (1999) *The Yoga Tradition of the Mysore Palace,* New Delhi: Shakti Malik.

Smith, B.R. (2007) Adjusting the quotidian: Ashtanga yoga as everyday practice, Available at HTTP:<http://wwwmcc.murdoch.edu.au/cfel/csaa_proceedings.htm> [accessed June 20, 2007].

Smith, D. (2005) Orientalism and Hinduism, in G.D. Flood (ed) *The Blackwell Companion to Hinduism,* Oxford: Blackwell. Also available as Chapter 6 of D. Smith (2003) *Hinduism and Modernity,* Oxford: Blackwell.

Strauss, S. (2000) 'Locating Yoga, Ethography and Transnational Practice; In: A. Vered (ed.) *Constructing the Field: Ethnography in the Contemporary World,* London: Routledge.

Sundareśan, V. (2000) The Jyotirmaṭha Śaṅkarācārya Lineage in the 20th Century, Available at HTTP: <http://indology.info/papers/sundaresan/> [accessed July 24, 2007].

Thoreau, H.D. (1968) *The Writings of Henry David Thoreau,* Walden Edition, 20 vols., New York: AMS Press.

van Buitenen, J.A.B. (1981) *The Bhagavadgītā in the Mahābhārata: Text and Translation,* Chicago: University of Chicago Press.

van der Veer, P. (1989) The power of detachment: disciplines of body and mind in the Ramanandi order, *American Ethnologist,* 16: 458–70.

Vivekananda, S. (1896) *Rāja Yoga,* London: Longmans, Green and Co.

Walliss, J. (2002) *The Brahma Kumaris as a "Reflexive Tradition": Responding to Late Modernity,* Aldershot: Ashgate.

White, D.G. (1996) *The Alchemical Body: Siddha Traditions in Medieval India,* Chicago: University of Chicago Press.

—(ed) (2000) *Tantra in Practice,* Princeton, NJ: Princeton University Press.

2 Yoga *Shivir*

Performativity and the Study of Modern Yoga

Joseph S. Alter

Mind, Body, and the Spectacular: Yoga *Shivir*

Though the precise history is difficult to reconstruct, the now common practice of organizing yoga camps (*shivir*) for the general public and for specific institutions—prisons, the police, government workers in various departments, school groups and the like—most likely dates back to the early twentieth century when the yoga teachings of Swami Vivekananda and Sri Aurobindo were being integrated into the practice of postural, embodied yoga. At the turn of the century, advocates of postural yoga sought to consciously dissociate embodied forms of practice from the magical, mystical, and sexual alchemy of *haṭha* yoga, as *haṭha* yoga was coming to public awareness as a consequence of the translation of medieval texts (Ayangar 1893; Brahmananda 1889; Vasaka 1877; Vasu 1996) and the publication of works on *tantra* in general (see Urban 2003). In tandem with this, however, there was a concern on the part of postural yoga practitioners that embodied yoga not simply be practised as a form of physical fitness training and that mental self-discipline, in conjunction with what they viewed as the metaphysical cum "spiritual" aspects of training, also be highlighted. Though one can argue that yoga in general and postural yoga in particular exhibits a distinct mind-body synthesis, it is important to point out that as a consequence of the way in which the practice of yoga has evolved over the past century—becoming ever more a kind of fitness regimen—advocacy for yoga as an embodied philosophy in fact exhibits a degree of anxiety and ambivalence about the inherent unity of mind, body, and spirit. In many respects, yoga *shivir* reflect this anxiety and ambivalence by seeking to synthesize yoga and construct a seamless, coherent body of practice.

Shivir is a term derived from Sanskrit and is most often translated as "camp." It is used to refer to events in which a combination of lectures, demonstrations, and group participation is used to promote yoga and other "cultural" traditions. As such, the term is most often used in contexts where various groups and institutions are involved in promoting "Hindu ideals" or "Vedic heritage" (or both). In other words, usage—and the performance that is linked to usage—is inflected with nationalism, though not necessarily, therefore, with communal sectarianism. Though various organizations and groups often hold yoga "days" (*diwas*) and "functions" (*smāroḥ*), *shivir*, which usually last from several days to a week, are conceptualized as occasions when those who participate are provided with basic training in a mass-drill format. The emphasis is on collective, group participation in a public venue.

On the basis of its Sanskrit derivation, the term *shivir* has martial connotations, and though most *shivir* are not conducted like boot camps, there is certainly a degree of ritualized communitas—and disciplinary regimentation—reflected in the way in which participants collectively follow the instructions of the person leading the event. The result is *ad hoc*, choreographed regimentation. *Āsana* and, to a lesser degree *prāṇāyāma*, require that practitioners have a clearly delimited space to sit, stand, and lie down in various postures, and typically *shivir* are conducted with participants seated on rectangular blankets or mats arranged in neat, symmetrical rows and columns. The person giving instructions and providing commentary and explanation usually sits or stands on a low dais where he or she is clearly visible to the assembled group. This configuration defines the basic parameters of the performance, insofar as the performance is often staged for an audience that is at a second-degree remove from the instructor and the regimented participants: Yoga camps invite participation, but participation, usually on a large scale, is designed to be seen by a larger group than is actively participating. In some instances, there is a "third-degree" remove in that the instructor, participants, and "real-space" audience is filmed for broadcast on television and photographed for various forms of print media distribution. *Shivir* are, in a sense, purely spectacular events and, in a number of instances, as we will see, the spectacular is, unto itself, an integral feature of performativity.

Performativity, the Public Sphere, and Yoga

Before describing and analyzing several different *shivir*, it is necessary to consider some problems that relate to the study of yoga in general and yoga *shivir* in particular. Unless one is a complete cynic, it must be accepted that individuals and groups who organize and sponsor *shivir* are being honest and sincere in their desire to promote yoga, accurately represent its history and philosophy, and teach people how and why to engage in various forms of practice. *Shivir* are, by definition, events in which yoga is defined in terms of absolute truth and irrefutable fact. What is problematic, though, is that however sincere these truth claims are, many—if not all—do not stand up to historical scrutiny. In other words, one can hold up the *Haṭhayogapradīpika*, a medieval manual on *āsana, prāṇāyāma*, alchemical sex, and magic, against what a contemporary practitioner of yoga claims and force the issue of dissonance and discontinuity, either in terms of logic, truth, or politics or a combination of all three. One can, of course, take a radically relativist stand and simply hold that all claims about yoga—medical, magical, or mystical—are equally true. However, this position lacks intellectual integrity, avoids the fundamental issue, and is not very critically astute. Therefore, a key methodological issue, which has a direct bearing on theory as well, is how to exercise ethnographic relativism, historical perspectivity, and intellectual skepticism all at the same time.

Beyond methodology, there are important ethical questions that relate to the problem of intellectual skepticism and representation: It is rather disingenuous to "take the natives point of view" to gather ethnographic data, knowing full well that an intellectual history of ideas renders ethnographic truth rather suspect. This is not a problem that is necessarily unique to the study of yoga and is one that anthropologists have struggled with over the years, but as yoga involves embodied practice, rigorous self-discipline, and structured training of the mind—not to mention conviction about efficacy and value—the ethical problem of questioning truth claims while trying to understand how and why they are made is one that is especially charged with passion and politics and fraught with parsimonious claims to intellectual property rights (Alter 2000; Clifford and Marcus 1985; Rabinow 1977).

On one level, *shivir* are simply rich and textured examples of culture being constructed and reconstructed through institutionalized practice. Precisely as a consequence of this, they are also performances and require an analysis that is attuned to the reiterative dynamics of performativity (Butler 1997). As I argue here, the problematic methodological and ethical issues mentioned above can be mitigated if not completely resolved by means of an analytical approach that focuses on performativity. *Shivir* are, in a sense, meta-commentaries on the nature and meaning of yoga in practice and are, therefore, representations that reference the "real," disciplined practice of yoga but are not designed to be the "real thing" as such. In these terms, yoga *shivir* performances are structurally the mirror opposite of "yogic truth," as this truth is articulated—but never really articulated—as a profound, esoteric secret that is communicated only by an enlightened guru to an adept disciple. This secret is the structural feature of yoga's history that has given those who have come to believe in it unmitigated hope that yoga can lead to a greater truth than is experienced in the world as we know it. A *shivir* is a reflection of that hope, as that reflection is magnified through public performance, and "brought down to earth" in terms of people's concern for better health, less stress, and generalized wellness. One must have faith in that hope, as it is what takes one beyond performance to something that is real, if only in the embodied imagination.

Shivir are not the only context in which yoga gets performed, as any yoga class or yoga demonstration is, in some sense, a performance. Perhaps the clearest example of this is B.K.S. Iyengar's performance—and documentation of performance (1993)—of *āsana* as embodied art wherein the aesthetics of form is a manifestation of perfected practice. In this context, the beauty of perfected form precisely reflects the mystical secrecy invoked time and again in the medieval literature but also turns secrecy on its head, so to speak, by means of a public—and widely publicized—spectacle. In any case, my argument is that *shivir* performativity is a self-conscious form of embodied discourse involving various degrees of ambivalence about the relationship between mind and body, worldly concerns and transcendence. The goal is not to "do" yoga, but to constitute it through reiterative performances involving an identified adept master, who conducts the *shivir*, and an audience whose participation serves to make manifest, in the public sphere, what by the very nature of yoga is not manifest and mystical. Though completely ritualized in terms of structure, *shivir* do not function as rituals, in the sense that rituals constitute the grounded reality of abstract, ineffable beliefs. *Shivir* metonymically index a set of practices that transcend reality, and it is the indexicality of performance that is—ethnographically speaking—"genuine" in this context. The more spectacular the performance, the more genuine the indexicality and its various entailments of well-being and health.

In the following, I describe and analyze two examples of *shivir*. The first is a *shivir* organized by the Aurobindo Society in the town of Mussoorie; the second is a series of *shivir* staged by the Bharatiya Yog Sansthan and described in detail in the organization's quarterly magazine.

Yoga Shivir, *Mussoorie, May 2007*

Located midway between the two primary pilgrimage routes to Jamnotri and Gangotri—ironically two iconic sites where yogic sages are said to reside—Mussoorie is a tourist resort town in the Himalayas that was established as a colonial Hill Station in the 1820s. Though tourism is the base of the town's economy, there are also a significant number of educational institutions, many of which are English-language boarding schools. Mussoorie has a large middle and upper-middle class population, and many individuals and groups are active in community and cultural organizations. Yoga in contemporary India is very much a middle- and upper-middle-class activity and, consequently, in Mussoorie as in most other cities throughout India, there are often lectures on yoga and yoga *shivir* organized by various temple societies and civic groups.

A *shivir* was organized for a week in May-June 2007 while I was in Mussoorie conducting research on medical and health institutions. There were banners across the main thoroughfare, posters pasted on walls and lamp posts around the town, and advertisements in the local paper indicating that the *shivir* would provide participants with information and training on how to live healthier, stress-free lives. Having previously conducted research on yoga, I was interested and decided to attend.

The *shivir* was organized by the local center of the Aurobindo Society, a national umbrella organization based in Pondicherry, which has regional, state-level branches and local, urban centers throughout the country. Though sponsored by the Aurobindo Society, the *shivir* was conducted under the auspices of the Patanjali Yogpeeth Trust of Haridwar and coordinated by the *Patanjali Yoga Prashikshan Samiti*.

The Patanjali Yogpeeth Trust was established by the very popular—but controversial—Swami Ramdev Maharaj who had earlier, in 1995, established a parent organization, the Divya Yog Mandir Trust, on the grounds of Kripalu Bagh Ashram built in 1932 by Param Pujya Swami Kripalu Dev Ji Maharaj. The

Patanjali Yogpeeth Trust has established several institutions for propagating yoga and self-help Āyurveda for health and wellness, most recently a large research hospital and pharmacy in Bahadrabad about twenty kilometers from Haridwar. The facilities at Bahadrabad are quite remarkable, and the Trust is set up to cater to wealthy patrons on a massive scale (Divya Yog Mandir 2007a). Swami Ramdev is perhaps best known because of his numerous "yoga science camps" conducted on a regular basis for mass audiences throughout India and, more recently and to a lesser extent, in England and the United States (Divya Yog Mandir 2007b). He also is the on-air personality for a number of yoga and popular Āyurveda shows broadcast on at least five different national and international television channels (Divya Yog Mandir 2007c).

Swami Ramdev Maharaj's yoga science camps and his broadcast teachings will require more detailed analysis at some other time. However, it is clear that the yoga camp in Mussoorie was modeled on these camps, though conducted on a smaller scale with more modest ambitions. The collaboration, albeit indirect, between The Aurobindo Society and the Patanjali Yogpeeth Trust reflects the way in which yoga in practice functions to conflate a spectrum of different histories and philosophies of yoga. It is this conflation that is also manifest in the *performance* of yoga in the context of a *shivir*.

The Aurobindo Society had arranged to use a large meeting room in a new wing of the old Radha-Krishna temple located near the center of Mussoorie. The meeting room was still under construction but was functional if rather spartanly appointed. The opening ceremony for the *shivir* was telling in terms of how these events are designed as community-based activities linked both to institutions of civil society and government. The chief guests at the *shivir* were Mr. Jod Singh, the local district Member of the Legislative Assembly and therefore an important political figure in the state of Uttaranchal, and Mr. Manohar Mall, the chairman of the City Board. After welcoming the members of the Aurobindo Society and making some brief, general remarks for the benefit of members of the public about how and why the society seeks to promote the teaching of Aurobindo and the Mother, a senior member of the Society made a formal introduction of the chief guests and other dignitaries, including two men in their late sixties who had been invited to conduct the camp. After each of the dignitaries was introduced, they were presented with a bouquet of flowers by a different member of the Aurobindo Society.

Once everyone was introduced, the master of ceremonies continued to speak, going into some detail on the nature of Integral Yoga (Aurobindo 1976) and the evolution of the super mind (Aurobindo 1977). However, the MC also made extensive reference to the *Bhagvadgītā*, discussing the relationship between *bhakti yoga* and *karma yoga*, primarily making the point that yoga as such should be an encompassing way of life, based on a solid foundation of devotion to god and commitment to work but with a studied disregard for the fruits of one's labor. On the whole, it was a pragmatic and "realist" interpretation of teachings that have been given more radical interpretations by others. In this context, it was interesting to note that one of the points made in the preamble was that though the society had arranged two sessions for each day of the week-long *shivir*, they were eager to respond to a request from women participants that a third session be added in the early morning—six to seven a.m. This would allow mothers to return home and make preparations for their children to attend school. In essence, on one level, the entire *shivir* was oriented toward practical, day-to-day concerns; on another level, however, these concerns were all couched in terms that referenced a range of works in the corpus of classical and neo-classical yoga philosophy.

After the opening speech by the MC, the *shivir* was formally inaugurated and opened through a ceremony that involved each of the dignitaries' lighting one wick of a meter-tall brass *āratī* lamp. As each person used matches to try to get his wick burning, photographers from the local press and television station jockeyed for ideal positions to take pictures. The lighting of the final wick was greeted with applause from those of us assembled, approximately 120 strong after a half-hour's activity.

With the event formally opened, the MC again introduced the two men who were going to conduct the *shivir*, Mr. Gupta, a sixty-eight-year-old expert in *āsana* (yoga postures) and *prāṇāyāma* (yogic breathing techniques), and a professor from Haryana[1] who had made a study of yoga philosophy and practice. Mr. Gupta stepped up to the front of the room with the group of us seated on the floor on durries (cotton mats) in front of him. There was a low stage just to his rear, and the chief guests and dignitaries sat in plastic chairs on either side of the stage.

Mr. Gupta's presentation was quite different from the "lectures" that had come before, insofar as it was more personal and also more interactive. He asked everyone to be seated in a *padmāsana* (lotus posture) and explained that the *āsana* would enable one to sit comfortably for a long time to meditate and do *prāṇāyāma*. He also performed the *āsana*, showing how each foot had to be placed on top of the opposite thigh and the hands placed on the knees with the thumb and ring figure touching in the appropriate *mudrā*. Speaking in a very confident and reassuring tone, he had us take a deep breath and then exhale while intoning "OM." His intonation continued much longer—and with more force—than did that of most of the rest of us, and there was a sense in which he was demonstrating his level of accomplishment while giving us instructions. This was most clearly apparent when, after having been seated in a *padmāsana* he placed his feet back on the ground and stood up without needing to support himself or push himself up with his hands. Having performed this feat, he said, "See, I am 68 years old and still have the strength to do this."

After having talked at some length about the general health benefits of *āsana* and *prāṇāyāma*, Mr. Gupta introduced his eight-year-old granddaughter and explained that she would demonstrate several *āsana*. He explained that if it were possible for a child to learn *āsana* and *prāṇāyāma*, it should be possible for anyone to do so. As his granddaughter performed several *āsana*—*dhanurāsana, tadāsana, bhujaṅgāsana*— Mr. Gupta explained the finer points of technique and indicated some general rules concerning breathing and posture. In doing so, he pointed out that we should be careful about doing *āsana* and *prāṇāyāma* directly on the durries and should each bring a blanket or sheet, as this would prevent us from breathing in the dust from the floor. At one point, Mr. Gupta provided an anecdote to support his claim that the regular practice of *āsana* helped to make one's bones "as strong and supple as bamboo." One day he was on his scooter going about forty kph when he had an accident that sent him flying over the handlebars. Though bruised and scraped, he was not seriously hurt. After going to the hospital to get a tetanus shot, he was able to leave as scheduled for an appointment in Delhi. He was certain that various bones would have been broken had he not been doing *āsana* for many years.

After the opening day, the *shivir* settled into a standardized routine whereby Mr. Gupta would teach various *āsana* and *prāṇāyāma* techniques for about an hour. On this level, the only thing that distinguishes a *shivir* from a scheduled class is the fact that it is open to the public and is, in some sense, staged as a performance that is designed to expose people to yoga in the hope that they will continue to learn and practice on a regular basis in some more permanent venue. In other words, a *shivir* is, in many ways, an advertisement for yoga as such and, as an advertisement, it is a strategically staged performance. Though clearly Mr. Gupta and other *shivir* leaders are sincere and committed to what they believe to be the essence and integrity of yoga, they are clearly aware of their situational role as on-stage performers and the way in which their performance constructs yoga as a popular activity. This is even more apparent in the elaborately staged *shivir* events organized by the Bharatiya Yog Sansthan.

The Bharatiya Yog Sansthan

Though there are countless groups and organizations that promote the practice of yoga for health and welfare, the Bharatiya Yog Sansthan (BYS) is in many ways unique, as I have indicated in more detail elsewhere (Alter 1997). It was founded in the late 1960s in part to develop a program of yogic public health promotion. Though oriented toward a goal of health and wellness, the broader motivation for founding the BYS was political: The men involved were closely associated with the Rashtriya Swayamsevak Sangh (RSS; see Alter 1994).[2] The founders of the BYS were disillusioned by what they regarded as a general deterioration of Hindu cultural values in the post-independence decades and sought to promote yoga as a form of healthy self-discipline with a solidly "Vedic" pedigree.

Though many organizations promote yoga in various ways, the approach of the BYS is quite novel. After first meeting in a public park in Old Delhi and teaching themselves *āsana* and *prāṇāyāma*, the founders branched out and established independent units in other parks in the city. As these units increased in size and participants learned and perfected the hour-long routine of postures and breathing exercises, designated leaders branched off and established new units in other parks. The yoga routine of the BYS is structured such that one moves through a series of seated, prone, and standing postures that are ergonomically choreographed. Though rigidly structured, the routine is not difficult to follow, and once one has gone through the sequence several times, it becomes a matter of second nature. The structure of practice is self-consciously performative, as each unit stages its routine in a designated public park precisely to advertise the Sansthan (society or institute) as an organization that is open to the public, free, and based, exclusively, on voluntary public participation. The strategy of geometric growth has resulted in thousands of units being established throughout urban north India and, more recently, several in Australia, Canada, and the United Kingdom.

At base, the success of the BYS is a function of its simplicity, both in structure and in practice. Each unit meets in a public park at 5:00 a.m. and goes through an hour-long routine that is the same day after day. Technically, the organization requires no leadership or headquarters and is completely self-sustaining, and this is very much an ideal that is maintained in publicity and promotional material. In fact, though, the BYS is run by a small and very well-organized cadre of men based in a small apartment-sized office in Shalimar Bagh in north Delhi. Recently, the organization succeeded in fulfilling a long-standing ambition and constructed a five-story Yogashram and Research Center in one of the expanding suburbs of west Delhi. Among other things, the new facility has a large hall designed to accommodate yoga performances and is intended to enable the BYS to hold national and regional meetings. The organization has grown significantly since the late 1960s, but though the structure has changed somewhat, insofar as there is a small but powerful center of operations, the basic principle underlying the organization has not changed. As the BYS Web site puts it:

> Bharatiya Yog Sansthan (Regd.) came into being on 10th April 1967, it is non-sectarian, social, cultural and non-profit making organization. It firmly believes in Bharatiya cultural heritage and aims to re-establish protect and preserve it. It draws its inspiration from the lofty human ideals of Bharatiya culture viz "Vasudhaiv Kutumbkam"—Entire Universe Is Our Family—and "Loka Samasta Sukhino Bhavantu," "Sarve Bhaventu Sukhina"—may all be happy, may all being rejoice in joy and happiness and the like as "Live 'N' Liven"—may all live for the service of humanity and inspire others to live in the service of Almighty. To fulfill this aim Sansthan has chosen Yog as its means. The genesis of Yog have been adopted on the lines enshrined by Maharishi Patanjali. It has eight fold steps—Yam, Niyam, Asan, Pranayam, Pratyahar, Dharna, Dhyan and Samadhi (Bharatiya Yog Sansthan 2007).

Though the morning park-based units are designed as public events to attract attention and increase participation—much like a *shivir*—the BYS also organizes numerous camps throughout northern India. Many of these are on a very large scale, with several hundred attendees. Periodically massive camps with several thousand participants are held—or, more properly, staged—in large venues such as sports stadiums and playing fields. Though these are not quite on the scale of the camps organized by Swami Ramdev, where tens of thousands take part, the principle is largely the same: the larger the number of people who can be enlisted to participate, the better it reflects on the health and vitality of the sponsoring organization. Therefore, all camps, but the massive camps in particular, are staged and strategically choreographed performances.

In conjunction with its other activities, the BYS publishes a quarterly magazine titled *Yog Manjari*, which, in addition to carrying articles and the text of speeches and lectures given at camps, always contains several pages of color photographs taken at the ceremonial establishment of new park units and at various camps. Thus, the magazine gives a degree of permanence to these large-scale performances, which highlights the way in which they are public events that are meant to attract attention. Along these lines, it is important to note that camps almost explicitly invert the standard injunction found in many of the medieval manuals—that one should practice yoga alone in an isolated hut built far from other people in the middle of a forest. Though one could obviously develop a somewhat cynical critique of contemporary practice based on this, an alternative perspective allows one to appreciate the way in which spectacular, mass-drill public performances play off the simple logic of enumeration and the social consequences of endlessly repeating the mathematics of one-plus-one to translate an antisocial exercise into an eminently public activity. Such public activity has meaning unto itself but also indexes the profound significance of the all-alone-adept lost in the Himalayas secretly practicing yoga in complete isolation. The benefit of the former derives, in part, from the elusive possibility of the latter.

Patañjali, Embodied Character, and the Union of Mind and Body

Anyone familiar with the *Yogasūtra* of Patañjali is aware that it is not a treatise from which one can draw "life lessons," much less a work of philosophy in which the body figures very prominently. As Ian Whicher has recently pointed out (1998), the Classical Yoga of Patañjali is based on a materialist ontology, but the *Yogasūtra* itself is oriented toward transcendence, magic, and immortality, not the ethics and morality of everyday life. Conversely, Patañjali does outline five moral observances (*yama*: nonviolence, truthfulness, not stealing, chastity, greedlessness) and five restraints (*niyama*: purity, contentment, asceticism, study, devotion) that together establish the foundation of practice. Significantly, *yama* and *niyama*—along with the other six "branches" of *aṣṭāṅga* (lit. "eight limbs"), which include *āsana* and *prāṇāyāma*—should be understood as means to the end of enstatic[3] transcendence rather than socially valued ends unto themselves, even though, as we will see, this is exactly how they have come to be interpreted and how they factor into *shivir* rhetoric. Following this logic, yoga becomes a means to develop morals, standards of good character, and civic-mindedness, and the performativity of the *shivir* lends itself very well to advocacy for social and moral reform based on the "virtues" of *yama* and *niyama*.

As in the relatively small camp organized by the Aurobindo Society in Mussoorie, at BYS camps the primary goal is to get participants to perform *āsana* and *prāṇāyāma* in a mass-drill format. However, in both contexts the person, or persons, leading the *shivir* gave lectures stressing the way in which yoga can bring about positive sociomoral reform. In the case of the BYS, versions of these lectures are often published in the quarterly magazine. Several examples will provide a perspective on the tone and orientation of the lectures.

The BYS has been publishing *Yog Manjari* for almost thirty years and periodically publishes special theme issues. One issue published in 2005, for example, is devoted to the problem of greed and the virtue of greedlessness. The cover consists of a photographic montage at the center of which is a visibly distressed man, shackled to a wide range of expensive and iconically modern consumer goods—a wide-screen TV, limousine, expansive house, gold bars, and a computer. Several essays in the issue make points that are often repeated during *shivir* lectures.

> In society today one can see that everyone is trying to outdo everyone else. The root cause of this problem is greed. To purify this contaminated social environment it is absolutely essential that people renounce their desires and practice greedlessness (Bharati 2005: 3).

> For the members of the Bharatiya Yog Sansthan the most basic meaning of greedlessness is to perform your work with energy and full commitment but to dispassionately give away the fruits of one's labor so as to benefit society at large. Not only does this benefit people in general, it also has the effect of giving you peace of mind (Meenu 2005: 15).

> It is dharma (duty) of every wise man to adopt aparigraha [greedlessness] in his life in order to lead a happy and prosperous social and individual life. If people adopt aparigraha in their lives then the problem of conflict between the rich and poor will be solved to the maximum extent. Such a society in which there is fair distribution of money and material is called socialist pattern of society for which all the saints and seers of the world preach (Sharma 2005: 30).

The issue of *Yog Manjari* commemorating the fortieth anniversary of the founding of the BYS is also a special issue on celibacy. The cover shows several images of iconic celibates: Vivekananda, Hanuman, and Buddha. As in the case of *aparigraha, brahmacarya* (celibacy) is often spoken about in terms of its social value and virtue.

> Today we see different kinds of problem erupting day-by-day and no solution in sight. The human beings have lost the power of Brahmacharya, hence lost longevity, glory, strength, knowledge, wealth etc.... The question is why we were so powerful in the golden age period? The answer is, it is the power of celibacy which had given us that kind of strength to be a strong and powerful nation. It is said that at one time our nation was like

> a lighthouse or Dharm Guru for the whole world.... We were so systematic in those days because of the wisdom acquired through adopting celibacy (Rajeev 2006: 23–4)

Beyond the injunctions of *yama* and *niyama*, *shivir* lectures often use Patañjali's *Yogasūtra* and the *Bhagavadgītā* as points of reference for the articulation of a broad range of issues that have a bearing on the development of character, civic-minded public service, work ethics, and what might generally be regarded as "life skills." In most basic terms, the logic that is employed is that the practice of yoga involves self-discipline and mental control. The second aphorism of the *Yogasūtra*—*yogaścittavṛttinirodha*—which indicates the need to control fluctuations or modifications of the mind, is interpreted in various different ways to mean specific things in various contexts: Students should control their minds to learn more effectively, young people should control their minds so as to remain "single-mindedly" focused on productive work, employees should control their minds so as to get more work done, and the like. In other words, specific features in the philosophy of yoga can be given very broad pragmatic interpretation such that yoga becomes the antidote to a spectrum of different individual, social, moral, ethical, and interpersonal problems.

Unto itself, this is an interesting phenomenon, but what is particularly noteworthy, and what most likely answers the question of why *shivir* are popular, is the way in which a generalized rhetoric of reform anchored in the *Yogasūtra* is explicitly linked, through performance, to *āsana* and *prāṇāyāma*, and how the mass-drill format for *āsana* and *prāṇāyāma* produces a sense of community with a common purpose. This is most clearly reflected in the performance of a *prāṇāyāma* exercise wherein individuals seated in *padmāsana* are instructed to collectively throw their arms in the air and laugh as loudly as possible. I was told on a number of occasions—and have heard about it in the context of *shivir* lectures—that this puts everyone into the same refreshed, uninhibited frame of mind and helps to promote a positive outlook on life. However, even when there is no explicit connection made between rhetoric and a specific *āsana*, the implicit correlation of the two in performance has the effect of giving to the physical practice of yoga an amplified and specified mental significance.

Conclusion

Since yoga has become extremely popular the world over, it is becoming increasingly important to understand the context and form of practice, because the notion of "doing" yoga or "learning" yoga does not capture very well the many different ways in which yoga can be performed and taught. Along with this, it is also important to understand the way in which yoga, as represented in the classical and medieval literature—which reveals differences and delineations in the form, structure, and meaning of practice—tends to get blurred together with modern and postmodern formulations.

Even though many people assume that by performing *āsana* and *prāṇāyāma* they are doing yoga, variability in contexts of performance begs the question of meaning and the coherence of meaning across space and time. As I have argued elsewhere (Alter: manuscript), it is impossible to draw a firm line above which all forms of practice are "legitimate" and below which they are not. Given this situation, what is crucial is that any analysis of practice must be critically historicized and that all claims to both originality and orthopraxy be scrutinized so as to understand why the claims are made rather than whether they are true. Here my concern has been to extend this reasoning by showing that to escape from the recursive paradox that is produced by the question of authenticity, one can focus on yoga's performativity, and the way in which performativity indexes the possibility, rather than the realization, of a "pure and authentic" form of practice. Performativity also enables one to take seriously interpretations of meaning—such as many of those discussed here—that a radical historicization of practice would not.

Notes

1 Indian state to the West of Delhi.

2 The RSS is a militant Hindu organization that conceptualizes itself as providing social services and community reform and moral leadership. Though ostensibly apolitical, in terms of leadership it has been closely affiliated with the (BJP) Bharatiya Janta Party and exerted considerable political influence in the late 1990s.

3 A term coined by Mircea Eliade to indicate the way in which yoga produces an internalized, embodied experience of externalized ecstasy.

Bibliography

Alter, J.S. (1994) Somatic Nationalism: Indian Wrestling and Militant Hinduism, *Modern Asian Studies*, 28 (3): 557–88.

— (1997) A Therapy to Live By: Public Health, the Self, and Nationalism in the Practice of a North Indian Yoga Society, *Medical Anthropology*, 11: 275–98.

—(2000) *Knowing Dil Das: Stories of a Himalayan Hunter*, Philadelphia: University of Pennsylvania Press, Series in Contemporary Ethnography.

—[Manuscript] Uninhibited Modifications of the Mind: Reflections on Yoga, Sex, and the Politics of Knowledge.

Aurobindo, S. (1976) *The Synthesis of Yoga*, Pondicherry: Sri Aurobindo Ashram.

—(1977) *The Life Divine*, 10th edn, Pondicherry: Sri Aurobindo Ashram.

Ayangar, T.R.S. (1893) *Haṭhayogapradīpikā of Svātmarāma Svāmin*, Bombay: Tookaram Tatya.

Bharati, Swami A. (2005) Aparigraha, *Yog Manjari* 28: 3.

Bharatiya Yog Sansthan (2007) Available HTTP <http://www.yogsansthan.org/enter.asp> (accessed September 2007).

Brahmananda Baba (1889) *Hathayogapradipika of Svatmarama Svamin*, Bombay: No Publisher.

Butler, J. (1997) *Excitable Speech: A Politics of the Performative*, New York: Routledge.

Clifford, J. and G. Marcus (1985) *Writing Culture: The Poetics and Politics of Ethnography*, Berkeley: University of California Press.

Divya Yog Mandir (2007a) Available HTTP <http://www.divyayoga.com/patanjali.htm> (last accessed September 2007).

—(2007b) Available HTTP <http://www.divyayoga.com/YogScienceCamp.htm> (accessed September 2007)

—(2007c) Available HTTP <http://www.divyayoga.com/TVProgram.htm> (accessed September 2007).

Iyengar, B.K.S. (1993) *The Art of Yoga*, New Delhi: Indus (HarperCollins).

Meenu (2005) Aparigraha ka Samajik Pahlu, *Yog Manjari* 28: 15.

Rabinow, P. (1977) *Reflections on Fieldwork in Morocco*, Berkeley: University of California Press.

Rajeev (2006) Celibacy (Brahmacharya), *Yog Manjari* 29: 23–4.

Sharma, O.P. (2005) Aparigraha and Its Practice, *Yoga Manjari* 28: 30.

Urban, H. (2003) *Tantra: Sex, Secrecy, Politics, and Power in the Study of Religion*, Berkeley: University of California Press.

Vasaka, B.C. (1877) *Gheranda Samhita*, Bombay: Theosophical Society.

Vasu, S.C. (1996) *The Siva Samhita*, Delhi: Munshiram Manoharlal.

Whicher, I. (1998) *The Integrity of the Yoga Darsana: A Reconsideration of Classical Yoga*, Albany: SUNY Press

3 "Adapt, Adjust, Accommodate"

The Production of Yoga in a Transnational World

Sarah Strauss

Introduction

The Divine Life Society (DLS) is a spiritual organization founded by Swami Sivananda of Rishikesh, India. Sivananda's DLS, including associated centers across India and abroad, has figured prominently in expanding the role of yoga as a tool for the development of modern India.[1] The DLS presents a well-defined example of the transformation of yoga's place in Indian society. In addition to contemporary ethnographic data, I use Sivananda's own poetry and the many pamphlets and books produced by both Sivananda, his contemporaries, and his successors through the twentieth century in India to understand some aspects of how the promotion and practice of yoga has contributed to the ongoing Indian nationalist project, as well as the transnational or global forces that became dominant in the latter half of the twentieth century. A comparison with the yoga institutions founded by a few of Sivananda's contemporaries highlights general trends and specific differences in the uses to which yoga has been put during the twentieth century.

The significance of the DLS as a spiritual institution in India owes much to Sivananda's noted predecessor, Swami Vivekananda, who came from India to Chicago for the 1893 Columbian Exposition's Parliament of the World's Religions. Vivekananda's presentation of yoga to the Western public and his subsequent re-presentation of yoga to his countrymen in India four years later[2] marks a turning point in the way in which this ancient system of ideas and practices has been understood. Poised between worlds, Vivekananda drew on both his experiences as a privileged child of the Calcutta *bhadralok* ("respectable people"), a well-educated son of a judge, and his commitment to Sri Ramakrishna, devotee of the Goddess and Hindu exemplar-saint for the alienated middle-class youth of Calcutta (Sarkar 1992). Since Vivekananda's time, the term *yoga* has taken on a life of its own, coming to signify everything from the "Wonder That Was India" (*pace* Basham 1954) to a method for universal salvation. Sivananda used Vivekananda's division of the yoga tradition into four major orientations—*Rāja, Bhakti, Jñāna, Karma*—as the basis for most of his own writings about yoga, and Vivekananda's organizations, the Ramakrishna Math and Mission and the Vedanta Societies in the West, as models for his own Divine Life Society in

Rishikesh. Though all four of Vivekananda's yogas are taught at the DLS, here I am primarily concerned with *Rāja*_Yoga, the "kingly" yoga, which comprises both moral and physical practices. *Rāja* yoga is also known as "Classical Yoga", as codified by Patañjali approximately 1,700 years ago.

The Rise of the DLS

In the 1920s, the not-yet-famous historian of religions, Mircea Eliade, sought out Sivananda at his ashram in Rishikesh. Eliade was one of the earliest foreigners to seek training from Sivananda; many other disciples from that time were educated Brahmans from southern India (DLS 1987), Tamil, or Malayali speakers who were also well educated in English. By 1936, the group had become large enough and Sivananda's reputation wide enough that he felt it necessary to create an official organization, the Divine Life Society. The Swami wrote many different works and was known to compose little poems and songs to express his feelings; one such poem describes his reasons for founding the DLS when he did:

The Critical Juncture

Students became irreligious,
They lost faith in religion,
Under the influence of Science,
They neglected Dharma,
They began to smoke and gamble,
Girls became fashionable,
Officers became materialists,
Health of people deteriorated,
People shunned the scriptures,
Materialism had its sway.

At this critical juncture,
To revive the Glory of the Lord,
To disseminate knowledge of Yoga,
To preach the Yoga of synthesis,
To instill devotion and faith in people,
To work for spiritual uplift of mankind,
To bring peace and bliss to every home,
I established the Divine Life Mission
And founded the Yoga-Vedanta Forest Academy,
In a sacred, charming spot in the Himalayas,
On the banks of the Holy Ganges in Rishikesh
(DLS 1987: 22)

This poem sets up a classic opposition between religion and science; as a Tamil Brahman[3] medical doctor trained in the methods of Western science, Sivananda was in the position of speaking for both sides, or more precisely, of seeking middle ground by reconciling the two. Sivananda directly links the influence of Western science on the development of a "materialist"perspective and the subsequent decline in health status. Despite Sivananda's general references to "people," "mankind," and "every home," we can imagine that the lower castes and classes in India were not particularly likely to have become the military officers and fashionable ladies described in this poem. Indeed, later official descriptions of the DLS reveal the target population for the mission outlined above: "The Society offers a peaceful haven wherein is provided ample opportunity and actual help for the restoration of peace to the troubled, conflict-ridden and psychologically traumatized personality of the modern man" (Sivananda 1988: 174), and "[t]he Society also functions as an ideal place of retreat for the *educated citizen of the world*, wherein he can renew himself and recreate and refresh his being, physically, mentally, morally, and spiritually" (Sivananda 1988: 172; emphasis added).

As part of the commemorative volume for Sivananda's birth centenary celebrations in 1986, DLS President Swami Chidananda spoke directly to Sivananda's purpose in founding the institution. In his essay, titled "Sivananda—An Answer to the Need of the Time" (DLS 1987:14–17), Chidananda blames the state of the nation on the alienation of the educated classes from traditional Hindu values. He comments that,

> the once orthodox upper class, the once jealous custodians of the scriptures, themselves now fell a prey to the advent of new ideas and ideals from the Occident...*The systematic adoption of English as the medium of instruction following Lord Macaulay's Minute of 1835, converted the once exclusive custodians of Sanskrit lore into a new English-knowing educated class that supplied the Company with qualified scribes, interpreters, assistants, etc...the role of reviver and reclaimer of scriptural knowledge and of spiritual life, devolved upon one who was himself of this new class.* And the irony of it all lay in the fact that he had necessarily to do this work in the very language that had brought on the decadence which he was to arrest (DLS 1987: 15; emphasis added).

Two interesting points emerge from this essay. First, Chidananda situates the work of his master Sivananda in a long line of people, including Tulsidas, Ekanath Maharaj, and Annie Besant, who made key texts and teachings such as those of the *Rāmāyaṇa* and the *Bhagavad Gītā* available to the general populace in vernacular languages as a way of restoring lost heritage; however, he does not mention Vivekananda, whose activities were among the most comparable to Sivananda's own, especially with regard to the use of English to accommodate the "educated classes." Perhaps it is that very similarity that Chidananda hoped to avoid in proclaiming the unique suitability of Sivananda to his task of "saving the moderns." Second, though Chidananda describes the "decadence" that Sivananda is to arrest in terms of a "commercial and mercenary" attitude on the part of the entire Indian nation, it must be noted that Sivananda's own efforts to combat this attitude included a flood of English-medium publications offered specifically for sale.

The stated "aims and objectives" of the DLS have always included a heavy emphasis on distribution of written publications and, at various points, other media such as phonograph records, audiocassettes, photographs of Sivananda, and videocassettes. Every publication is available in English, but the most popular items are usually translated into at least Hindi and Tamil and sometimes into Bengali, Gujarati, Malayalam, or Marathi. In the late 1980s and early 1990s, a German couple associated with the DLS of Cologne began translating publications into German and distributing them, and representatives of other language groups have initiated similar efforts at various times.

The DLS presents itself today as a modern service organization that provides social, educational, and medical support to the local and global communities. The five current objectives are:

> 1) dissemination of spiritual knowledge through "publication of books, pamphlets and magazines dealing with ancient, oriental, and occidental philosophy, religion and medicine in the modern scientific manner...by holding and arranging frequent spiritual discourses and conferences...[b]y establishing training centers or societies for the practice of Yoga...[and] doing all such acts and things as may be necessary and conducive to the moral, spiritual and cultural uplift of mankind in general";
> 2) establishment and management of educational institutions "on modern lines and on right basic principles";
> 3) provision of aid to "deserving orphans and destitutes";
> 4) establishment and management of medical organizations; and
> 5) enaction of other measures which "may be necessary for effecting a quick and effective moral and spiritual regeneration in the world" (DLS 1987: 34).

Though many charitable works are indeed conducted by the DLS, the financial situation of the institution is extremely strong,[4] and many of its services and publications are not provided without a fee. Prices for audio and video cassettes in 1992 were in the $6–15 range when purchased directly at the DLS ashram. This is not to say that the DLS is primarily a commercial institution, for they are indeed involved in many charitable activities. Among their other activities, outreach from Rishikesh is significant. In the 1950s, Sivananda sent a number of his disciples, mostly Indians but also one returning Canadian, to the West with the explicit mission of teaching yoga. The disciples in the West, unlike the disciples who were sent to Malaysia, and other locations in Asia to set up new branches of the Divine Life Society, started their own organizations, most of which are still quite active today. The better-known of these include the Sivananda Yoga Vedanta Centres and the Integral Yoga Institutes, founded by Swamis Vishnudevananda and Satchidananda,[5] respectively.

The DLS today continues to provide free instruction to Indians and foreigners alike. Donations are welcome, but there is no pressure on the average person to give; statements of typical or expected amounts for lodging, meals, or instruction—

common at many ashrams—are here absent. Very few of the publications are available free of charge, but one can subscribe to the monthly journal or buy publications and products in Rishikesh at reasonable prices, though the same items at branch or affiliated institutions tend to cost much more.[6] Recently, there has been a trend toward publishing Sivananda's writings online.[7] Since its inception, the DLS has inspired both Indian and foreign interest in the practice of yoga and provided a nexus, first in India and now globally and virtually, where many different kinds of people could come together in the pursuit of spiritual enrichment. Sivananda created the DLS as a way to continue Vivekananda's work, both on the home front, strengthening India's citizens, and abroad, bringing India's rich traditions to a wider audience.

Independence: the DLS and the New Nation

With this general overview of the history of the DLS in mind, I focus now on the evolution of this institution during the period surrounding Indian independence, a "critical juncture" in the history of India and the DLS. The pre-Independence (1947) period saw an increase in the activities of the DLS, with ever more disciples and lay members from many countries joining the community. During this time, the DLS produced many books and pamphlets through the in-house press, the Sivananda Publication League, and Sivananda's reputation continued to spread. With the expansion of the DLS, we begin to see a tension arising between Sivananda's broad goal of global spiritual unity and his attention, however muted, to the politics of Indian nationalism. The events surrounding World War II, particularly the development of nuclear weapons technology, provided a rationale for many people, in India and elsewhere, to take up the practice of yoga. In the aftermath of the War, Sivananda's message of universal unity and brotherhood became still more appealing. The development of nuclear weapons created a world in which it was no longer possible to imagine completely detachable nations, able to withdraw into their own shells and remain unaffected by events on the other side of the globe (Omkarananda 1960: 94). Peace and security, wherever and however they could be found, were top priorities for many of the people who sought Sivananda's advice, whether in person or through his standing offer of a "postal"discipleship.

Word of Sivananda's teachings reached many foreigners through the availability of his English-medium pamphlets. In the 1940s, a German man named Boris Sacharow became a: "disciple-by-mail"; he never visited Sivananda in India but nevertheless did gain his recognition as a *"yogiraj"*(Fuchs 1990), or master of yoga. Sacharow began the first yoga school in Germany and is today considered one of the main forces in the development of professional yoga instruction in Europe. One of the cornerstones of his instruction was the so-called Rishikesh *Reihe* ("sequence") of postures, which he learned from Sivananda and which was often cited when I asked German yoga students in 1992 their reasons for coming to Rishikesh to study. The increasing number of disciples and correspondents from the West supplemented the growing popularity of the DLS in India (DLS 1985a). In

1945, Sivananda announced the creation of an "All-World Religions' Federation" and in 1948, the Yoga-Vedanta Forest Academy at the DLS headquarters. Both were designed to accommodate the "systematic spiritual training" (DLS 1987: 24) of residents and visitors alike. India's independence in 1947 created further opportunities for reflection on questions of religious freedom, political alignment, and the new United Nations and the importance of bringing India up to speed in the Modern World. India's position as a leader of the nonaligned movement (Gupta 1992) meshed well with the frequently heard assertion that India had a universal spiritual message to share.

The *Diamond Jubilee Commemoration Volume of Sri Swami Sivananda* was published on September 8, 1947 and contained many references to India's newfound independence (August 15, 1947), while retaining the organization's universalist message. Prefatory pages included two songs written by Sivananda, "The Universal Anthem" and "Mother India: A National Anthem." In the first, Sivananda extols,

> glory to Thee, O fair Mother Earth, common Parent of all,...Though conduct, actions and behaviour appear as diverse, One alone is the power that works in the Universe. Though words and languages differ in Peking or in Rome, One alone is the Primal Sound, the Root Vibration OM....As one Sun illumines the whole Earth outside, the One Spirit Universal in Man doth reside,...A Golden Cord Spiritual, the whole world to bind, in bonds of Love and Brotherhood and Unity Eternal (DLS 1947: xxx).

But on the next page, he strikes a different chord:

> May God bless Mother India, our sacred glorious Hind, The land of Rishis, Yogis, Sages of high spiritual culture. India is the only land where God-realization is the goal; India is the only land where Rishis, yogis abound...It is a land of Dharma, where people practice Yama and Niyama, It is a sacred land, where holy Ganges, Jumna, Sindhu flow; It is a peaceful land of broad tolerance, where all religionists dwell, Glory to India, glory to Hind...May India's fame extend fully all over the world! (DLS 1947: xxxi)

In the space of two pages, Sivananda demonstrates the two cornerstones of the DLS: universal unity, expressed in English as a transnational medium, and a national identity for India based on Patañjali's eight-fold path of *rāja* yoga, which takes *yama* and *niyama*, roughly translated as moral observances and self-discipline, as its first two steps. Sivananda's message, as we have discussed already, strongly echoes that of Vivekananda. There is no question that the Ramakrishna Mission and the writings of Vivekananda inspired the creation of the DLS, for both assert the value of yoga as a universal science and emphasize service in the world (or *karma* yoga) as a way to transcendence of it. In addition, the tension between the universalist and the Hindu nationalist positions that appears in Vivekananda's writings is also present in Sivananda's work. The tendency, as McKean describes so well in her analysis of the 1987 Sivananda

Birth Centenary celebration (1996: 212–75), is for the DLS to project outwardly an image of universal tolerance while simultaneously catering to the agenda of wealthy Hindu nationalists.

Even more explicit is an article by Sri Rajani Mohan Chakravarty, B.A., L.L.B., of Calcutta, from the same Diamond Jubilee volume, entitled "Spiritual Rejuvination [sic] of India," heralding Sivananda as the savior of modern civilization:

> Thus in this present age—the age of godless materialism, spiritual bankruptcy, of endless divisions of sects and classes, of struggles and strifes, God sent His Divine Messenger in the form of Swami Sivananda. He showed to the modern East, steeped in bigotry and narrowness, a new light of self-dependence and catholicity: and to the power-drunk West, believing in nothing but the power of the material sciences, the fundamental Truth of the Upanishadic Sages, the lofty ideals of the Vedanta, mellowed in the fiery furnace of Universality and Love for God....Let his appearence [sic] in the world be marked with the dawn of a new era of universal spiritual awakening and world-federation on a spiritual basis, and let his message of Truth and Love spread in ever-widening circles over the entire human Society for meeting the supreme demand of the age (DLS 1947: 171).

In such a tribute to Sivananda, we can see addressed many of the concerns particularly relevant to educated members of the Indian middle classes during the years following Independence, Partition, and the rise of the UN and other post–World War II international organizations: sectarian violence, the global mindset, and the relative importance of material well-being. At the end of the Diamond Jubilee publication, we learn that the,

> aims, objects and principles of the Divine Life Society are broad and universal. It expounds in a rational and scientific manner the Yoga of Synthesis, and propounds that any man can attain the Goal of life in his own station of life in the midst of varied avocations. It is real Spiritual Universality intended to free men from the thraldom of this painful Samsara; from the wheel of birth and death (DLS 1947; back cover).

In examining the writings of S. Radhakrishnan, vice president of India at the time this was written in 1947, one can see the same concerns highlighted (e.g., Radhakrishnan 1992 [1939]: 33, 48, 109, 383). Radhakrishnan also used Vivekananda's teachings to develop his political stance (Das 1992: 77). Such compatibility between the aims of the DLS and the aims of the Indian government as expressed through its elected officials has continued into the present. When I was living in Rishikesh in 1992, the current President of India came to visit the DLS to have the *darśan* (visual contact, understood as a blessing) of Swami Chidananda, and everyone in town knew about the visit. Another yoga-related export recently promoted by the government of India has been postage stamps.

Both Vivekananda, and more recently Sivananda, have been recognized for their contributions to the nation in the issuance of a postage stamp—the official "stamp of approval" (Figure 3.1). And an entire series of quite costly stamps depicting four different hat.ha yoga postures has also been produced for the international market (Figure 3.2).

Additional activities of the DLS explained in this 1947 publication are the training of students on site to be "highly useful to the world in some form or other," including the dispatching of students for "Propaganda Tours" to facilitate the "regeneration of youths" and the promotion of "Health and Long Life" through "classes on Asans, Pranayams, well-regulated diet, Satsang, well-disciplined life, nature-cure methods." Other services and products were gramophone records, movies, and Magic Lantern lectures on the lives of Saints, *āsana* demonstrations, and the life story of Sivananda; activities for "Rural Uplift" such as providing health care, financial aid, primary schooling, and spiritual lectures to the residents of neighboring villages; a way-station for pilgrims traveling to the high shrines of Badri and Kedarnath; "special poojas" and *yajñās* performed "frequently for the peace and prosperity of the world"; ongoing performance of the *māhāmantra* "by turns all the 24 hours every day

Figure 3.1 Postage stamp of Sivananda (Government of India issue, 1986)

Figure 3.2 Postage stamp of *yogāsanas* (Government of India issue, 1986)

from December, 1943 onwards" for the "peace and prosperity of the world, health and long life of the devotees, and for relieving the sickness of the persons who send their requests." Many of these events and services continue to be provided by the DLS today.

From September to November of 1950, Sivananda undertook his first and only major tour of India, establishing new branches of the DLS and making contacts in urban and rural areas alike. The All-India tour took Sivananda from Rishikesh east across Uttar Pradesh, through the cities of Lucknow and Banaras, through Bihar to Calcutta; south to Madras and then Cape Cormorin, the southernmost point in India; north up the center of the subcontinent through Bangalore and Mysore, west across to Pune and Bombay; and finally through Baroda and Ahmedabad to Delhi before returning home to Rishikesh—a total of more than 7,500 miles (DLS 1951: xi–xxiv).

Before setting out from Rishikesh, Sivananda and his associates participated in a farewell banquet at the Railway Station, to which all the "important personages of Rishikesh" were invited, including the station master, the postmaster, the police officer, the bank manager, some businessmen, a representative of the Tehri Royal family, and many senior *saṃnyāsins*. The official account states that the "service and the layout were in European style; but the spirit was thoroughly Indian, as also the dishes" (DLS 1951: 3). As Sivananda made ready to depart from the Rishikesh Railway station with his entourage, he spoke to the gathered crowd, saying, "If you want to enjoy peace and happiness, practice this simple Sadhana. Adapt, Adjust, and Accommodate. Lack of this divine quality of adaptability is the cause for disharmony, quarrels, riots and wars" (DLS 1951: 5). What a clear picture of the DLS this gives: The structure and material goods are European, but the substance, the spirit, and the food, are Indian—a truly transnational blend! Here we see no signs of radical activism. Instead, we have the essence of middle-class conformity, the perfect colonial-national subject-citizen, who never makes a fuss and expects that if one simply "adjusts, adapts, and accommodates," everything will be fine.

According to the tour volume's editor, Swami Venkatesananda (DLS 1951: xvi), the purpose of undertaking this tour of India was to preach tolerance, love, understanding, and harmony to counteract the religious intolerance that had swept the world. Certainly, the rift between Hindus and practitioners of Islam on the subcontinent, which had driven Partition and ripped apart the lives of millions, was a pressing concern at the time that this All-India Tour was planned. Sivananda's intention was apparently

> to spread the Gospel of spiritual evolution and universal peace and love... never was the need for peace and good-will among nations so great or so urgent as [then]. If the world [was] to save itself from the physical devastation, the moral degradation and the other calamitous consequences of a third world war, there [was] only one way... (DLS 1951: xxi).

His approach to solving the world's problems, as well as India's, was fundamentally grounded in personal reform, both physical and spiritual, and the notion that if each individual made him- or herself into a better person, the world would indeed be a better place. Two days after starting out, Sivananda spoke to two young boys who had come into his train compartment, telling them to "[s]erve, love, give, purify, meditate, realize—these few words give you the essence of Yoga and Vedanta. Be good, do good, be kind, be compassionate. This is what all the scriptures teach! If you do these simple things, the whole world will love you..." (DLS 1951: 7).

The Parliament of the World's Religions: Once, Twice, and Again

During this 1950 All-India tour, Sivananda presented his universalist message around the nation, in lecture halls and on trains, over the radio, and in the villages. The tour also set the stage for Sivananda's next venture, a reinvention of the Parliament of the World's Religions that had launched Vivekananda's rise in the public arena in 1893. That original exposition, held in Chicago, was organized by a committee composed of a variety of Christian denominations who had invited representatives of other world religions to join them in a global celebration. One theme that had contributed strongly to Vivekananda's popularity in 1893 was that of universal brotherhood, a community of like-minded folk transcending national boundaries. Vivekananda's suggestions for the development of a universal brotherhood resonated quite well with members of the American and European middle and upper classes, for whom the shortcomings of industrial society were becoming all too apparent; his program for change also suited the needs of the emergent nationalists in India, who were comfortable with his hybrid East-West discourse (Bharati 1970; Sarkar 1985).

In 1993, a centennial celebration of the 1893 Parliament of the World's Religions was held, once again in Chicago. The 1993 event came into being largely through the efforts of the Chicago Hindu community, including but not limited to the membership of the Ramakrishna Mission/Vedanta Society of Chicago. Though not explicitly stated, the success of the 1993 centennial endeavor seems to have been viewed as something of a turnabout—instead of Christian groups convening the event and inviting only those whom they chose, this time the Hindu community was instrumental in determining the agenda.

However, between the 1893 and 1993 world parliaments was another that was less well known. In 1953, sixty years after the first Chicago gathering, Swami Sivananda hosted his own Parliament of the World's Religion at the DLS headquarters in Rishikesh, India. Sivananda chose to use the format of a parliament to showcase the contributions his institution could make to both his country and the world. As with the 1947 Diamond Jubilee, the 1953 Parliament was simultaneously presented as a tribute to Indian nationhood and a step toward solving global problems. Because of their insistence on promoting what they claimed to be universal truths and solidarity across national and religious boundaries, the DLS was embraced by Congress politicians and other yoga organizations as demonstrating the spiritual path to the future. In the Commemoration Volume created for the 1953 event, Swami Sadananda comments that

> this Parliament of Religion was not held in response to the desire of religious organizations to establish a unity of religions or a common basis of understanding among them. It was the outcome of the overflowing love of a single person who has come into the world only for the purpose of saving mankind (DLS 1956: 19).

Again we can see how Sivananda actively modeled himself and his organization on Vivekananda and the Ramakrishna Mission; in the early years, before incorporation, the DLS was referred to as the Divine Life Mission, and many aspiring disciples were sent first to their local Ramkrishna Mission for training before coming to Rishikesh to stay. The production of a Parliament of Religions on site at Sivanandanagar clearly represents another step on this path, and in fact goes the extra measure of bringing the global focus home to India.

At the1953 Parliament, Sivananda focused on security for post-Independence India and a post-War world, making his feelings regarding India's superiority as a new nation evident. In his opening address, Sir C.P. Ramaswamy Aiyar, Vice Chancellor of Annamalai University in Madras, presented his analysis of the state of the world and the place of India and the Parliament of Religions in it:

> The 19th century dethroned reason for economic progress, industrial development. Economic progress was enthroned in the 19th century. In the twentieth century today, we are on a quest for security.
>
> Security from what, of what? Of mankind, from fear—fear against war, against economic enslavement, against creedal and ideological differences... in this stage, when the whole world is gripped by the domination of this fear, our Parliament of Religions, and especially the contribution of India to that Parliament of Religions, is and can be noteworthy; because if India stands for anything, it stands for freedom, liberation from fear, the realization of the supremacy of the Self and the oneness of the Self with all other selves—that is the contribution which India can make to world peace (DLS 1956:39).

By emphasizing the importance of security as synonymous with Berlin's (1958) negative freedom, that is "Freedom From" rather than "Freedom To," Sivananda and the other speakers at the 1953 Parliament exemplify the type of modern society characterized by attention to risks that has been the central focus for the work of Ulrich Beck (1992). Beck claims that many contemporary societies, rather than being classified as "post-modern," should be seen as fully modern "risk societies." For these primarily Western societies, but increasingly including the rest of the world (and clearly at least the English-speaking Indian civil and religious leaders associated with Sivananda and his Parliament), reflexivity concerning the conditions of modernity, under which "'the social production of *wealth* is accompanied by the social production of *risks*" (Beck 1992: 19, emphasis in the original), becomes the primary concern. One arena within which Beck notes a great deal of change as compared with earlier forms of modernity is that of community; he comments that

> as traditional forms of community beyond the family [begin] to disappear... newly formed social relationships and social networks now have to be individually chosen; social ties, too, are becoming *reflexive*, so that they have to be established, maintained, and constantly renewed by individuals (Beck 1992: 97—emphasis in the original).

One of the driving forces behind the new forms of community characteristic of such risk societies is the "commonality of anxiety" (Beck 1992: 49). It is for these shared fears of political strife at the international (cold war) or national (Partition) levels; of health impacts, whether at the global or local environmental levels; or in terms of the physical, mental, and spiritual stresses affecting the individual person, that the neo-Hindu Renaissance standard-bearers such as Vivekananda and Sivananda offer solutions.

The *Hindustan Times* of April 7, 1953 offered the following report of the closing session of the Parliament in Rishikesh: "Mr. Ananthasayanam Ayyangar, Deputy Speaker of the House of the People...appealed to the USA and the Soviet union to 'come together as early as possible, give up atomic weapons and utilize their energies for the common human welfare.'" This theme is also present a few years later, with the dedication of the International Vishwayatan Yogashram in Delhi. The *Times of India* reported on March 3, 1958 that, among others, Pandit Nehru, Indira Gandhi, and Morarji Desai were present for the opening comments by philosopher and Vice President of India, S.Radhkrishnan:

> The purpose of yoga, Dr. Radhakrishnan explained, was to enable man to achieve...harmony. Yoga, the Vice-President said, did not aim at promoting physical well-being only...but prompted us to adopt certain practices which enabled us to become integrated individuals and to serve the common purpose of cosmic evolution...

The presence of leading political figures at both Sivananda's Parliament and the Delhi yogashram opening, and the press coverage in major English-medium newspapers, attest to the significant relationship between yoga ideology and practice and popular ideas of national and international harmony.

Fifty years later, the concern shown for security and universal peace was also present in 1993 at the centenary celebration of the Parliament of the World's Religions. There, following on the heels of the collapse of Soviet socialism and the Rio Earth Summit in 1992, environmental security was the central concern, though nuclear weapons proliferation and other global security issues were also addressed. Of prime importance for many of the participants at the 1993 Parliament was the need for recognizing the mutual interdependence of peoples and nations. One of the keynote speakers at the 1993 Parliament was Swami Chidananda, Sivananda's successor as president of the DLS. The head of the Hindu Host Committee for the centenary celebration of the Parliament introduced Chidananda through a recitation of his spiritual lineage: from St. Francis, to Ramakrishna, Vivekananda, and of course Sivananda, and introduced him as the "honorary president of the Hindu faith"—a reference to the fact that Chidananda had been elected as head of the Hindu delegation to the Parliament afteer the sudden death of Swami Chinmayananda[8] by a heart attack in the week prior to the meeting.

The theme of universal brotherhood was woven throughout the 1993 Parliament, where it held together calls for world peace and global environmental action along with spiritual unity. For example, in Chidananda's piece entitled "Authentic Religion," he states that "We are non-different. We are children of the One Being. Essentially, we are all one. But it is a matter of great regret that up till now religion has failed in its global mission of unifying man" (Chidananda 1993). Though Chidananda, and indeed the contemporary DLS more generally, tend to focus on philosophical and religious ideologies of monism, Sivananda himself promoted unification through common practice, making it clear that belief was less important for creating community than was shared action. Through participation in common practices, both those carried out individually and as part of a group endeavor, Sivananda felt that differences among people could be overcome and the world be made a safer place. As Eliade comments in his essays on India, all of the swamis that he met at Swarag-Ashram in 1930, including Sivananda, told him the same thing: "They say, 'we are all One' and, this is the important thing, they never cease to put this affirmation into practice. They help one another, become selfless before their friends, and practice seva (service)" (Eliade 1988: 175).[9] Chidananda (1993) acknowledges these teachings but then stresses that prayer is the most important thing and that Sivananda's "true" intentions were to convey this sentiment.

I understand the shift from Sivananda's action orientation to Chidananda's contemplative one in two ways. First, the evolution of message is something that takes place in any religious tradition. New leaders must differentiate themselves by their interpretations without straying so far from the basic texts as to cause alienation. Second, the shift away from the practice of yoga was confirmed by my experiences with yoga classes at the DLS in 1992; though yoga classes are listed as part of the daily schedule at the ashram, teachers are often reassigned to other tasks, so cancellations are common. This shift tends to affect foreigners visiting the ashram more severely, as there tend to be more non-Indians interested in *haṭha* yoga classes at the DLS. The result of the shift, also supported by other policy decisions discussed below, is that the DLS is made less appealing or accessible for foreigners, a stance that is in accord with the shift toward Hindu nationalism in North Indian politics over the last few decades.

"Scientific Yoga": Strong Bodies for a Strong Indian Nation

Yoga was a useful tool for breaking free of the Raj in the early decades of the twentieth century. From the decade or so before Sivananda first arrived in Rishikesh in 1924 through to Independence in 1947, many other organizations and ashrams overtly emphasized—or at least covertly embodied—nationalist ideas. As a technique for achieving freedom from political bondage, yoga was particularly evident in the works of Sri Yogendra and Swami Kuvalayananda, who founded yoga centers in the Bombay region in 1919 and 1924, respectively, and were both involved in developing programs of yoga specifically geared toward youth and school curricula. Kuvalayananda was also one of the main proponents of the scientific analysis and validation of yogic techniques. In both cases, yoga was promoted as an ancient Indian solution to a contemporary problem created by Western contact, thus staying well within the framework for understanding yoga established by Vivekananda.

Swami Kuvalayananda founded the Kaivalyadhama Institute of Lonavla in 1924. This institution's use of yoga to promote the nationalist cause was extremely prominent:

> An ardent lover of freedom and independent spirit... [Kuvalayanda] got great inspiration from ardent nationalists like Shri Aurobindo and Lokamanya Tilak. He wanted to generate the spirit of freedom and patriotism in the youths of India and to make them fit in every way--bodily, mentally and intellectually for the struggle that lay ahead... (Kaivalyadhama Institute 1975: Ch. 5–n.p.)

Kuvalayanada and Sivananda, whose lifetimes overlapped nearly completely—1887–1963 for Sivananda and 1883–1966 for Kuvalayananda—both drew inspiration from the life and writings of Swami Vivekananda but developed their own organizations following two distinctive tracks. Both highlighted the importance of education and the dissemination of written materials about yoga. Sivananda, though a medical doctor interested in the health benefits of yoga practice, asked his disciples to focus on the provision of selfless service, or *karma* yoga as it had been defined by Vivekananda and demonstrated by the activities of the Ramakrishna Mission. Kuvalayananda, however, emphasized the scientific validation of yoga practice as a health-promoting program through scientific research and experimentation. Both were concerned with the development of good citizens of the nation and the world and of the universality of yoga as a technique for promoting world harmony, peace, and freedom, issues that also appear first in Vivekananda's writings. Sivananda presented these ideas directly to the middle-class householders and travelers who came to the ashram in Rishikesh and sent his disciples out to open affiliated centers for promotion of his teachings around India and the world. Kuvalayananda took a very different direction. Though he, too, taught householders and disciples at his ashram in Lonavla and his clinic in Bombay, he spent a great deal of energy organizing teacher training programs for public school teachers.

Swami Kuvalayananda was born J.G. Gune of Gujarat; before he renounced worldly life (around 1920), he was a physical education teacher, a reporter for Lokmanya Tilak's *Kesari* periodical, and generally an ardent nationalist activist (Kaivalyadhama Institute 1975). While principal at the National College in Amalner, he began to focus on yoga. Continuing with Chingle's account, begun above, Kuvalayananda felt that yoga,

> was veiled and shrouded in mystery as also it was over-laid [sic] by numerous crusts of blind beliefs and irrelevant superstitions. In one word it was unscientific. Hence it had scant appeal to the modern mind. Shri Swamiji fully realized that its scientific presentation was indispensable to put it in the right perspective for the benefit not only of India but of the world at large...No wonder men with modern education were attracted towards him (Kaivalyadhama Institute 1975: n.p.).

Like most of the well-known proponents of yoga since Vivekananda, Kuvalyananda's primary concern was to present yoga as a science, comparable to any of the various Western sciences. The essentialist view of India as the seat of world spiritual wealth, in opposition to the material wealth concentrated in the West, rests in an oblique relationship with another oppositional pair, that of religion and science, usually reduced to faith (intuition, feeling, emotion) and reason (rationality). However, the goals of these swamis did not involve choosing one side or the other in any of these face-offs; rather, the creation of a synthesis, or at least the denial of any need to choose between them, drove their campaigns. It was therefore possible to make claims about yoga that were supported by a sense of the intrinsic value of both systematic and intuitive styles of knowing. Another prominent concern, linked to the promotion of yoga as a science, was to show yoga's relevance for modern lives. All of these issues brought discussions of yoga quite far from its earlier context in the philosophical-religious domain of isolated ascetics.[10]

Today, the campus of the Kaivalyadhama Institute is large and pretty, though perhaps not as well maintained as it had once been. Comprising many different sections, including a research laboratory, a literary-philosophical division focused on text translation and elucidation, a publications department, a College of Yoga, a library, a hospital, and an ashram, the Institute as a whole is committed to the promotion of yoga in India and internationally. The joint director of research, a physiologist by training, told me about some of their laboratory research; projects ranged from measurement of O_2 consumption during the performance of *yogāsanas* and *prāṇāyāma*, to electroencephalography and electrocardiography studies of individuals carrying out the same *yogāsana* in three different ways, from very tense to very relaxed. The textual division is attempting a complete concordance of the terminology used in all of the known yoga texts, and annotated translations (and re-translations) of all of the major published and unpublished texts—quite a task, to say the least. The Yoga College seeks to educate primary and secondary schoolteachers to be competent yoga instructors.[11] The emphasis here is definitely on bodies, and Indian bodies at that. Though foreigners participate in some of the activities and the staff were most gracious to me and supportive of my research, the Nationalist soundings of the Institute's founder still resonate most clearly through the Lonavla hills.

Like the DLS, the Kaivalyadhama Institute also has affiliated centers outside of India, though on a much smaller scale. In America, the SKY foundation (named for Swami Kuvalayananda) and its research branch, the Yoga Research Society, are headquartered in Philadelphia. In keeping with Kuvalayananda's emphasis on scientific validation, the Yoga Research Society sponsors a newsletter and an annual conference highlighting scientific analyses of yoga practice.

A second example of yoga's role in Indian nationalism is that of one of Kuvalayananda's main competitors for the contemporary Bombay regional yoga market, so to speak: Sri Yogendra, the so-called "householder yogi" who in 1919 founded the Yoga Institute of Santa Cruz.

Yogendra's story, too, includes prominent nationalists and, like Vivekananda, foreign travel. Born Manibhai Haribhai Desai on November 18, 1897 in a village near Surat, the future Sri Yogendra was the son of a Brahmin schoolteacher who taught his young son to be "rational about superstition and religious rituals" (Rodrigues 1983: 10). Manibhai's father hoped that the boy would take the Civil Service exams and so rise to higher ranks of colonial society than he himself had. Thus, the boy was sent at the age of seventeen to St. Xavier's College in Bombay, one of the premiere colleges in the country. A classmate introduced him to Madhavadasji, and from then on, Manibhai could think of nothing else. He withdrew from college to live with his guru. There he began to write poetry and discovered the work of Rabindranath Tagore, from whom he requested and received permission to translate works from Bengali to Gujarati. This connection with Tagore eventually led to other significant encounters, most importantly with Homi Dadina, the son-in-law of Dadabhai Naoroji (Rodrigues 1982: 72). Dadina began to take yoga lessons from the young Manibhai, and helped to sponsor the creation of the Yoga Institute in December of 1918. The following year, the two traveled together on a tour of Europe and the United States "to get this ancient lore accepted by the best medical brains and then propagated by the omnipresent mass media" (Rodrigues 1983: 79). On his way back to Bombay in 1921, Manibhai, now known as Sri Yogendra, met the Bengali philosopher S.N. Dasgupta, with whom Eliade would study only a few years later. This meeting resulted in a two-month stay with Dasgupta at his residence in Calcutta, where the two discussed the relationship between theory and practice of yoga. After this visit, Yogendra fulfilled a promise to his father to marry and become a householder. He felt that by his own example, he could demonstrate the utility of yoga for ordinary people, both men and women. Rodrigues's biography concludes with affirmations of support for Yogendra and his Institute from the Indologist Heinrich Zimmer, S. Radhakrishnan, and Zakir Hussain, among many other Western and Indian scholars and politicians.

As at the Kaivalyadhama Institute, the main activities of the Yoga Institute have been therapeutic and educational, operating a clinic and developing teacher-training programs to disseminate yoga techniques to school children. Yogendra's status as a householder, rather than a renouncer, was quite unusual at the time; in contrast with Sivananda, for example, the prominent involvement of Yogendra's family with the activities of the Yoga Institute sends a completely different message from the DLS's insistence on the complete denial of sexuality to their founder (though given the evidence from Eliade and others, it seems to have been more scripted than accurate). Though the DLS also addresses an audience of householders and places an emphasis on the value of service—*karma* yoga—the fundamental framework of the institution is still oriented toward the individual male renouncer (Fornaio 1969).

The final institution I discuss is the relatively new Vivekananda Kendra (VK) of Bangalore. This organization again uses the language of science to validate its programs and practices. One of their publications, entitled *Yoga-The Science of Holistic Living* (Vivekananda Kendra 1988), includes articles addressing such topics as "Yoga—Science and Evolution," "Stress—The Basic Challenge and Holistic Solution," "Yoga to the Rescue of Modern Societies," and "Yoga and Ecology." The description of the Vivekananda Kendra Yoga Foundation, founded in 1986, states a plan of research that essentially follows that of the Kaivalyadhama Institute, with separate divisions for textual, therapeutic, and practical yoga research and instruction and a proposal for the development of research laboratories. The rationale for creating this organization rests on the belief that "Yoga is the solution to unearthing the hidden dimensions of man, strengthening him to face the challenge of STRESS and POLLUTION of this modern era of science and technology which has become mandatory even to survive in this globe" (Vivekananda Kendra 1988: 269; emphasis in original).

The director of the VK, Dr. H.R. Nagendra, has published articles on the therapeutic use of yoga in British, American, and Indian medical journals. I first learned about his research and the development of the VK from my friend Swamiji, a yoga teacher from Rishikesh whom I knew quite well. Swamiji had worked in Bangalore as a professional engineer for several years before deciding to renounce, and during that time, had become acquainted with Dr. Nagendra. Nagendra had set up a small clinic-yoga center in Bangalore but had not yet formally created the VK foundation. From 1977 to 1980, Swamiji had volunteered his engineering skills to help develop the physical facility. One day, Swami Vishnudevananda came to give a lecture there, and Swamiji became intrigued. This meeting led to a visit to the Sivananda Yoga Vedanta Ashram at Neyyar Dam in Kerala and ultimately to his decision to take *saṃnyās*. Swamiji felt that the work of Dr. Nagendra was the most comprehensive and scientific effort to promote research and practice of yoga, and for that reason, I should visit the VK Ashram.

What he did not tell me at first was that VK was in fact a spin-off of the well-known Hindu nationalist group called the Rashtriya Swayamsevak Sangh (RSS), founded in 1932 to promote the cause of a Hindu nation-state (McKean 1996: 70). The creation of the Vivekananda Rock Memorial at Kanyakumari, in the southern tip of India, had been proposed as a tribute to Vivekananda at the place where, legend has it, he gained enlightenment and a sense of purpose to bring spirituality to the West while improving the material conditions of Indian life. The statue of Vivekananda on the rock was completed in 1970, but the story of its creation is one bound up with the religious divisiveness of the subcontinent.[12] According to one of my Rishikesh discussants, Hans, a German man who had lived for several years at the VK center in Bangalore, a group of individuals, many of whom were affiliated with the Ramakrishna Mission, decided to build the memorial. However, because of local protest by Christians in the region, the RK Mission withdrew its support of the project. The local RSS affiliates picked it up and determined to carry through; they apparently received a substantial amount of financial support for the project from expatriate Indians. The VK was born for the purpose of coordinating development and construction of the statue. When the memorial had been completed, the group, rather than dissolving, looked for new activities and began to focus on the teaching of yoga to children and adults in short "camps." By 1986, the organization had sufficient support to incorporate as an official institution with a permanent base in Bangalore. Though the primary official purpose of the VK when Hans arrived in the late 1980s was the promotion of yoga, he was uncomfortable with the strident undertones of Hindu nationalism he found still to exist. He commented to me that, personally, he found such nationalism to be quite contrary to the writings of Vivekananda, and indeed to the professed universalist orientation of the VK administration. Of course, as we have seen, Vivekananda certainly did exhibit strong nationalist sentiments, particularly in his comments directed toward the people of India.

Hans's response is not atypical. Most non-VK yoga practitioners I have encountered, whether Indian or Western, focus their attention on Vivekananda's universalism as his primary message, downplaying the significance of the more partisan Hindu nationalist messages on which the VK capitalizes. There is little question that both nationalist and universalist goals have been espoused simultaneously through much of the history of the DLS as well. The 1990–1991 Annual Report of the Vivekananda Kendra Yoga Research Foundation shows the group to be active in many different areas; the organizational mission comprises a "five-fold approach to National Reconstruction" (Vivekananda Kendra 1991: 2); according to this document, the VK is "spreading the message of man-making and nation-building" (ibid.: 5). The five areas of research for the umbrella organization include yoga, education, rural development, natural resources development, and publications. The VK Yoga Research Institute addresses three of these fundamental concerns, emphasizing "Yoga for modern society to propagate the science of holistic living for happiness, health, harmony and higher efficiency" and for medical and stress management applications. In addition to the regular clinic operations and yoga instruction, staff of the VK also put on "Citizenship Training Camps" for college students; nation building in all forms remains an explicit aspect of their organization.

Communities of Practice: Citizenship through Yoga

In a similar vein, Swami Chidananda of the DLS has also made an interesting contribution to the cause of citizenship. The November 1991 issue of *The Divine Life* magazine includes a piece by Chidananda that purports to be a National Code of Conduct "to serve as an ethical standard of conduct for the citizens of India." He continues with the exhortation "God bless our Motherland with noble citizens with ideal good conduct in their private and public life! May the citizens bring a good name to the country and restore its resplendent greatness as the land of Dharma!." This National Code, which had been translated into several other Indian languages and sent around the country by the time it appeared in the DLS monthly magazine, includes twelve rules for serving India. One of the most interesting features of the Code is that though Chidananda admitted authorship, the actual statement reads "Compiled by Lovers of the Country"—thus, most who would see it would not be aware of its association with the DLS. Many DLS stock phrases are used in the Code, including "Health is wealth" and "simple living and high thinking." The Code suggests that support of nation and God are the two most important aspects of a citizen's life and that the way to serve the nation best is to serve God, be of unassailable character, and stay healthy. After those primary obligations come the remaining guidelines relating to avoiding alcohol, dishonesty, damage to public property, and violence and to promoting equal support for all religions, being frugal, upholding social justice, and teaching your children to do the same. Prior to Indian independence, the notion of freedom was of course primary, but in the estimation of the DLS of the 1990s, maintaining good health is the central duty of the true citizen.

As a medical doctor, Sivananda was extremely concerned about promoting both the physical and spiritual health of individuals but, from the earliest days of the DLS, a nationalist rationale for such practices as yoga is also clearly present in his teachings. Sivananda, through his publications, institution, and staged events, continues to plead Vivekananda's case for universal brotherhood and national integration. He fuses claims about individual liberation—*mokṣa*—with an entire range of freedoms deriving from India's aspiring and then actual status as an independent nation. In a 1947 paean entitled *Siva—The Prophet of the New Age,* disciple A.B.N. Sinha describes Sivananda in glowing terms:

> *He stands today the herald of a liberated India*—liberated from the tyranny of caste and creed, liberated from ignorance of its own scriptures and customs...*having fully realised that the individual is free and liberated only if it has the will,* that India must live to unfold its great destiny and that religion has a value all its own in the making of a nation. He stands today the great prophet of daring and peace, teaching people...to defy vices and overcome personal weaknesses while forgetting not that peace was so essential for development. *He stands today the Messenger of India to the world, propagating its mission of Vedanta and* Yoga...*If the portals of the glorious future are to be opened it is not the Key of atom bombs that will open it...The world of future* need have no labour-capital troubles, need have no religious persecutions, need have no secular bickerings; it *should be a world of equality with service as its motto...This world can easily open to the sesame of the preachings of Swami Sivananda...* (Sinha 1947: 143–44; emphasis added).

It is clear, however, that "preachings" alone were insufficient in Sivananda's mind. Most of the early DLS publications contain a substantial discussion of practice, *abhyās* or *sādhana* in Hindi; even quite small pamphlets often contain instructions for keeping a "spiritual diary" on a daily basis, one copy of which is to be sent to the guru for further advice. Many other books (e.g., *Triple Yoga, Yoga in Daily Life*) contain numbered lists of practices to be followed, often with supplementary hints, worksheets, and commentaries. One of the primary texts for DLS disciples, first published in the 1950s, is called simply *Sadhana*—it is a large handbook of practical advice, programs of study, and narrative exemplars designed to offer the aspirant specific techniques for achieving liberation (DLS 1985b). This and other volumes available for purchase or on-line provide not only a common textual base but a set of activities and a fixed sequence of practices that all DLS disciples may follow. Many have been translated into several languages, both Indian and European, and so they provide a unified framework for the translocal communities of yoga practice in the DLS style.[13]

A community of practice, as I define it, follows the basic definition given by Lave and Wenger that is "a set of relations among persons, activity, and world, over time and in relation with other tangential and overlapping communities of practice" (1991: 98). It is an imagined community in Benedict Anderson's sense, in that the majority of its members "will never know most of their fellow-members, meet them, or even hear of them, yet in the minds of each lives the image of their communion" (Anderson 1983: 15). This community of practice is *translocal*; its membership includes individuals from several different nations and very different regions within specific nations, many of whom have had direct experience with one another's native places and practices. When we imagine a translocal community, we avoid the tendency to assert a global-local dichotomy by highlighting instead the interwoven nature of this community. The work of maintaining community is itself a type of practice that can be subdivided into many different aspects, each specific to the variety of social tie being constructed and maintained. For example, the activities associated with establishing and sustaining a yoga community of practice include both the set of physical practices embodying a particular ideology (e.g., the *yogāsanas*, or postures, and the variety of other bodily techniques, rituals, and prayers associated with their execution) and the set of maintenance practices associated with teaching, critiquing, and promoting those core physical practices (e.g., teaching styles and techniques, literary conventions, advertising strategies, organizational development, and the like). Without the core practices, there is nothing on which to base the maintenance activities.

We can see how Sivananda promoted the development of a community of practitioners as a subset of (or precursor to) a broader global community by examining one of his more popular books. This volume (published for commercial audiences by D.B. Taraporevala Sons & Co. Pvt. Ltd., Bombay) is entitled *Yogic Home Exercises: Easy Course of Physical Culture for Modern Men and Women*; it shows how Sivananda linked the concepts of personal health with global security. Though originally published in 1959, it has been reprinted several times, most recently in 1983. This volume is "[d]edicated to the men and women of East and West, who desire to possess wonderful health, charming and powerful personality, longevity, abundant energy, muscular strength, and nerve-vigour through the practice of Yogic Exercises" (Sivananda 1983: iv). The first chapter of this treatise is titled "Health and Freedom," and it asks "what is that precious thing that makes life worth living? It is health" (xiv). Sivananda extends the answer to this question by quoting the author of the *Caraka Samhitā*, a well-known āyurvedic medical text: "'Health is the best cause of virtue, wealth, desire and emancipation, and is the blessedness of life'" (Sivananda 1983: iv). In this introductory chapter explaining the value of yoga for the modern men and women of the book's title, Sivananda makes it quite clear that the practice of yoga is important not only for the physical and spiritual health of individuals but for the nation and, indeed, the entire planet:

> Sattwic ahara or good wholesome food rich in vitamins, or a *well-balanced diet, systematic practice of Asan and Pranayam, right and simple living and right thinking are the important prerequisites for the preservation of health* and the attainment of a high standard of vigour and vitality. These are the sublime principles on which the Rishis and Yogins of yore lived a long peaceful life. *These are the important methods on which they based the system of Yoga to achieve perfection in health of body and mind. These are the supports on which the sinking nation must fall back if it wishes to regain her lost glory and splendour.*

> The world needs good healthy mothers, healthy and strong boys and girls. What do we find these days in India? India, the land which produced Bhishma, Bhima, Arjuna, Drona, Aswattama, Kripa, Parashuram and countless other chivalrous warriors...now abounds with effeminate impotent weaklings. Children beget children. The laws of health are ignored and neglected. *The nation is suffering and dying. The world requires numberless brave, moral, Adhyatmic soldiers who are equipped with the five virtues [of* yoga*]. Those who possess health and strength...those who have knowledge of the Self, they alone can secure real freedom for the world* (Sivananda 1983: xiii–xiv; emphasis added).

The primary thread that we see running through all of these statements is that the realization of the oneness of the Self with all other selves or, in other words, the affirmation of universal brotherhood, is the key to individual bliss and world peace and the freedom deriving from these.[14] India as the locus of true freedom, and yoga as the path that leads there, also appear as a central concern for Eliade in Yoga: *Immortality and Freedom* (1973). In Eliade's work, as in the early writings of Vivekananda or Sivananda, elements of *tantra*, affirming the positive aspects of life in the body, offer a counterpoint to the less corporeal classical tradition. However, Eliade's interest in freedom is in terms of the ultimate liberation of the self—there is nothing social about it. Recall that Eliade learned to practice yoga from Sivananda many years before the founding of the DLS and the definition of the service orientation of that organization. Though Sivananda's own actions may have been directed toward helping others, Eliade's practice had little, if anything, to do with such social work. His autobiography and other writings indicate that he wished to follow in the footsteps of more "traditional" or "authentic" ascetics, like his ash-covered neighbors on the banks of the Ganges in Rishikesh. Eliade did seek Sivananda because he was known to accept foreign, English-speaking students, but he also stated, in several different places, that he did not think it a good idea for his Western reading audience to try yoga: "We have no intention of inviting Western scholars to practice Yoga (which, by the way, is not so easy as some amateurs are wont to suggest)..." (Eliade 1963: 125–6). He spoke of his own practice only under the guise of fiction.

Eliade wrote that he wanted to become a "real Indian," assuming that authenticity as an Indian derived from a particular brand of ascetic practice. Sivananda, however, following the lead of Vivekananda, wanted to apply the teachings of yoga to the solution of practical problems. Bharati sees Sivananda as occupying a centrist position in the neo-Hindu Renaissance that began in the nineteenth century, espousing the basic tenets of what Bharati terms the Hindu Apologetic:

> India has forgotten her marvellous past; this past contained not only material and cultural wealth, it also offered a complete solution of all problems of the individual and of society...The modern world--the West, that is, has usurped the things that India has lost...In matters of the spirit, India has retained its

> superiority—the West has failed, it has misused its powers. India now can and should have both the worlds... (Bharati 1970: 276).

Supporting that understanding of the neo-Hindu renaissance goals is an article about the 1953 Parliament of Religions in Rishikesh from the *Sunday Standard of Bombay*, commenting that,

> The DLS...has thrown open its doors to seekers of truth, irrespective of their religion and race. It initiates them into the cult of Yoga to make the human body a fit instrument for realizing the higher purpose of religion and truth. Although some of the members of the society are experts in Yoga culture, they are precluded from indulging in exhibitionism or cheap shows which have made the noble institution of Yoga misunderstood. The dynamic energy which yoga releases in the human body is to be dedicated to the service and happiness of mankind (Divine Life Society 1956: 641–2; *Sunday Standard*, Bombay, April 5, 1953).

An interesting aside to these remarks is that as of 1993, the secretary of the DLS, Krishnananda, has closed the doors, at least to non-Indian nationals who desire membership in the DLS. This action again reflects the tension inhering in the DLS since its inception, that of nationalist versus universalist orientation, and the shift from practice to prayer mentioned above. As McKean has shown (1996: 253–5), financial support for the DLS, at least since the 1980s, is often linked in some way to the support of Hindu nationalism, even as the official rhetoric of the organization speaks to the universalist agenda (McKean 1996: 165).

Reorienting Yoga

To Indians, the type of yoga reoriented by innovators such as Vivekananda and Sivananda suggests empowerment, using an imagined shared history to create a progressive, self-possessed, and unifying identity. In this light, yoga can be understood as part of a methodology for living a good life. Because of its basis in bodily practice, the yoga tradition is easily linked with physical health maintenance at the level of the person. The physical development of the person was seen by many as the first, necessary step to be taken in the service of improving a larger community, whether local, national, or global. Yoga reoriented is *new* theory with *old* practice. Experientially based, it offers individuals hope that through the practice of yoga, they might be freed from the constraints of "taking sides," because yoga suggests the possibility of transcending such essentializing dichotomies as East-West, religion-science, mind-body, or nation-world.

By going between the horns of the dilemma, being free to choose the elements from each side that make the most sense to them as individuals, these middle-class yoga practitioners seek a globally relevant model for living a good life. This model is not static but dynamic. Yoga offers a literate, historically grounded tradition, critical for people who rely heavily on the print media for transmission of authoritative knowledge, and an active set of practices that, if followed, promise tangible results—spiritual "progress" made visible because embodied. The development of yoga in India through institutions such as Swami Sivananda of Rishikesh's DLS has been a way of promoting the struggle for freedom at the national level, by helping strengthen the minds, spirits, and bodies of colonized subjects for the difficulties of modern independent life.

Acknowledgments

This chapter was previously published in *History and Anthropology* (2002) 13 (3): 231–51, and is here reprinted with permission. The research on which the chapter is based was funded by a Fulbright-Hays Doctoral Dissertation Award (1992) and a grant from the School of Arts and Sciences at the University of Pennsylvania (1993). A version of this chapter was given in October, 2001 at the University of Wyoming Colloquium on History, Culture, and Society. I thank the members of the Colloquium, especially Mark Potter, Michael Brose, and Janice Harris, for their thoughtful comments and queries. Finally, I owe particular debts to my dissertation supervisor, Arjun Appadurai, whose insights about transnational processes shaped my outlook on history in general and on India in particular, and to my colleague Lin Poyer, whose expert editorial eye and sage advice have been invaluable over the years.

Notes

1 The DLS has been studied by several researchers (e.g. McKean 1996; Miller 1989; Fornaio 1969) but never from the perspective of yoga practice. The differing agendas of these other studies range from the political to the philosophical, all of which complement the present research. Yoga is a topic about which much has been said; there have been very many organizations and teachers devoted to the promotion of yoga over the last century, and more continue to appear every day. Of these, dozens could justify book-length treatments on their own. Perhaps most conspicuous in their absence from the discussion below are the Integral Yoga of Sri Aurobindo and Paramahansa Yogananda's Self-Realization Fellowship. It is not my intention to present an overview of this vast set of organizations but only to contrast Sivananda and his Divine Life Society with some other examples of the wide range of yoga presentations available to the contemporary spiritual consumer.

2 Rolland 1988[1931]; also see for example Vivekananda's letter of July 14, 1896, from England: "...the *Rāja-Yoga*, by Longman Green and Co. You can get it at Bombay. It consists of my lectures on Rāja Yoga in New York" (Vivekananda 1989: 298).

3 Tamil Brahmans are considered by many Indians to be among the most observant of Hindus.

4 See McKean 1996. During the course of field work in Rishikesh, I also became well acquainted with a local bank manager who indicated that the DLS accounts were more than healthy.

5 Satchidananda, whose main ashram is in Virginia, is the guru of the popular physician, Dean Ornish, who recommends that the use of meditation, yoga, and a strict vegetarian diet can reverse coronary disease, among other things.

6 Sivananda/DLS publications available at the Sivananda Yoga Vedanta Center in New Delhi cost approximately three times as much as the same items in Rishikesh and even more at the DLS centers in Europe and the United States.

7 For example, see <http://www.SivanandaDlshq.org/teachings/teachings.htm> or <http://www.sivananda.org/teachings/index.htm>l.

8 Chinmayananda, interestingly enough, was one of Sivananda's earliest young admirers, though he ultimately left the DLS to take sannyas from another holy man.

9 Translation by author. In the original: "Ils disent "nous sommes tous Un" et, ce qui est important, ils ne cessent de mettre en pratique cette affirmation. Ils s'entraident, se depersonnalisent devant leurs amis et pratiquent le seva (service)" (Eliade 1988: 175).

10 The practice of yoga thus becomes a life strategy for ordinary householders and for Dumont's individualist world renouncers (Dumont 1980). These ascetics can now be brought back into the social world, still immersed in their *vairagya* (renunciation) and *yogābhyās* (yoga practice) but with the added twist of a responsibility to help others, a concept quite absent from, for example, Patañjali's description of the quest for *kaivalya* (isolation) through yogic practice (Aranya 1983:406).

11 To this end, they run a nine-month (forty students) and a six-week (100 students) yoga instructor's course each year; of the participants, about twenty percent are non-Indian, and the gender ratio is approximately fifty percent women; these figures represent a deliberate attempt at balance on the part of the administration.

12 But see also Sangi 1990.

13 The yoga-oriented community of practice associated with Sivananda and his disciples is a fluid group of individuals who recognize in each other certain commonalities of value orientation, particularly those focused on health and freedom, and of self-selected physical practice and mediated ideology. Such shared ideas and activities predispose these yoga practitioners to feeling comfortable in one another's company, affording them the same kind of group identification and solidarity that members of any other imagined community, whether nationally or otherwise determined, enjoy. For a more in-depth discussion of this community of practice and the relevance of the concept for ethnographic fieldwork, see Strauss 2000.

14 For another extended example of the relationship between yoga practice and broader concepts of self and national or global reform, see Alter's (1987) study of the Delhi-based organization called Bharatiya Yog Sansthan, founded in 1967, and his contribution to this volume.

Bibliography

Alter, J.S. (1997) A Therapy to Live By, *Medical Anthropology*, 17: 309–35.

Anderson, B. (1983) *Imagined Communities: Reflections on the Origin and Spread of Nationalism*, London: Verso Editions and NLB.

Aranya, Swami H. (1983) *Yoga Philosophy of Patañjali*, Albany: SUNY Press.

Basham, A.L. (1954) *The Wonder that was India*, New York: Grove.

Beck, U. (1992) *Risk Society: Towards a New Modernity*, trans M. Ritter, London: Sage Publications.

Berlin, I. (1958) *Two Concepts of Liberty*, Oxford: Oxford University Press.

Bharati, A. (1970) The Hindu Renaissance and its Apologetic Patterns, *Journal of Asian Studies* 29: 267–87.

Chidananda, Swami (1993) *Timely Wisdom*, Published for the 1993 Parliament of the World's Religions, by the DLS Maryland, Inc.

——(1991) National Code of Conduct, *The Divine Life* 5 (9): 252.

Das, A. (1992) *India Invented: A Nation-in-the-Making*, Delhi: Manohar Publications.

Divine Life Society (1947) *Diamond Jubilee Volume.* Rikhikesh: Sivananda Publication League.
—(1951) *All-India Tour Volume,* Rishikesh: Sivananda Publication League.
—(1956) *World Parliament of Religions Volume,* Rishikesh: Sivananda Publication League.
—(1985a) *Sivananda: His Life and Works, vol. 1: Biography of a Sage,* Rishikesh: DLS.
—(1985b) *Sadhana,* Rishikesh: DLS.
—(1987) *The Master, His Mission, and his Works,* Rishikesh: DLS.
Dumont, L. (1980) *Homo Hierarchicus: The Caste System and Its Implications,* revised English ed., trans M. Sainsbury, L. Dumont and B. Gulati, Chicago: University of Chicago Press.
Eliade, M. (1963) Yoga and Modern Philosophy, *Journal of General Education,* 15: 124–37.
—(1973 [1958]) *Yoga: Immortality and Freedom,* trans. W.R. Trask, Bollingen Series, Princeton: Princeton University Press.
—(1988 [1934]) *L'Inde.* Mayenne: Les Editions de L'Herne.
—Fornaio, R.J. (1969) *Sivananda and the Divine Life Society: A Paradigm of the "Secularism," "Puritanism," and "Cultural Dissimulation" of a Neo-Hindu Religious Society* [Ph.D. dissertation], Syracuse: Department of Anthropology, Syracuse University.
Fuchs, C. (1990) *Yoga in Deutschland: Rezeption-Organisation-Typologie,* Stuttgart: Kohlhammer Verlag.
Gupta, A. (1992) 'The song of the Non-Aligned World: Transnational Identities and the Reinscription of Space in Late Capitalism', *Cultural Anthropology* 7 (1): 63–92.
Kaivalyadhama Institute (1975) *Golden Jubilee Souvenir Volume,* Lonavla: Kaivalyadhama.
Lave, J. and Wenger, E. (1991) *Situated Learning: Legitimate Peripheral Participation,* Cambridge: Cambridge University Press.
McKean, L. (1996) *Divine Enterprise: Gurus and the Hindu Nationalist Movement.* Chicago: University of Chicago Press.
Miller, D. (1989) The Divine Life Society Movement, in R.D. Baird (ed) *Religion in Modern India,* 2nd revised ed., Delhi: Manohar, 81–112,
Omkarananda, Swami (ed) (1960) *Sivananda Literature, vol I.,* Rishikesh: Divine Life Society.
Radhakrishnan, S. (1992 [1939]) *Eastern Religions and Western Thought,* Delhi: Oxford University Press.
Rodrigues, S. (1982) *The Householder Yogi: Life of Sri Yogendra,* Santa Cruz: Yogendra Publications Fund, The *Yoga* Institute.
Rolland, R. (1988) *The Life of Vivekananda and the Universal Gospel,* trans. E.F. Malcolm-Smith, Calcutta: Advaita Ashrama.
Sangi, V. (1990) *All India Travel Companion,* trans L. Mazumdar, Calcutta: Asia Publishing Company.
Sarkar, S. (1985) *Modern India, 1885-1947,* Madras: Macmillan India Limited.
—(1992) "Kaliyuga," "Chakri" and "Bhakti": Ramakrishna and His Times, *Economic and Political Weekly,* July 18: 1543–66.
Sinha, A.B.N. (1947) *Siva—The Prophet of the New Age,* Life and Teachings Series #12. Rishikesh: Sivananda Publication League.
Sivananda, Swami (1983 [1959]) *Yogic Home Exercises: Easy Course of Physical Culture for Modern Men and Women,* Bombay: D.B. Taraporevala Sons & Co. Pvt. Ltd.
—(1988) *Essence of Yoga.* 13th ed., Rishikesh: Divine Life Society.
Strauss, S. (2000) Locating Yoga: Ethnography and Transnational Practice, in V. Amit (ed) *Constructing the Field,* London: Routledge, 162–94,
Vivekananda Kendra (1988) *Yoga—The Science of Holistic Living.* Bangalore: VK.
—(1991) 1990–91 *Annual Report of the Vivekananda Kendra,* Bangalore: VK.
Vivekananda, Swami (1989) *Letters of Swami Vivekananda,* Calcutta: Advaita Ashrama.

Part II

Posturing for Authenticity

4 The Classical Reveries of Modern Yoga

Patañjali and Constructive Orientalism[1]

Mark Singleton

> [O]h, in the midst of such heart-rending scenes, how must your glowing classical reveries appear as incongruous as would the songs of boisterous merriment amid requiems for the dead!
>
> (Alexander Duff on witnessing "some of the leading superstitions and idolatries of Eastern India," in Duff 1988 [1840]: 223).

Today, Patañjali is routinely invoked as source-authority and figurehead of a diverse range of techniques and belief systems commonly termed *yoga*. His *Yogasūtra* (hereafter YS) is popularly regarded in many modern and transnational milieux as the ur-text of yoga and is used to sanction and legitimize contemporary practice. Often taken as the quintessential expression of "Classical Yoga," the YS has come to symbolize, among other things, the ancient authenticity of modern aspirations and the fidelity of contemporary practices to the "yoga tradition," in spite of the often-radical divergences between text and praxis. In this chapter, I examine these notions in relation to certain expressions of popular, anglophone yoga in the late nineteenth and early twentieth centuries and suggest some ways in which the YS has been mediated and reinterpreted in modern times. I consider the changing status and function of the YS in its encounter with nineteenth-century Orientalist and modern Indian scholarship and the ways in which these interpretations enabled and directed the conditions of the text's assimilation into the practical (and international) reformulations of yoga that followed.

The installation of the YS as the Classical Yoga text in the modern age is bound up with several dialectically interlinked, ideological currents. These include colonial translation projects intended to inculcate the critical habits and values of European philosophy in Indian minds via Hindu scripture and subsequent reclamations of these texts by Indian cultural nationalists seeking to identify and interpret the definitive canon of modern Hinduism. The refurbishment of the YS as the exemplary expression of *practical* Indian philosophy culminates in Vivekananda's innovative translation and commentary in his *Rāja Yoga* of 1896, a publication that was to be prototypical for many subsequent English-language formulations of yoga in the twentieth century. Vivekananda's creative interpretation is partially based on an understanding of spiritual life informed by Western esotericism and the para-Christian, metaphysical frameworks pervasive in some quarters of late-nineteenth century America (De Michelis 2004). These and other influences contribute to the "modern" quality of Vivekananda's work, and many forms of popular transnational yoga today bear the imprint of this eclectic revisioning.

I suggest that Vivekananda's presentation of Patañjali in *Rāja Yoga*—and in the many subsequent expressions of popular, anglophone yoga—rests on a broader reinterpretation and elevation of the YS within the Orientalist and (emergent) cultural nationalist contexts and that the notion of a Classical Yoga is in many respects a cultural production of modernity itself. In many transnational settings today (particularly those in the West), the YS is often accorded the virtual status of revealed scripture (*śruti*),[2] and Patañjali himself revered as the quasi-deity of yoga as a whole. This situation was made possible, in part, by a distinct *relocation* of Patañjali within neo-Hinduism from the mid-nineteenth century.

I begin by briefly considering Patañjali's place within yoga practice traditions, suggesting that the virtually hegemonic status enjoyed by the YS in some modern yogas by no means reflects the text's status and function in premodern Indian yoga traditions. I go on to consider the construction of Patañjali-as-philosopher in early modern translations of the YS and the subsequent identification of the text as symbolic source-authority for modern yoga enthusiasts. Then, with reference to parallel, contemporaneous efforts in modern Indian music and dance, I suggest that the construction of the Classical within yoga reflects a wider process of political and cultural legitimization within India at the time. Finally, on the basis of this evidence, I consider several examples of the relocated Patañjali in contemporary transnational yoga. Also subtending my argument throughout is the assumption that the modern elevation of the YS as the (imagined) quintessential text of yoga entailed the *exclusion* of unseemly, heterodox elements within India's yoga traditions, such as tantric-oriented *haṭha* yoga.

Patañjali and Yoga Practice Traditions

It is by no means self-evident, as many modern practitioners assume, that the YS has always been the ultimate authority on the practice of yoga, nor indeed that Classical Yoga has ever really constituted a distinct practice lineage in its own right. Though one must not ignore the intrinsic place of the YS and its commentaries in previous traditions of "Hinduism,"[3] it may be that the monolithic deference to the authority of the YS as a "practice text" is itself a modern phenomenon and that the manifold yoga practice traditions of India do not necessarily owe any significant debt to the work. Vasudeva (2004) argues that this is overwhelmingly the case in traditions of Śaiva scripture and practice, wherein Patañjali is rarely a significant presence (237). When the influence of the YS *is* felt, it is often as "no more than just one of many competing systems of yoga and not yet necessarily as the most prominent one"

(186). Outside of Śaivism, the lesser status of Patañjali is also suggested by the eighth-century (C.E.) syncretic yoga works of the Jaina convert Haribhadra (alias Bhavavirahasūri), which draw on Sāṃkhya, Buddhist, Śaiva, and Mahāvratin (Pāśupata) systems, but "rarely take note of Patañjali's views" (186, n.3). If such examples are representative, it may be inappropriate to project the impression of a Patañjalian theoretical hegemony during the "extraordinarily rich and diverse" (Whicher and Carpenter 2003: 1) course of yoga's development. The fact that such an impression holds sway in popular yoga circles today may be more helpfully considered as the result of modern Orientalist scholarship on the one hand and the popular presentation of Patañjali by Vivekananda (and his more or less self-conscious emulators) on the other.

To what extent, in fact, should we then consider the YS to represent a "yoga tradition" as such? Johannes Bronkhorst has argued that the YS was never the basis for an autonomous yoga tradition but rather a complementary system associated with a range of distinct philosophies (1981: 317). If the YS does not have its own lineage but is simply a source-text for competing philosophical and soteriological systems (most notably Sāṃkhya and Vedānta but also Nyāya and Vaiśeṣika), then the notion of a unified tradition of "Classical Yoga" flowing from the authority of the text must be questioned. Moreover, the text itself seems composed of elements from several distinct religiophilosophical schools, including Sāṃkhya,[4] Buddhism,[5] and a variety of *śramana* traditions.[6] Given the lack of evidence to support the idea of a consistent tradition of Classical Yoga founded on the YS, it is remarkable that contemporary practitioners of yoga so consistently assume both the existence of such a tradition and the provenance of their own practices from this source. Norman Sjoman deems the identification made by modern students between their own practices and actual Patañjalian practice traditions not only tenuous but careless too, in so far as it ignores that "[t]he textual tradition from Patañjali from an estimated 150 BC is a dead textual tradition" (1996: 37). He notes in this regard that "Vyāsa, the first commentator on Patañjali, is generally considered to have lost touch with the tradition already—if there was one" (ibid.), a viewpoint also mentioned by Bronkhorst (1985; 2005), Grinshpon (2002), and Sarbacker (2005).[7] This brings us back to our main question of how and why this impression of a "Classical" Pātañjala yoga tradition occurred and how it came to form the ideological bedrock for some of the most popular, export-yogas of the early twentieth century.

In this regard, Elizabeth De Michelis states that "occultist definitions of yoga have gained enormous ascendancy in Modern Yoga circles because the full authority of the *Yoga Sūtras* has been mistakenly attributed to them" (2004: 179) and, indeed, a large portion of her book is devoted to the analysis of such definitions as they appear in Vivekananda's *Rāja Yoga*. However, the "full authority" of the YS is by no means a given here, and the mistaken attribution of it to modern occult definitions of yoga may be a doubly compounded error. That is to say, the assumption of a full authority that can be "mistakenly attributed" may itself be an inaccurate assessment of the status of the YS as authoritative text. On the contrary, it seems clear that the particular status enjoyed by the YS in the modern age itself derives greatly from various endorsements of the text's authority by early modern translators and scholars on the one hand and by Vivekananda himself on the other. In this view, the "mistake" that De Michelis discerns in "Modern Yoga circles" was itself enabled by a major current of Indological thought that predated it and continued to provide philosophical validation for it well into the twentieth century.

Could it be, then, that the vision of the YS as the source of a timeless tradition of Classical Indian Yoga is in fact an *idée recue* of the modern era, and that the "mistake" of popular yoga was inbuilt from its very inception? As I attempt to demonstrate in the following section, it seems clear at the very least that from the mid-nineteenth century the YS was accorded a status and context within Indian intellectual life that it did not have before. However, whether we conceive of this as a *disjunction* from an authentic, extant, living tradition at the heart of Hinduism (the position of some Western practitioners and modern Hindus),[8] a *revival* of a substantially defunct one, or an *invention* of a new one, this remains secondary to the fact that in the modern period, we are dealing with an altered Patañjali—reinterpreted to fit the aspirations and constraints of the age.

Patañjali as Philosopher: Early Modern Translations of the YS

In the modern period, there are examples to suggest that the YS was expressly installed as yoga's "textbook" through a collaborative effort on the part of British Orientalists and Indian Pandits and thereby salvaged from a state of *practical* desuetude. James Ballantyne's "constructive Orientalism" project during his tenure as principal of Benares Sanskrit College in the mid-1900s is one such case. This project was conceived as

> a pedagogy which was intended to demonstrate to the learned Hindu elite that the truths of European philosophy and science, while constituting a significant advancement upon Hindu learning, might also be reached by way of the latter's sound, yet undeveloped, premises (Dodson 2002: 258).

Via the medium of Sanskrit, Western philosophy and science were to be presented to students "as the development of the 'old truth' contained in the Hindu shastra" (ibid.: 280), and to this end Ballantyne commissioned new translations of the orthodox Hindu *darśanas* by Benares Pandits that collectively came to be known as the "*navya vidya*" or "new knowledge" (ibid.: 295). Crucially, however, Ballantyne's translation project nearly foundered when it reached the *yogadarśana*. In the introduction to what is the earliest known English translation of the YS, Ballantyne records that though there were many scholars in Benares willing to learn English and help with the textbook project, there was great difficulty in finding anyone to carry out the *yoga* translation, because "[i] n these days no pandit claims to be teaching this system" (Ballantyne 1852: ii). This seems to indicate that among mid-nineteenth century orthodox Benares

Pandits, Pātañjala yoga was simply not a living philosophical system, let alone the scriptural basis of an extant practice tradition. This is not to say that there were not living traditions of yoga in Benares at that time but that those that were in existence were effectively decoupled from the authority of Patañjali (or, possibly, that their representatives—unlike the other, *participating* Pandits—were simply unwilling to partake in Ballantyne's project). We should also consider the possibility outlined above that Ballantyne's search for exponents of an autonomous yoga tradition was ultimately misguided insofar as the YS may have functioned as a "floating *darśana*" that merely complemented other philosophical systems. Ballantyne and his team of pandits only translated the first two *pādas* of the YS,[9] but his work should be seen as part of a wider enterprise, based on "an interaction between the Western Orientalist and the brahmanical pundit" that contributed to the "specific nature" of modern Hinduism (King 1999: 90) and, *mutatis mutandis*, to certain modern expressions of yoga.

A similar difficulty was faced by Rajendralala Mitra some thirty years later when he began to seek practitioner-collaborators for his 1883 translation, with Bhoja's commentary, in the respected Bibliotheca Indica series, entitled *Yoga Aphorisms of Patanjali*. When he first undertook the project, he records in his introduction, "I had hopes of reading the work with the assistance of a professional Yogī; but I was disappointed. I could find no Paṇḍit in Bengal who had made the Yoga the special subject of his study" (Mitra 1883: xc). This would seem to support the notion that the YS was simply not an apparent part of an active tradition at that time, at least not among the orthodox of Bengal. Mitra eventually finds a suitable candidate in Benares, but unfortunately this *yogī* "was most exorbitant in his demands" in that he wanted Mitra to live with him as a *cela* (disciple) and learn in the traditional way (Mitra 1883: xc). The incident illustrates that even where there are traces of a living, oral tradition of Patañjali, the new translations that began with Ballantyne are effectively decoupled from it. What we see in these translations is the formation of a new Patañjali in dialogue with Western philosophy and neo-Hinduism but self-consciously cut off from traditional learning.[10]

Mitra's translation runs in much the same ideological grain as Ballantyne's larger project, insofar as it seeks to present the YS as a textbook of comparative philosophy.[11] Much of his lengthy preface is concerned, indeed, to align the text with Western philosophers—most notably Schopenhauer, Berkeley, the Epicureans, and the Greeks more generally—and thereby to save the "Yoga doctrine" from a reputation that has, he notes, "been hitherto exceedingly unfavourable among Anglo-Oriental scholars" (lv).[12] He protests, furthermore, that "it is unfair to associate it with the vagaries of fanatical, deluded mendicants, or with the modifications and adaptations which it has undergone in the hands of the Tāntrics and the Puraṇics" (lvi). This desire to rescue Patañjali from irrational Tantric zealots such as the *haṭha* yogis and to "restore" it to its perceived status as (neo-classical) philosophy also provides one of the most prominent rationales in many subsequent formulations of popular practical yoga.[13] Mitra's edition is an important landmark in this restoration process, insofar as the "tenets" it sets out are explicitly intended to "show to the unbiased enquirer that they are closely similar to those enunciated by some of the greatest metaphysicians of ancient Greece" (lvii), and to revive Patañjali in this neo-classical light. As one of the very few English translations available at this time and published in a widely disseminated, reputed series, Mitra's views (like those of Ballantyne before him) are an important marker in the development of the YS's modern intellectual context.[14]

Other early translations of the YS reflect an identical determination to represent the text as a fit participant in an explicitly European hermeneutic and philosophical colloquy. A particularly poignant example of this is afforded by a translation that appeared serially in 1877 in the monthly *Saddarshana-Chintanikâ, or Studies in Indian Philosophy*, a journal dedicated (as the sub-subtitle announces) to an explanation of "the Aphorisms of the Six Schools of Indian [i.e. *Hindu*] Philosophy."[15] The intended readership, suggests the introduction to the first number, is " [t]he modern Hindu," and the journal's purpose to "inculcate principles which have all the freshness of modern European thought and possess truths of which no nation ought to be ashamed" (n.a 1877, vol. ii). At least two things strike one about these statements. First is the evocation of an impending sense of *national shame* regarding the intellectual validity (and "freshness") of Indian forms of knowledge. The second is that to avert this sense of shame, it is necessary to establish the validity of the *saddarśanas* in terms of the *Western* tradition—not the Indian—and to implant this model in the consciousness of the present generation (which is defined in terms of modernity and Hinduism). In other words, since Western philosophy provides the standard on which Indian (Hindu) thought must be judged, it becomes culturally imperative that it be assimilated by modern citizens of India. Even the critical apparatus of the journal is designed with this pedagogical project in mind:

> *N.B. It is our intention to indicate the modern philosophical ideas of Europe in foot-notes as occasion arises either by way of comparison or contrast so that they may be popularized in this country, and that our country-men may adopt them. We need not state that modern philosophy and the material prosperity of Europe are inseparably connected* (ibid.: xv).

There is a lot riding on the *saddarśanas*: They are not only the flagship of the intellectual neo-Hindu enterprise but the merchant navy, too, holding out the prospect of material prosperity through ideological commerce. The *darśanas*, as King points out, are during this period increasingly conceived as complementary and commensurable "perspectives on a single truth," of which Vedānta is the highest expression (1999: 137). Within this philosophical framework, Yoga is not only naturally subordinate to Vedānta but Patañjali is himself recast as a Vedāntic sage.[16]

Practical Modern Patañjali

Patañjali, then, has taken such prominence in the scholastic imagination largely thanks to what Joseph Alter refers to as "Orientalist studies of Yoga as philosophy, as distinct from indigenous commentaries on Yoga as Truth" (Alter 2004: 6).[17] What is more, the centrality of (an excerpted, modernized) Patañjali to Vivekananda's yoga and to subsequent practical yoga formulations is also due—at least in part—to the wider reforms within Indian education and the concomitant projection of the YS as the founding text of yogic "philosophy." Certainly, this is the light in which the text is presented by Vivekananda, who declares, following Ballantyne and Mitra, that the aphorisms are precisely "the highest authority on Raja-Yoga and form its *textbook*" (Vivekananda 1991 [1896]: vii, my emphasis) and that "the other philosophers, though occasionally differing from Patanjali in some philosophical points, have, as a rule, acceded to his method of practice a decided consent" (ibid.). These statements become questionable, of course, as soon as we admit the possibility that the text was neither authoritative for most yoga systems nor a functional *practice* tradition as such. On the contrary, such statements more accurately reflect the way that Patañjali had been, and was being, restored, refashioned, and elevated within Orientalism and the Indian education system of which Vivekananda himself was so much a product. What Vivekananda perceives as "consent" might therefore be more profitably considered an active and current "commensurization" of the YS with the "Hindu tradition." This, combined with his American audience's clamoring for an efficient, and Indian, *method of practice*[18] goes some way to explaining the latter-day hegemony of Patañjali within contemporary yogas. In producing an eminently practical (and public) system for a new audience, indeed, Vivekananda was to some degree in accord with the intentions of Ballantyne himself, who conceived his translation project, after all, as a way to turn Indian knowledge away from excessive speculation and toward "useful truth" (Dodson 2002: 287). The desired result—"the material, social, intellectual and of course moral 'progress' of India" (ibid.)—is largely exemplified by Vivekananda's own life and work, both of which evince parallels with the method and the goal of Ballantyne's project, and with the ideological tenor of most other early translations of the YS.

Vivekananda's schooling in Calcutta institutions founded (respectively) by the educational reformists Ishvarachandra Vidyasagar[19] (1820–1891) and Alexander Duff[20] (1806–1878) exposed him to comparable (though by no means identical) efforts to discern the essential characteristics of Indian philosophy to pedagogical ends. Vidyasagar's translation of Mādhava's *Sarvadarśana Saṃgraha* of 1853—published under the patronage of the East India Company and subtitled *An Epitome of the Different Systems of Indian Philosophy*—is part of this wider project to essentialize, codify, and systematize Indian intellectual traditions as philosophy. As early as 1850, Vidyasagar advised the Calcutta Sanskrit College to change the name of the *Nyāya* class to "Darshana or Philosophy Class" and to discontinue the study of difficult *navya-nyāya* texts.

In their place, he recommended the study of *Sāṃkhyapravācana, Pātañjala darśana, Pañcadasi,* and *Sarvadarśana saṃgraha* (Bandyopadhyaya 1948: 80). One of Vidyasagar's primary, explicit aims through this curricular overhaul was to facilitate a more informed comparison of Indian and European philosophy, albeit (unlike Ballantyne) to the end of perceiving the single, self-contained truth of the Indian systems (ibid.).[21] As in Benares at precisely the same historical moment, the trend in Calcutta was toward establishing the philosophical credentials of Indian thought via the thorough reformation of the university syllabi. The name of this Indian project of philosophy has most often been, notes Halbfass, "*darśana*" (1988: 287).[22] It was through efforts such as these that the YS was established as yoga's textbook for the English-educated proto-nationalist *bhadralok* elite such as Vivekananda. Indeed, it seems reasonable to speculate that Vivekananda's first exposure to Patañjali may have come via Vidyasagar's *Sarvadarśana Saṃgraha*[23] (itself installed as a university textbook), or one of the other "philosophical" translations that were available at the time.

In terms of a modern intellectual lineage for the YS, we must also mention here the YS translation by M.N. Dvivedi of 1890, published under the auspices of the Theosophical Society in Bombay. As in Vivekananda's work six years later, the emphasis in Dvivedi's translation is on yoga as a *practical science* rather than a merely theoretical one, and his book is explicitly intended to be "suited to the wants of the general reader" in a way that Mitra's is not (Dvivedi 1890: i). In this sense, Dvivedi's work stands out from the earlier translations that stressed the element of "pure theory" in the text: a feature that, as Halbfass notes, was regarded by the European historians of philosophy, along with critical reasoning, as the "criteria of 'real' philosophy" (Halbfass 1988: 264).[24] Alongside this, and crucial to an understanding of Vivekananda's immediate ideological and intellectual precedents, is Dvivedi's equation of *rāja* yoga with the Vedānta and his assertion that the YS is predominantly a *rāja* yoga (and hence Vedāntic) text (an identification that occurs first in Dvivedi's own *Rāja Yoga* of 1885).[25] De Michelis (2004) has pointed out that such assertions also color the practical yoga initiated by Vivekananda in *his Rāja Yoga* of 1896, and it seems reasonable to posit a direct borrowing by him here from Dvivedi and his spiritual and intellectual alma mater, the Theosophical Society. *Rāja* yoga, moreover, is defined by Dvivedi against the "more physical" *haṭha* yoga (1890: vi) in a way that anticipates Vivekananda's polarization of the terms (De Michelis 2004: 178–80) and recapitulates Mme. Blavatsky's own influential dichotomization. Though there is none of the overt hostility toward *haṭha* yoga characteristic of Vivekananda and Blavatsky themselves,[26] Dvivedi claims that Patañjali perceived the "inutility" of "physical *Yoga*" (i.e. *haṭha*) and so "set up the practice of mental yoga [i.e. *rāja*] as both practical and easy" (ibid.). These features of Dvivedi's vision of yoga—in the YS edition of 1890 and in his *Rāja Yoga* of 1885—are immediate precursors for Vivekananda's identically entitled, seminal work of 1896 and help to explain the broader ideological context of his yoga system's emergence.

In this regard, we must also ask which editions Vivekananda relied on during the crucial period of *Rāja Yoga*'s composition in New York in 1895. Bharati asserts that *Rāja Yoga* is based on "a not too good late nineteenth century translation of the *Yogasūtras* of Patāñjali [sic]" (1976: 154) but neglects to mention which. Though it is possible that several of the above-mentioned translations were consulted by Vivekananda, we should consider which were most readily available to him during that particular year in America. The most likely candidate, under this criterion, is the Theosophist William Quan Judge's "interpretation" of the YS, completed in 1889 and widely circulated in a fourth edition of 1893 by the New York Theosophical imprint, The Path.[27] Based on the 1885 edition of Ballantyne and Shastrideva's translation (see note 8 below), Judge's book aims to simplify Patañjali's text "for the greater number of readers" and to "clear up" its ideas for use by "earnest students" (Judge 1965[1889]: iv). "The endeavour," he continues, "has been to interpret it to Western minds unfamiliar with the Hindu modes of expression, and equally unaccustomed to their philosophy and logic" (v). Less extensive in its commentary than Vivekananda's *Rāja Yoga*, the text's practical purpose nevertheless accords in many respects with Vivekananda's own. Though there is no space to examine such continuities in detail, it is clear that Vivekananda's project was the latest in a series of attempts to render Patañjali user-friendly to esoterically minded Westerners and to present "his" yoga to the West as India's exemplary cultural artefact. Judge's inexpensive, intentionally populist text—by an American, for Americans—may well have served as a barometer in Vivekananda's experiments to render yoga palatable and interesting to his audience.

Alongside his association with popular Western esotericism, then, Vivekananda operated in a related and markedly modern context in which *darśanas* are cast as Indian "philosophy" (Pahlajrai 2004), and "philosophy"—as Vivekananda himself expresses it—is cast as "the very essence of religion" (1992 [1901]: 72). In this framework, as Halbfass demonstrates, "philosophy" is not only part of a process of assimilation and "Westernization" but a vehicle of "self-affirmation against the West insofar as it is conceived as an intrinsically *Indian* project that provides a *practical* spiritual path unavailable in the purely theoretical Western model (1988: 287–310). It was from this recent intellectual configuration that the YS rose to the (thenceforth) unassailable imagined status of source-authority for, and essence of, yoga as a whole.

Corruption, Reformation, and *True Ground*

The colonial encounter turned the YS into a focus of self-conscious identity for modern Hindus. As a function of this encounter, within many Indian cultural nationalist circles and within some exported forms of yoga that arose from them, the YS was projected as the timeless, pristine, and unitary expression of India's yoga tradition.[28] Intrinsic to this construction was a new kind of "Classical" rhetoric, with all its resonances and connotations of seriousness, intellectualism, proportion, taste, and aesthetic—European—golden ages. As Nile Green has noted, in the period around the dawn of modern yoga,

> appeals to antique scripture[29] were part of a wider neo-classical ethos that evolved through the interaction of Indian scholars with European Orientalists, a movement whose invention of a "classical" era involved no less a denigration of a marginalised "middle" ages than its European counterpart (Green forthcoming: n88, 40).

In terms of yoga, this ethos occasioned a denigration of certain classes of practitioner, such as tantric *haṭha* yogins, who were deemed antagonistic to, or unworthy of, these classical values (Singleton 2007). Max Weber's narrative of yoga history in his *Religion of India* of 1909—with its accent on the refinements of orthodox Brahminical thought and a concomitant depreciation in importance of nonintellectual, "irrational" systems—is a particularly illuminating example of the restitution of the classical in modern times, through a process of linguistic and scholastic overkill. Classical Yoga is presented by Weber as a "rationally systematized form of methodical emotional asceticism, and therein somewhat comparable to the exercises of Ignatius" (1958 [1909]: 166)—that is, a proportioned, ordered, intellectual pursuit incorporating a measured element of devotionalism, analogous to the great contemplative traditions of Christendom. Indeed, just as Christianity condemned heathen idolatry, so too "Classical Yoga rejected the irrational mortification, the *atha Yoga* [sic.] of pure magical asceticism" (ibid.). Non-Brahminical yoga techniques, recognizes Weber, presuppose "an irrational psychic experience available by irrational means which allegedly have nothing to do with rational, demonstrable knowledge," and it is for this very reason that they could not be countenanced by "Classical Brahmanical intellectualism" (1958 [1909]: 164) with its protoscientific empirical procedures. The techniques of these casteless, non-Vedic magician-yogis, he relates, were historically "superseded by *the classical Brahmanical holy technique*" (ibid; my emphasis) and "Classical Brahmanical contemplation" (ibid.) in which rationality, gnosis, and "classical soteriology" (166) regain their rightful ascendancy. In the hands of the Brahmin intelligentsia, yoga becomes "a supreme form of a specific, intellectualistic conquest of the godly" (164) and is thereby restored to something akin to what Weber later calls "*the true ground of the classical viewpoint*" (192; my emphasis). Weber's sketch of yoga draws on the neo-classical idealism of his Orientalist peers and recapitulates the theme of a golden age of Indian philosophy characterized by "proud and rather rational conceptions of thinkers who were consistent in their ways" (177). His narrative of the origin, corruption and restoration of Classical Yoga rehearses the para-historical accounts of Orientalists such as Max Müller and is probably derived from them.[30] As Girardot points out, this oft-repeated religious theory of the "gradually corrupted, and periodically reformed" is itself made up of an odd mixture of elements "which collectively amount to a reworking of various Reformation, Enlightenment, and Romantic perspectives on religious development" (2002: 238). It is unsurprising, perhaps, that such a model would have spoken to Weber, who is best known as a theorist of the Protestant ethic. The ideal of a classical Indian canon, situated on the intellectual *true ground* of religion, held a strong ideological appeal for those who—like the "father" of modern sociology Weber—sought to grasp the fundamental characteristics of Hinduism (as well as other "religions" such as Confucianism, Taoism, and Buddhism) for comparison and contrast with the Judeo-Christian tradition. The appeals to classical rationality throughout this text also bear the distinct trace of the Platonic *logos*. Though the tendency to endorse certain strands of thought against others recapitulates currents present through Indian religious history,[31] such divisions are magnified under the "classical" lens of Indologists and Indian intellectuals in the modern period who seek to isolate and identify (for their respective ends) the phenomenon of Hinduism.

The notion of the Classical, endorsed and reinforced by the European intelligentsia, was used as a foundation, alibi, and authority for those seeking to establish a clear identity, and a sense of dignity, for India's cultural productions. Nowhere is this more apparent than in popular yoga. European Orientalists and anglicized Indian Pandits were wont to run down yoga's *popular, practical* manifestations,[32] and the reappropriation of the Classical, via the YS, by late-nineteenth-century exponents of practical yoga was a means to legitimize and elevate their own formulations in the face of such attitudes.

The Construction of the Classical in Indian Music and Dance

The stages of the "construction of the Classical" in yoga can be illuminated with reference to Indian music and dance during the period under discussion, insofar as, like in yoga, they are vital components in a project to reclaim and restore Indian cultural values during the colonial period. The field of dance in particular offers a revealing analogy for our consideration of yoga. My discussion is based mainly on two articles by ethnomusicologist Matthew Harp Allen, which summarize most concisely the main features of my argument. In his 1998 study of the influence of colonialism upon South Indian music, Allen notes that the classical/non-classical dyad derives from "a multiple intellectual lineage, incorporating colonial European alongside indigenous Indian modes of thought" (Allen 1998: 23). This was seized on, moreover, as a workable concept by cultural nationalists wishing to counter colonial claims of (British) intellectual and artistic superiority, and certain musical forms were thereby elevated as "simultaneously sophisticated, systematic, ancient and sacred" (ibid.)—much as in the case of yoga. As we have also seen with reference to yoga, such an elevation was assisted by the Orientalist project generally, with its concern to promote an ideal of "spiritual India" (see Alter 2004: 7). As Regula Qureshi notes, " [s]omewhat ironically, it was British Indology which showed the way to reclaiming the spiritual status of music" (Qureshi 1991: 160). Similar instances, indeed, can be found across the expressive arts of modern India,[33] and a particularly pertinent example is the "revival" of the quintessentially

Indian dance form, *bhārat nāṭyam*. As Allen points out elsewhere, in the Indian context, the very term *revival* "is a drastically reductive linguistic summary of a complex process—a deliberate selection from among many possibilities" (Allen 1997: 63), and *bhārat nāṭyam* is paradigmatic of this process. He identifies the constituents of this revival as (1) *re-population* (where one community appropriates a practice from another); (2) *re-construction* (altering aspects of repertoire and choreography); (3) *re-naming* (in this case from "*nautch*" and other terms to "*bhārat nāṭyam*"); (4) *re-situation* (from temple to stage); and (5) *re-storation* (in which performances are grafted together to give the impression of an ancient whole; ibid.: 63–4). To illustrate his thesis, he considers the case of the queen of modern Indian dance, Rukmini Devi (1904–1986), who—though drawing substantial inspiration from the dance traditions of the "hereditary community of artists" (63)—effectively enacted a divorce between her style of dance and those of these lower caste performers. Rukmini's dancers were drawn solely from the Brahmin community and brought with them "an explicit agenda involving appropriation based on a worldview which considered the hereditary keepers of the tradition as unworthy" (ibid.: 66). This unworthiness was, of course, both moral and hereditary: The eroticism and prostitution associated with the *devadāsī* temple dancers[34] and the *nautch* girls[35] had no place in this new cultured milieu. The operation of severance, furthermore, necessarily involved a *reconstruction* of the dance itself and an effective exclusion of those elements that connoted the *nautch* world: As N. Pattabhiram glowingly states, Devi's "unique contribution was to destroy what was crude and vulgar in the inherited traditions of dance and to replace them with sophisticated and refined taste" (1988: 24). In other words, the classical/non-classical dyad was thereafter firmly established in a manner that parallels the history of the constitution of post-Vivekanandan transnational yoga. In yoga, however, the crude and vulgar element was of course not the *nautch* but the *haṭha* yogin (Singleton 2007).

It was (as Joan Erdman tells us in her study of international Indian dance star Uday Shankar) the noted Madras Sanskritist Professor V. Raghavan who changed the name of the form to *bhārat nāṭyam* to convey its new status as the essential artistic expression of *Indian* identity and to point to a presumed Hindu golden age (Erdman 1987: 64). This new and eminently respectable mode of dance no longer took place in the temple but on the stage, and the complete authority of the teacher was replaced by the cash tuition format (Allen 1997: 67), a *re-situation* that once again matches yoga's shift from the *maṭha* (cloister, monastery) to the fee-paying classroom (De Michelis 2004: 187)—and the transition of the *guru* into a remunerated, professional yoga instructor and the *śiṣya* into client.[36] Rukmini's weltanschauung, moreover, was conditioned by her close association with the Theosophical Society (Allen 1997: 70), an organization that did perhaps more than any other to spread a distinct brand of esotericism packaged as yoga. Rukmini's family house, indeed, was situated just outside the Society's headquarters in Adyar (Chennai), and the dancer herself was twice proclaimed "World Mother" by the group (once in 1925 and again in 1928), in an appointment intended to parallel Krishnamurthy's ill-fated status as "World Teacher" (ibid.: 70).

To come to the final element of Allen's subdivisions of the *bhārat nāṭyam* revival, in Rukmini Devi's hands Indian dance was *restored* as the ancient, essential expression of Indian culture, parallel to yoga's own restoration from Vivekananda onward. At the same time, the modern (and even foreign) derivation of certain techniques and syntheses was repressed. Dance historian Priya Srinivasan summarizes as follows:

> Indian dance history does not acknowledge the importance of American and European Oriental dancers in India in the 1920s and 1930s, a presence which contributed to the revival of the "classical" forms of India. This continues as Indians have migrated to western countries where they wish to preserve their "authentic" Indianness and guard it against the pressures of assimilation. Bharatanatyam practitioners continue masking their own inventions as "tradition" in their new environments, which is complemented by Modern dancers who mask their appropriations of Asian dance forms as "new" inventions (Srinivasan 2004).

The turn-of-the-century "Oriental dance" genre pioneered by women such as Ruth St. Denis and Maud Allen was part of a more generalized assimilation of Asian-inspired techniques such as Transcendentalism, Theosophy, neo-Vedānta and, of course, yoga. The craze for Indian dancing did much to bolster the reputation and self-esteem of "indigenous" artists such as Rukmini Devi and Uday Shankar, who (as Srinivasan and Erdman, respectively, argue) adopted many of the innovations of their Western impersonators in an ongoing operation of exchange and translation. Both sides claimed to be teaching and performing the original, authentic dance of India. Much the same can be said, clearly, for the role of Vivekananda (and those who followed him) in the restoration of yoga in the modern era. The same socioeconomic group of white, mainly Protestant women who lauded Vivekananda and enthusiastically took up the practice of yoga in their own homes (see Syman 2003) were also dabbling in mystical dance. And their endorsement of Vivekananda's yoga—which, as De Michelis (2004) has demonstrated, fed back to them a version of their very own esoteric convictions—was instrumental in establishing Vivekananda as an authoritative spiritual and political voice in his homeland.[37] What is more, the European and American yoga teachers who emerged at the same time claimed to be presenting the original, authentic yoga of India, in spite of many patent innovations. As we have already seen, this was largely possible owing to the attribution of the "full authority" of the YS to modern yoga's innovations (De Michelis 2004: 179). Yoga and Indian dance are clearly both players in "a drama of appropriation and legitimation within a pan-South Asian framework of nationalist aspiration and cultural regeneration" (Allen 1997: 69) and dominant currencies of spiritual and cultural capital in the romanticized Asian marketplaces of the West.

It would be wrong to assume that because "classical" Indian dance was lifted out of the sacred environs of the temple and resituated in the classroom and on the stage, it lost any pretension toward the "spiritual." What did occur, in fact, was a self-conscious recreation of a "spiritual" aura within these secular contexts. And it is here that we return more directly to the figure of Patañjali. As for modern yoga, modern Indian dance came into being in (sometimes violent) reaction against the purportedly primitive, mystical practices of the original exponents of the "art" and, in certain instances, replaced them with a modern, Enlightenment ethos of personal, secular spirituality.[38] One of the ways in which Rukmini Devi accomplished this transition was by placing an icon of the "dancing Śiva" Naṭarāja on stage while she performed, a device intended to recapture some of the mystery of the very temples she had cut herself off from (Allen 1997: 79). She thereby created a kind of second-order religiosity, based on the imitation of an original context that had needed to be rejected. Given the ubiquitousness of the Naṭarāja icon today—as a symbol not only of dance but of "Indian spirituality" in general—it is remarkable that Rukmini's innovation was probably the first time that a Naṭarāja had presided over a dance performance in this way (ibid.). Indeed, according to Allen, the notion of Naṭarāja as "god of the dance" took hold of the public imagination thanks to A.K. Coomaraswamy's 1918 essay, "The Dance of Shiva" (in Coomaraswamy 1948), which promoted the deity as an emblem of cultural nationalism (Allen 1997: 79). Coomaraswamy developed

> an overriding concern with Hindu India's "classical" heritage in the arts—a concern both to demonstrate the existence of an ancient sophisticated heritage based on ideals of *Vedanta* and *yoga* and to revive that heritage in the present day (ibid: 85),

and the reclamation of the figure of Naṭarāja as a symbol of that heritage was one product of this concern. Given the historical contiguity of modern dance and modern yoga and the fact that Coomaraswamy and cultural nationalists like him were energetically engaged in "an elaborate exposition on the links between art, asceticism and *Yoga* in the Indian tradition" (Guha-Thakurta 1992: 178), it is hardly surprising that Patañjali has come to occupy a (dis-re-located) place within modern yoga parallel to that of Natarāja in *bhārat nāṭyam* (in spite of the fact that Naṭarāja is indisputably a god, whereas Patañjali is not). Like Naṭarāja in classrooms and theaters of modern Indian dance, *mūrtis* of Patañjali now commonly grace the shrines of modern yoga studios in the West, as a focus of devotion and inspiration for practitioners. Both are modern adjuncts to contemporary body disciplines associated with Indian cultural-nationalist self-assertions on the one hand and transnational practice on the other.

Conclusion: The Classical in Contemporary Transnational Yoga

Patañjali and the "Classical Yoga" he symbolizes are today pervasively used to underwrite the authenticity of techniques engaged in by modern transnational practitioners. A recent Google search for the phrase *trained in Classical Yoga* returned approximately 353,000 hits, a large number of which appeared to be advertisements for Western teachers imparting the blends of postural stretching, relaxation, and "meditation" characteristic of popular transnational yoga today. It is clear that within the global marketplace of early-twenty-first-century yoga, the label "Classical" functions as an affirmation of a technique's soundness and verifiability. Even—perhaps especially—in the *āsana*-heavy systems that have become synonymous with yoga for many Westerners, the YS is today habitually invoked as a source and authority for practitioners, in spite of the infrequency of material on *āsana* in the YS and its commentaries (beyond terse references to static meditation "seats") and the fact that there is "no evidence" for an "ancient tradition" of *āsana* practice (Bühnemann 2007: 160). This lacuna can often be a cause of consternation for Western practitioners of modern, dynamic postural sequences (such as Ashtanga Vinyasa yoga), who take up study of the YS on the assurance that it is the foundational document of their own practice lineage.[39]

Such views have been endorsed and amplified by transnational gurus such as B.K.S. Iyengar, who has been a significant impetus in the establishment of Patañjali as a devotional focus within international postural yoga. From his seminal *Light on Yoga* of 1966 (the *vade mecum* of several generations of *āsana* enthusiasts), through *Yoga Vṛkṣa: Tree of Yoga* (1988) and *Light on the Yoga Sūtras of Patañjali* (1993), Iyengar has been concerned to align his posture system with the YS. Iyengar yoga classes worldwide typically begin with a chant to Patañjali, and an icon or photograph of him not uncommonly adorns the yoga room. Most remarkable, however, is the 2004 establishment by Iyengar, in his native village of Bellur (Karnataka), of what is claimed to be India's first Patañjali temple.[40] The temple, promoted by his organization as "a place of pilgrimage for all the Iyengar students" (B.K.S.Iyengar.com 2006), represents not only a reassertion of Iyengar's own devotional roots—albeit significantly reoriented from more traditional Śrī Vaiṣṇava devotional foci—but the latest expression of Patañjali's elevation as the central symbol of devotion and respect within health- and physical culture-oriented, transnational yoga. A similar elevation of Patañjali's standing can be seen in the "Vedic" chanting of the YS in the teachings of T.K.V. Desikachar (student and son of Iyengar's guru, T. Krishnamacharya). As Klas Nevrin points out, such chanting "considerably elevates the status of the text by treating it as if it were a Vedic or Tantric text with mantras to be chanted and not sūtras to be memorized" (Nevrin, forthcoming). On many accounts," Nevrin continues,

> we are witnessing innovation, both in terms of the role played by reciting YS (using Vedic chanting techniques), as well as the way in which the

devotionalism of *Sri Vaishnavism* (i.e. *bhakti-yoga*) is coupled with an unprecedented emphasis on practicing Ashtanga Yoga (ibid.).

Examples such as these are representative of the kind of "category shift" that has characterized the treatment of Patañjali and the YS within some of the most popular global forms of yoga today. Given space, many more instances of the shifting and varied function of the YS could be adduced, especially within acculturated transnational yoga communities today, where practitioners increasingly demand authentic (viz. Sanskritic) authority for their practices. In many cases, such modern practitioner rationalizations are inherently tautological, insofar as the modern category of "Classical" has functioned to lend a new kind of canonicity to certain texts, which then lend their authority to the very exponents of yoga who helped to establish said texts within modern expressions of yoga. In this sense, some forms of transnational yoga operate in a closed, circular, and *self-authorizing* system. Of course, contemporary transnational practitioners are no longer engaged in the same way with the ideological nexuses of constructive Orientalism and cultural assertion that shaped the interpretations of the early modern rehabilitators of the YS. Many other intervening factors would need to be examined to understand Patañjali's status and function in twenty-first-century global yoga. However, it seems clear that the widespread acceptance of the YS as the origin and fountainhead of transnational yoga practice today was made possible by the installation of Patañjali as the *logos* of yoga during the heyday of European Orientalism.

Notes

1 Thanks to Brian Hatcher and Peter Schreiner for their comments on earlier versions of this chapter.
2 See Nevrin (Forthcoming).
3 See Alter 2004: 6–8 for a useful historical summary of these commentaries.
4 See Larson 1989 and 1999; Bronkhorst 1981.
5 Larson 1989 gives a useful survey of the "hybridity" debate and a lexical comparison of the YS and Vasubandhu's *Abhidharmakośa*. Bronkhurst (1993) goes so far as to argue that the YS is theoretically dependent on Buddhist sources.
6 Sarbacker (2005: 101) includes Sénart, de la Vallé Poussin, and Oldenburg as scholars who assert this latter.
7 Sjoman does, however, oddly speculate that the Tattva-Vaiśāradī of Vacaspati Miśra (ca. ninth century C.E.) and the commentary of twentieth-century *Sāṃkhyayogācārya* Hariharānanda Āraṇya may be somehow connected to a "living" Patañjalian tradition, though he admits that the situation is ultimately "enigmatic" (1996: 38).
8 See Classical Yoga Hindu Academy (2007) for one modern Hindu vision of Patañjali's status.
9 The translation was eventually "completed" thirty years later in 1882 by Shastrideva, and published by the Bombay branch of the Theosophical Society (see Shastrideva and Ballantyne 1885).
10 Mitra, significantly, declares himself to be "No Yogi myself, nor anywise interested in the doctrine" (lxiii), in what seems to be a thinly veiled profession of his own credibility as a scholar.
11 "And we have enough in these facts and reasons to infer that the Yoga text-book is posterior to the Sankhya text-book and that both the text-books are later than

Buddha" (xxiii). It is also worth noting that the very choice of the term *aphorism* in the title (from the earliest YS translations a standard gloss on "sūtra") already serves to implicitly align the YS with a specific, Western philosophical format.

12 Much of the introduction and appendix to Govind Shastrideva's 1885 "completion" of Ballantyne's partial translation of the YS (prefaced by Olcott) are similarly dedicated to a rapprochement between Patañjali and Western philosophers, ancient and modern. Note also the common slur on "[t]he painful postures and sometimes revolting practices" of *haṭha* yoga (1885: vi).

13 See Singleton 2007 for a fuller account of the exclusion of *haṭha* yoga from "neo-Classical" modern yogas.

14 Ramchandra Bose, in his 1884 exposition of the orthodox *darśanas*, *Hindu Philosophy Popularly Explained*, praises the work of "our illustrious countryman" Mitra who, he declares, "has done so much to popularize the knowledge enshrined in the sacred literature of the country" (160).

15 The editor's name is not apparent from the journal itself, and in the written endorsements that accompany each volume (which include letters from Max Müller and M. Monier-Williams) he is referred to mysteriously as Mr——. However, Bose (1884: 160) names him as "Professor Kunte."

16 Also pertinent here is Col. Olcott's preface in Shastrideva's 1885 "completion" of Ballantyne's YS translation, where the "six schools of philosophy" of "Ancient India" are claimed to have had "their counterpart in Greece" (i). *Haṭha* yoga, conversely, is "strongly denounced by all the philosophers" (iii). This opinion is also quoted (without attribution) in Sarkar's YS commentary of 1902 (54).

17 On the topic of "Indian Philosophy," Larson 1989 makes a similar distinction between "spiritual methodologies 'vierge du métaphysique'" (La Vallé Poussin's phrase) and systematic reflections that seek overall coherence (131). He cautions, moreover, against considering every textual occurrence of the terms *Yoga* and *Sāṃkhya* as expressions of the latter approach (ibid.). My point here is not that it is somehow illegitimate to consider the YS as philosophy in this sense (though many have of course questioned its overall coherence and cohesion) but simply that it was assimilated, as philosophy, into an explicitly ideological project within nineteenth century colonialism.

18 See De Michelis 2004: 116–19.

19 Vidyasagar was, notes Halbfass, "[o]ne of the greatest educators and most efficient 'reformers'" of the day (1988: 247). He was "one of the first Indians to apply Western historical and critical methods" and "never abandoned his confidence in what he considered to be superior European learning and rationality" (ibid.). He is not to be confused with Pandit Jibananda Vidyasagara, superintendent of the Free Sanskrit College in Calcutta, who in 1874 published a Sanskrit edition of the YS, with the Vyāsa commentary and Vacaspati Miśra gloss, entitled, *The Patanjala Darshana, or The Aphorisms of Theistic Philosophy*. This book, incidentally, suggests that there was also an interest and a market for editions of the YS that were not geared toward English-language philosophers.

20 "Both men embodied powerful intellectual positions attempting to synthesize tradition and modernity, both were convinced rationalists, but most of all both fostered a secularist spirit in their charges" (De Michelis 2004: 94). As the epigraph to this section may suggest, Duff was a tireless crusader for the "Classical" (that is to say, graeco-Christian) within Indian religion. His 1840 "unfoldment" of the "grand theory of Hinduism" (vi) is a self-consciously selective rendering which seeks to isolate 'the real genius and spirit of the system' (242) uniquely within high-caste orthodox Brahminism. Religious expression outside this orthodox framework is treated to a lengthy denunciation that is both lurid and pious by turns.

21 Thanks to Brian Hatcher for alerting me to this report by Vidyasagar.

22 "Since the first half of the nineteenth century, and in particular since the introduction of English as the language of higher education (1835) and the inauguration of English-

language universities (after 1854), philosophy in the European sense and, moreover, the word and concept of 'philosophy,' has taken up an ever firmer place in Indian religious life" (Halbfass 1988: 287). On one hand, European thought was adopted by Indians, but at the same time "India's own, indigenous tradition has also been rediscovered and interpreted as philosophy, and it has thus been presented anew, and related to Western philosophy in a multitude of ways, involving comparison, identification, parallelization, or contrasting and neutralization" (ibid.). See also Hartog 1929 for a brief history of the Indian university.

23 Or perhaps that of Cowell and Gough of 1874–78 (published in Trubner's Oriental Series, 1882).

24 This is not to say that Dvivedi was not also deeply involved in the project to further the rapprochement of Western philosophy and (Vedāntic) Hinduism. The extensive introduction to his *Rāja Yoga, or The Practical Metaphysics of the Vedanta* of 1885, for example, is in fact mainly taken up with establishing the case that Western philosophy and science are "mainly in accordance with, and lead logically to, the teachings and precepts of Eastern Adwaiteesm" (31). Dvivedi's practical Patañjali should be considered as the intellectual child of the Theosophical Society and is the first in an extensive series of practical renderings of the YS. Other important examples of this trend are Sarkar (1902); Johnston (1912); and Stephen (1914).

25 The precise intellectual maneuver by which Patañjali is "vedānticized" by Dvivedi is most clearly encapsulated in a passage from his *Rāja Yoga*: Patañjali, he asserts, "abolished the idle distinction between inseparable Purusha and Prakriti as an inconvenient bar in the way of any action for Moksha as such, and declared that the whole universe was all Purusha, or Brahma" (1885: 45). See De Michelis (2004), White (2004), and Schreiner (2007) for discussion of the academically controversial term *rāja yoga*.

26 See Vivekananda 1992 [1894] 184; 1992 [1896]: 20; 1992 [1900]: 225; 1992 [1902]: 242. And Blavatsky 1982a: 462–4; 1982b: 160, 604, 615; 1982c: 51, 113. See also Singleton 2007 for a further analysis of this attitude in relation to modern yoga.

27 The fact that Mitra's, Dvivedi's, and Shastrideva's translations were published only in Bombay at that time does not of course preclude Vivekananda's consultation of them.

28 Vivekananda expresses this vision of timelessness and completion well in *Raja Yoga*: " [f]rom the time it was discovered, more than four thousand years ago, Yoga was perfectly delineated, formulated and preached in India [...] the more ancient the writer, the more rational he is" (Vivekananda 1991 [1896]: 134).

29 As Girardot points out, from the nineteenth century, the term *scripture* was "for the first time used in a generic and pluralistic way," within the context of comparative religion, to refer to "holy" texts from other, in particular Oriental, traditions, rather than exclusively to Biblical writings of the Hebrew and Christian traditions (2002: 232). The YS certainly came to be perceived as possessing this less-restricted status of a sacred document (especially within modern yoga) in spite of its not traditionally belonging within the category of *śruti*, or divinely revealed knowledge. This was facilitated by the comparative perspective that British Orientalism made possible, combined with a pick-and-mix romanticism regarding sacred India and its literature that characterizes certain expressions of modern yoga. In short, I am using Green's statement on the assumption that the point it makes also holds good for the YS, which was elevated to canonical status in the modern period within just such a neo-classical ethos.

30 See Müller (1899: 458–65) for an example of this and related narratives. A virtually identical account is given in E. Washburn Hopkins's important *The Religions of India* (1970 [1885]: 351).

31 For example, White diagnoses "the centuries-old error of identifying the aphorisms of the philosophico-psychological portion of the YS—i.e., the bulk of the contents

of the first, second, and fourth *pādas* of the work—as Classical Yoga,'" pointing out that it is Advaita Vedāntins who are in the main responsible for this identification. The mistake is compounded in the modern period, he points out, by Vivekananda in his amalgamation of "Classical Yoga" with "rāja yoga" (2004: 623). White's thesis is further confirmation that Orientalist assertions regarding the status of the YS (such as Müller's rejection of the *aṣṭāṅga* section in *pāda* 2 and the miraculous *vibhūti* of *pāda* 3 as inauthentic, degenerate late additions [1899: 458]) recapitulate themes and trends that were already present within the Indian tradition. This "recapitulation" of Orientalist themes in the Indian tradition is the topic of Sheldon Pollock's controversial essay "Deep Orientalism? Notes on Sanskrit and Power Beyond the Raj" (1993).

32 E.g. Müller (1899: xx and 458). Müller, incidentally, deplored the 1893 Chicago Parliament of World Religions at which Vivekananda made his sensational American debut (Girardot 2002: 234 n.42). See also De Michelis 2004: 9–12 on the similar kind of disdain evinced by the Orientalists Raymond Schwab and Mircea Eliade regarding "esoteric" elements within Indology.

33 Highly relevant in this regard is the case of Indian painting. See Mitter 1994.

34 In the 1920s, there was even a campaign to abolish the ill-reputed *devadāsī* system (Allen 1997: 67). See Kersenboom (1987) on this topic and on the collapse in modern times of the traditional "mythopoetical universe" that sustained the *devadāsī*. The system persists, however, to the present day, and it is estimated that there are 25,000 devadāsīs in Karnataka alone (Grammaticas 2007).

35 Indian dancers were collectively referred to as "nautch girls" by the British and were often brought to Europe and America by impresarios such as P.T. Barnum (of circus fame) as part of the simultaneously exotic-erotic and grotesque carnival of Indian culture (Srinivasan 2004). See Reed 1998 on the "'native dancers' featured prominently in Carl Hagenbeck's profitmaking ethnological displays in nineteenth-century Europe" (509). The amateur British yogi-fakir Victor Dane, in his colourful popular ethnography *Naked Ascetic* (1933), offers a vivid vignette of an erotic nautch performance attended by him in colonial India (257).

36 This observation is in no way intended to imply a general judgment about the modern remunerated teacher's integrity, nor to suggest that financial gain should be considered the prime motivating factor in modern yoga teaching. Despite yoga's relatively recent association with corporate business, cynicism is not a prevalent feature in most modern yoga milieux.

37 Peter van der Veer similarly argues that Vivekananda's cultural nationalist project could not have emerged without his having devized classes on ancient Indian wisdom for Bostonians: "This was one of the first and most important steps in systematizing 'Indian spirituality' as a discipline for body and spirit, which has become so important in transnational spiritual movements of Indian origins. Vivekananda's success in the United States did not go unnoticed in India. He returned as a certified saint" (1994: 118). See also Bharati's now-famous analysis of the "pizza effect" in transnational Hinduism, in Bharati 1970.

38 By this I intend the kind of "unchurched" religiosity described at length in Fuller (2001).

39 See Maehle (2006) for a recent, and particularly clear, endorsement of this line of reasoning in Ashtanga Vinyasa yoga.

40 The British ethnographer Briggs refers to a Patañjali āśrama in Haridwar (Briggs 1938:4), and there seems to exist examples of a cult of (the composite grammarian and yogi) Patañjali in certain locations in South India, as Younger (1995) has shown. It is therefore necessary to consider the possibility that Patañjali played a devotional role within some (mainly Vaiṣṇava?) sectors of Indian society, prior to and independent of what I have framed as his "installation" by scholars and yoga revivalists such as Vivekananda. However, I have not found any evidence to counter

Iyengar's claim that the Bellur temple is India's first to be dedicated exclusively to Patanjali.

Bibliography

Allen, M.H. (1997) Rewriting the Script for South Indian Dance, *The Drama Review* 41 (3): 63–100.

——(1998) Tales Tunes Tell: Deepening the Dialogue between "Classical" and "Non-Classical" in the Music of India, *Yearbook for Traditional Music* 30: 22–52.

Alter, J.S. (2004) *Yoga in Modern India : the body between science and philosophy*, Princeton: Princeton University Press.

Bandyopadhyaya, G. (ed) (1948) *Kalikata Samskrta Kalejer Itihasa, Part One*, Kolkata: Sanskrit College.

B.K.S.Iyengar.com (2006), Inauguration of the WORLD'S FIRST "Sage Patanjali" Temple at Bellur, Karnataka, India. Available HTTP: <http://www.bksiyengar.com/modules/Institut/Yogini/temple.htm.> (accessed July 12, 2007).

Ballantyne, J.R. (1852) *The Aphorisms of the Yoga Philosophy of Patanjali with Illustrative Extracts from the Commentary by Bhoja Raja*, Allahabad: Presbyterian Mission Press.

Bharati, A. (1970) The Hindu renaissance and its apologetic patterns, *Journal of Asian Studies* 29 (2): 267–88.

——(1976) *The Light at the Center, Context and Pretext of Modern Mysticism*, Santa Barbara: Ross-Erikson.

Blavatsky, H.P. (1982a) *Collected Writings Volume II, 1879-1880*, Wheaton, Ill., Madras: Theosophical Publishing House.

——(1982b), *Collected Writings Volume VI, 1883-1885*, Wheaton Ill, Madras: Theosophical Publishing House.

——(1982c), *Collected Writings Volume VIII, 1887*, Wheaton Ill, Madras: Theosophical Publishing House.

Bose, R.C. (1884) *Hindu Philosophy Popularly Explained, The Orthodox Systems*, New York: Funk and Wagnalls.

Briggs, G.W. (1989 [1938]) *Goraknāth and the Kānpaṭa Yogīs*, Delhi: Motilal Banarsidass.

Bronkhorst, J. (1981) Yoga and Seśvara Sāṃkhya, *Journal of Indian Philosophy* 9: 309–20.

——(1985) Patañjali and the Yoga Sūtras, *Studien zur Indologie und Iranistik* 10: 191–212.

——(1993) *The two traditions of meditation in ancient India*, Delhi: Motilal Banarsidass Publishers.

——(2005) The Reliability of Tradition, *Boundaries, Dynamics and Construction of Traditions in South Asia*. F. Squarcini. Firenze, Delhi: Firenze University Press and Munshiram Manoharlal, 63–76.

Bühneman, G. (2007) The Identification of an Illustrated Haṭhayoga Manuscript and Its Significance for Traditions of 84 Āsanas in Yoga, *Asian Medicine, Tradition and Modernity—Special Yoga Issue* 3 (1): 156–76.

Classical Yoga Hindu Academy (2007). The True Facts About Yoga, Available HTTP: <http://www.classicalyoga.org/true_facts_about_yoga.htm> (accessed June 1, 2007).

Coomaraswamy, A.K. (1948) *The dance of Shiva : fourteen Indian essays*, Bombay: Published for Asia Pub. House by P. S. Jayasinghe.

Dane, V. (1933) *Naked Ascetic*, London: Rider.

De Michelis, E. (2004) *A History of Modern Yoga : Patañjali and Western esotericism*, London: Continuum.

Dodson, M.S. (2002) Re-Presented for the Pandits: James Ballantyne, "Useful Knowledge," and Sanskrit Scholarship in Benares College during the Mid-Nineteenth Century, *Modern Asian Studies* 36 (2): 257–98.

Duff, A. (1988 [1840]) *India and Indian Missions: Including Sketches of the Gigantic System of Hinduism both in Theory and in Practice*, Delhi: Swati.

Dvivedi, M.N. (1885) *Raja Yoga, or The Practical Metaphysics of the Vedanta*, Bombay: Sobhodha-Prakasha Press.

—(1890) *The Yoga-Sutra of Patanjali*, Bombay: Tookaram Tatya for the Bombay Theosophical Publication Fund.

Erdman, J.L. (1987) Performance as Translation, Uday Shankar in the West, *The Drama Review* 31 (1): 64–88.

Fuller, R.C. (2001) *Spiritual but not Religious, Understanding Unchurched America*, Oxford: Oxford University Press.

Girardot, N.J. (2002) Max Muller's "Sacred Books" and the Nineteenth-Century Production of the Comparative Science of Religions, *History of Religions* 41 (3): 213–50.

Grammaticus, D. (2007) *Slaves to the Goddess of Fertility*, Available HTTP: <http://news.bbc.co.uk/2/hi/south_asia/6729927.stm> (accessed June 8, 2007).

Green, N. (forthcoming) Breathing in India, c.1890, *Modern Asian Studies*.

Grinshpon, Y. (2002) *Silence Unheard : Deathly otherness in Patanjala-yoga*, Albany: State University of New York Press.

Guha-Thakurta, T. (1992) *The Making of a New "Indian" Art. Artists, aesthetics and nationalism in Bengal, c.1850-1920*, Cambridge: Cambridge University Press.

Halbfass, W. (1988) *India and Europe : an essay in understanding*, Albany: State University of New York Press.

Hartog, P.J. (1929) The Indian Universities, *Annals of the American Academy of Political and Social Science* 145 (2): 138–50.

Hopkins, E.W. (1970 [1885]) *The Religions of India*, New Delhi: Munshiram Manoharlal.

Iyengar, B.K.S. (1966) *Light on Yoga*, London: Allen & Unwin.

—(1988) *Yoga Vṛkṣa: Tree of Yoga*, Oxford: Fine Line.

—(1993) *Light on the Yoga Sūtras of Patañjali*, London: Aquarian/Thorsons.

Johnston, C. (1912) *The Yoga Sutras of Patanjali, The Book of Spiritual Man*, New York: Charles Johnston.

Judge, William Q. (1965 [1889]) *The Yoga Aphorisms of Patanjali, An Interpretation by W.Q. Judge*. 4th ed., New York: The Path.

Kersenboom, S. (1987) *Nityasumangali : Devadasi tradition in South India*, Delhi: Motilal Banarsidass.

King, R. (1999) *Orientalism and Religion : Post-colonial theory, India and the mystic East*, London: Routledge.

Larson, J.G. (1989) An Old Problem Revisited: the Relation between Sāṃkhya, Yoga and Buddhism, *Studien zur Indologie und Iranistik* 15: 129–46.

—(1999) Classical Yoga as Neo-Sāṃkhya: A Chapter in the History of Indian Philosophy, *Asiatische Studien* 53 (3): 723–32.

Madhava, trans. I. Vidyasagara (1858 [1853]) *Sarvadarsana sangraha, or, An epitome of the different systems of Indian philosophy*, Calcutta: Asiatic Society of Bengal.

Madhava, trans. E.B. Cowell, et al. (1882) *The Sarva-Darsana-Samgraha*, London: Trubner.

Maehle, G. (2006) *Ashtanga Yoga: Practice and Philosophy*, Innaloo City: Kaivalya

Mitra, R. (1883) *The Yoga Aphorisms of Patanjali with the Commentary of Bhoja Raja and and English Translation*, Calcutta: Asiatic Society of Bengal.

Mitter, P. (1994) *Art and Nationalism in colonial India, 1850–1922*, Cambridge: Cambridge University Press.

Müller, M. (1899) *The Six Systems of Indian Philosophy*, London, New York, Bombay: Longmans, Green and Co.

n.a. (1877) *The Saddarshana-Chintanikâ, or Studies in Indian Philosophy. A Monthly Publication Stating and Explaining the Aphorisms of the Six Schools of Indian Philosophy, with their translation in to Marathi and English*, Poona: Dnyan Prakash Press.

Nevrin, K. (forthcoming) Performing the Yogasutra: Towards a methodology for studying recitation in modern Hatha Yoga, *Chakra*.

Ohtani, K. (1991) "Bharata Nāṭyam," Rebirth of Dance in India, *Studia Musicologica Academiae Scientiarum Hungaricae* 33: 301–8.

Pahlajrai, P. (2004) Doxographies-Why six *darśanas*? Which six? students.washington.edu/prem/Colloquium04-Doxographies.pdf. August. (Last accessed June 1, 2006).

Pattabhiram, N. (1988) The Trinity of Bharatanatyam: Bala, Rukmini Devi and Kamala, *Sruti* 48: 23–4.

Pollock, S. (1993). Deep Orientalism? Notes on Sanskrit and Power Beyond the Raj, in C. Breckenridge and P. van der Veer (eds) *Orientalism and the Postcolonial Predicament, Perspectives on South Asia*. Philadelphia: University of Pennsylvania Press, 76–133.

Qureshi, R. (1991) Whose Music? Sources and Contexts in Indic Musicology, in V. Bohlman and B. Nettl (eds) *Comparative musicology and anthropology of music : essays on the history of ethnomusicology : Conference entitled "Ideas, concepts, and personalities in the history of ethnomusicology" : Papers*, Chicago: University of Chicago Press, 152–68.

Reed, S. A. (1998) The Politics and Poetics of Dance, *Annual Review of Anthropology* 27: 503–2.

Sarbacker, S.R. (2005) *Samādhi : Numinous and Cessative in Indo-Tibetan Yoga*, Albany: State University of New York Press.

Sarkar, K.L. (1902) *The Hindu System of Self-Culture, or the Patanjala Yoga Shastra*, Calcutta: Sarasi Lal Sarkar.

Schreiner, P. (2007) Le rāja-yoga dans une perspective historique, in S. Berti Rossi and D. Chaille (eds) *L'héritage spirituel de l'Inde: Des Védas à la Bhagavad-Gita*. Gollion: Infolio éditions, 15–76. (vol. 1 of *Raja Yoga : Histoire et tradition*, 7 vols.).

Shastrideva, G. and J. Ballantyne (1885) *The Yoga Philosophy, being the Text of Patanjali with Bhoja Raja's Commentary; with their translations in English by Dr. Ballantyne and Govind Shastri Deva, and Introduction by Col. Olcott and an Appendix*, Bombay: Tookaram Tatya for the Bombay Theosophical Fund.

Singleton, M. (2007) The Body at the Centre: Contexts of Postural Yoga in the Modern Age, [Unpublished Ph. D dissertation], Cambridge: Faculty of Divinity, University of Cambridge, 228 pages.

Sjoman, N.E. (1996) *The Yoga Tradition of the Mysore Palace*, New Delhi: Abhinav Publications.

Srinivasan, P. (2004) Dancing Modern/Dancing Indian/Dancing...In America. The Myths of Cultural "Purity" *Ballet-Dance Magazine*.

Stephen, D.R. (1914) *Patanjali for Western Readers, The Yoga Aphorisms of Patanjali Paraphrased and Modernised from Various English Translations and Recensions*, London: Theosophical Publishing Society.

Syman, S. (2003) Boston Brahma: How a group of turn-of-the-century Cambridge women made America safe for yoga, *The Boston Globe* (Friday August 8), Available HTTP: <www.boston.com/news/globe/ideas/articles/2003/08/24/boston_brahma?mode=PF> (accessed July 10, 2004).

van der Veer, P. (1994) *Religious Nationalism, Hindus and Muslims in India*, London: University of California Press.

Vasu, S.C. (1895) *The Gheranda Sanhita, A Treatise on Hatha Yoga*, Bombay: Bombay Theosophical Publication Fund.

Vasudeva, S. (2004) *The Yoga of the Malinīvijayottaratantra : chapters 1-4, 7-11, 11-17*, Pondicherry: Institut Francais de Pondichery, Ecole Francaise D' Extreme-Orient.

Vidyasagara, I. (trans.) (1858 [1853]) *Sarvadarsana sangraha, or, An epitome of the different systems of Indian philosophy*, Calcutta: Asiatic Society of Bengal.

Vidyasagara, P.J. (1874) *The Patanjala Darshana, or The Aphorisms of Theistic Philosophy, with the Commentary of Maharshi Vedavyasa and the gloss of Vachaspati Misra*, Calcutta: Satya Press.

Vivekananda, S. (1991 [1896]) *Raja Yoga, or Conquering the Internal Nature*, Calcutta: Advaita Ashrama.

—(1992 [1894]) Miracles, *The Complete Works of Swami Vivekananda*, Calcutta: Advaita Ashram, 183–5.

—(1992 [1895]) Epistle LXII, *The Complete Works of Swami Vivekananda*, Calcutta: Advaita Ashram, 361–3.

—(1992 [1900]) Concentration, *The Complete Works of Swami Vivekananda*, Calcutta: Advaita Ashrama, 218–26.

—(1992 [1901]) *Karma Yoga*, Calcutta: Advaita Ashrama.

—(1992 [1902]) Conversations and Dialogues XXIII, in *The Complete Works of Swami Vivekananda*. Calcutta: Advaita Ashram, 239–44.

Weber, M. (1958 [1909]) *The Religion of India*, Glencoe, IL: The Free Press.

Whicher, I. and D. Carpenter (2003) *Yoga : The Indian tradition*, London: Routledge/ Curzon.

White, D.G. (2004) Early Understandings of Yoga in the Light of Three Aphorisms from the Yoga Sutras of Patañjali, *Du corps humain, au carrefour de plusieurs savoirs en Inde. Mélanges offerts à Arion Rosu par ses collègues et ses amis à l'occasion de son 80e anniversaire*. E. Ciurtin. Paris: De Boccard, 611–27.

Younger, P. (1995) *The Home of the Dancing Śivan, The Traditions of the Hindu Temple in Citamparam*, Oxford: Oxford University Press.

5 The Reflexivity of the Authenticity of *Haṭha* Yoga

Kenneth Liberman

The "Origin"of *Haṭha* Yoga

In yoga today, there is a widespread assumption that once, long ago, there was a pure and original yoga. This tradition is thought to have passed through a long lineage of adepts with a modest amount of change until it reached us in the modern era, where it has become contaminated with European Christian (or Buddhist or Muslim) notions and by the general tendency of contemporary capitalist culture to commodify everything. The sincere concern is voiced that what is sold as "yoga" in the West today is a derivative yoga that has transformed, and thereby lost, the core insights of the original yoga to the point that yoga and *bhoga*[1] are not readily distinguishable. The concern is a diligent one, were it not complicated by the fact that many of the assumptions that underlie it are erroneous. Yet the intuition that animates this concern must be kept in play but with the condition that it becomes better informed about the actual circumstances of yoga and its evolution.

There never existed a "pure" yoga; rather, yoga, like every other social production, was syncretic from the outset. As we have learned from Jacques Derrida (1974: 61), absolutely everything in this world is derivative, and most talk of "origins"is illusionary. The notion of an original yoga is a just-so story that is constructed about the cultural context of yoga, which is transmitted (often by ill-informed students) at the time practices are taught. The aspect of yoga that involves extensive physical discipline and the exploration of the anatomical-physiological bases of spiritual practice, that is, the yogic tradition known as *haṭha* yoga, was never a major part of "classical" yoga, if we can even speak of classical yoga, given the paucity of historical records, which are mostly shrouded in mythology or iconography; *haṭha* yoga was actually a "medieval" phenomenon[2] in that it did not develop until the tenth to twelfth centuries. Even these yogis used *āsana* not for meditation or better health but to awaken the *kuṇḍalinī* and gain such *siddhis* as human flight, alchemical abilities, and escaping death (White 2003: 221).

Before the period of these great ascetics and yogis of the northern jungles of India during those relatively recent centuries of innovation, yoga consisted primarily of contemplation and mantra (for example, the use of the *bīja* "Om" is ancient), and the principal aims were to achieve a sense of mental equilibrium, a degree of control over the baser (*tamasic* and *rajasic*) energies of the nervous system, selflessness, and a sustainable reconciliation with being. The few *āsana* known and practiced in classical times, such as *siddhāsana* and *padmāsana*, were designed to facilitate meditation or to pacify the body generally and did not constitute anything like a physical culture. Patañjali's *Yogasūtra* barely discusses *āsana*, except as a means of gaining stability (*sthira*) and makes no mention of *nāḍīs* or *cakras*. Austerities and *tapas* were practiced, but their purpose was to facilitate renunciation and to restrain desire, disciplines essential for spiritual freedom. In brief, they emphasized mental practices more than physical ones.

Whereas the yoga of Patañjali has *Sāṃkhya* metaphysics at its basis, the "yoga"of the Nāths, Kānphaṭas, or *yogis* of north India in the tenth to twelfth centuries was a syncretic amalgam of tantra with aspects of Mahāyāna Buddhism, Śaivism, alchemy, and magic. It was these yogis, generally driven to the East and into the jungles by the Muslim migrations, who experimented with *āsana* and *prāṇāyāma*, vastly extending their pertinence in yogic practice. These ascetics rejected the rigid principles of the Hinduism of their day, including the caste system, and many of the original teachers were Buddhist, including their founder Matsyendranāth (tenth century),[3] for whom the *āsana* "*matsyendrāsana*" is named and who in Nepal was associated with the Buddhist deity Avalokitesvara. Matsyendranāth was also known as Minanāth (Mallik 1954: 10), a name that relates to a practitioner of Buddhist tantra, or simply as the Ādi Vajrācārya ("the preceptor of *Vajrayāna*," the Mahāyāna form of tantric worship; Mallik 1954: 17). White (2003: 24) writes, "The earliest accounts of the *cakras* as 'circles' or 'wheels' of subtle energy located within the yogic body are found in the *Caryāgīti* and the *Hevajra* tantra, two circa eighth-century Buddhist Tantric works that locate four *cakras* within the human body at the levels of the navel, heart, throat, and head."

The two sons of Matsyendranāth are Jain saints. The term *Nāth* itself means "Lord"and has its origin in Buddhism, and it is usually adopted as the surname for male Kānphaṭas (Bhattacharya 1968 (1896): 318).[4] These ascetics specialized in learning practical techniques for awakening *kuṇḍalinī śakti* through elaborate daily bodily practices (*kāyasādhana*) and relied more on personal experience than on textual traditions. The earliest uses of the term *kuṇḍalinī* occurred in the tenth to eleventh centuries, but it was not until the twelfth to thirteenth centuries "that *kuṇḍalinī* becomes the vehicle for fluid, rather than phonematic transactions and transfers" (White 2003: 232). It is to the *Nāths*' innovative research into physical austerities and disciplines, including special attention to the cultivation of a healthy spine and concentration on the various *cakra* along with an extension of the uses of *kumbhaka* or retention of breath, to which we owe most of what is popular about yoga in the contemporary West. The *āsana* they discovered and that were first recorded in their principal texts, *Siddhasiddhāntapaddhati* (eleventh century), *Gorakṣaśataka* (eleventh or twelfth century) and *Haṭhayogapradīpikā* (fourteenth century), form the core of the *āsana* that we know and practice today. These are the texts that elaborate how to cleanse the nerves, how to control and restrain *prāṇa*, and how to kindle the digestive fires, and the like, that is, the practices with which yoga is now inseparably associated.

The earliest datable evidence of a full-blown tantric religion appears in the seventh century, and no *haṭha* yoga text can be dated before the tenth century (Lorenzen 2002: 26, 33). Though the historical record is too obscure to determine anything definitive about the course of evolution of tantric ideas in and among South Asian cultures, one possibility is that the Mahāyāna Buddhists developed tantra as we basically know it today. The yogi practitioners expanded it, and when these cults became Śaivite in the twelfth to fourteenth centuries, the new tantric practices entered mainstream Hinduism. These activities would have begun about the fifth century and would have been completed by the fourteenth century.

Matsyendranāth initiated Goraknāth (eleventh century), who became the greatest Indian teacher since Śaṅkara (David Lorenzen 1987a: 77–8) and for whom many temples and shrines still exist. Gorakanāth amalgamated Buddhist *Vajrayāna* and Śaivism, and he collected his disciples among Buddhists, Hindus (especially from the *śūdra* caste), and Muslims. One disciple, Baba Ratan Haji, converted a number of Muslims to yogic practices. There was also substantial Sufi influence on the Kānphaṭas; one order today continues to use the Sufi title *pir* for the head of Caughera Monastery in Nepal (Fuller 1999: 634). The liberal Muslim Emperor Akbar was a practitioner of yoga, and Goraknāth is said to have brought about a degree of unity among Hindus and Muslims. He was also the patron deity of the Gorkhas of eastern Nepal who took his name (Khakhar 1978: 47). All this places the synthesis of yoga with Buddhism (and of yoga with Islam), suspect in some contemporary commentary, at a period long before the modern era.

Goraknāth's student Jālandharnāth was Buddhist, as were the ascetics Srigaripao and Ramanvajra, who were associated with Jālandharnāth's disciple, the famous renunciate and former king, Gopicandra; and the great Buddhist saint Tilopa had much association with Gopicandra's capital (Mallik 1954: 22). Both of the founding gurus of *haṭha* yoga, Matsyendranāth and Goraknāth, are mentioned as Buddhist teachers by the historiographer Taranāth (1970: 153), born in 1575. At the same time, Śaivites claim Goraknāth as an incarnation of Śiva. Another early biographer, Abhyadatt (1979: 50–3), also translated into Tibetan, provides an account of Goraknāth. According to Tibetan tradition, Goraknāth's followers were Buddhists who became Śaivites in the twelfth century (Briggs 1938: 248). Professor Hariprasad Dwivedi (1950)[5] calls the Nāths a crypto-Buddhist cult.

Some take it to be essentially a crypto-Buddhist or an esoteric Buddhist cult that later seceded from the Buddhist fold and transformed itself into a Śaivite cult. Others, conversely, are of the opinion that the Nāth a cult is essentially a Śaivite cult, which in the course of its evolution was assimilated within esoteric Buddhism, and it is for this reason that we find a hotchpotch of esoteric Buddhist and yogic Śaivism.

Of course, this "hotchpotch" is to be placed nine hundred years before us, and it is difficult to dismiss a hotchpotch when it was responsible for *haṭha* yoga.

The *Siddhasiddāntapaddhati* refers to a meditation on *śūnya* at the tenth door of the *śaṅkinī* nerve (Mallik 1954: 37), a duct through which *amṛta* flows out of a hollow in the palatal region (Dasgupta 1962: 239),[6] and the *Haṭhayogapradīpikā* gives reverence to the notion of *śūnyāśūnya*.[7] *Śūnya* is a reference to the doctrine of the emptiness of inherent essences promulgated by Mahāyāna Buddhists. The *Siddhasiddāntapaddhati* also mentions an important practice in Buddhist *Vajrayāna*, the concentration on the nerve centers known as *cakras* during the practicse of *vajroli mudrā* (Mallik 1954: 37), and the *haṭha* yoga texts give emphasis to this practice.

The most vital part of *haṭha* yoga is its investigation of the *nāḍīs* or nerves, which it derived from Buddhist Tantra, which in turn may have inherited it from animistic traditions. Bhattacharya (Briggs 1938: 275–6) holds that Buddhist Tantra preceded Hindu Tantra, especially the former's notions of *mahāsukha* (great bliss) and the worship of female energy in connection with that of the male (Ibid). The Tibetans use a synonym for tantra, known as *nang rig*,[8] (knowledge of internal processes), and this "knowledge"also includes the idea of ongoing "investigation"or "inquiry," an idea that is very much in sympathy with the research into "internal" experience undertaken by *haṭha yogis*. *Haṭha* itself means "forceful suppression" (Lorenzen 1987b: 214) or "violent union" (White 2003: 217), which refers to the control and manipulation of internal energies,[9] energies that were identified as sexual.

Later there were Vaiṣṇava *haṭha yogis*, including Gheraṇḍa, the author of another foundational *haṭha* yoga text, the *Gheraṇḍasaṃhitā*. Yet the rise of a stricter Vaiṣṇavism, along with the expansion of Islam in India, contributed to the decline of influence of the Nāths or Kānphaṭas after the fourteenth century, though some of their communities survived in northeastern and northwestern India and a number of Kānphaṭa adepts exist even today.[10] The temple of Goraknāth at Gorakhpur was destroyed twice by Muslims and rebuilt each time. In the sixteenth century, the Sikhs, who teach their own variety of *haṭha* yoga that includes an emphasis on the cultivation of *kuṇḍalinī*, further suppressed the Kānphaṭas; however, in many thickly forested areas, the Kānphaṭas were free to cultivate their yogic practices within their own decentralized spiritual institutions.

The Buddhist tantrism, which was the basis for some of the *haṭha yogis'* practices, is itself thought by many to be very ancient; in fact, it evolved well after the founding centuries of Buddhism. Max Weber (1958: 295) traces tantrism to the religious yearnings of the "lower strata," and lower-caste adepts certainly constituted the majority of the Kānphaṭa. Though some tantric elements seem to date from about 650 CE (Lorenzen 1987a: 77), most comprehensive written evidence of tantric methods commences with the tenth century (Varenne 1976: 182), though most certainly tantra did not emerge autochthonously. Zvelebil (1973: 26) writes:

> Tantrism undoubtedly contains very old elements, some of which belong to the religious protohistory and prehistory of India; but their introduction

> or rather intrusion into Buddhism and Hinduism in a more massive and systematic manner began relatively late—not before the first centuries of our era, probably only after the fifth–sixth century A.D.[11]

I have taken the effort to retrace all of this not to emphasize the historical connections of yoga to Buddhism but to make the vitally important point that the "yoga" that is known and practiced in the modern world is derived from *a tradition that was itself a derivative and syncretic form* of spiritual practice; moreover, it is a practice that is not really "ancient" but "medieval," being separated from us by one and not two millennia. It was indeed a hotchpotch of Buddhism, Śaivism, Vaiṣṇavism, with even Islamic influence and non-Hindu tribal asceticism. However, this would not surprise any modern Nepali, who lives a religious culture that continues to syncretize Hinduism and Buddhism without serious trouble.[12] At no time was there a "pure" yoga, except perhaps in the subjective experience of an accomplished practitioner. The principal disciples of the tenth to fourteenth centuries seemed to move freely between Mahāyāna Buddhist Tantrism and Śaivism. Mallik (1954: 24) describes it well when she writes, "The element of yoga as practised by both these schools, together with the rites and rituals were neither Buddhistic nor brahminical, they were a common heritage." So, in the absence of an original, pure yoga, we need to address more carefully what it can mean to have strayed from yoga.

The Nāths or Kānphaṭas, to whom we owe the basic practices of *haṭha* yoga, were "rough looking " (Gold and Gold 1984: 115) iconoclasts who rejected the mores of their society, including the notion of caste, grew their hair and nails long without pruning (Bhattacharya 1968/1896: 317), and occasionally smoked ganja. As a rule, the Kānphaṭas distrusted academic scholarship and believed that only practice and not discussions or reasoning produce results and that results were measured by the degree of mental equilibrium achieved. Gorakhnāth counseled his disciples to practice the four yogas (*lāya, haṭha, mantra, and rāja*) and locate the results for oneself, advising that just as no medicinal books can cure a patient, so no theoretical knowledge can make one a yogi (Mallik 1954: 45). Yet they wrote books and are known today primarily by their literary contributions.

The source of their genius was their practical investigation of their bodily experiences during extensive courses of deliberate *sādhana*. Jean Varenne (1976: 190–1) writes, "Yoga. .. requires both an unqualified adherence and a long apprenticeship; that is something clearly stated by the texts and continually repeated by the yoga masters." Their work involved treating the body as the epitome of the universe (Dasgupta 1962: 230), with special focus on the nerves and nerve centers; their research involved extensive exploration of the inner environments of the body and their effects on consciousness. Though texts played an important part in their tradition, it was held that the discursive practices should never be permitted to be aimless.[13]

Syncretic Dialectics in Classical Yoga

Even before the "medieval" period during which tantrism held sway, the yoga of the first millennium exchanged a great deal of perspective with the Buddhism of that period. The "pacification" referred to by the Buddha in his basic *sūtras* refers to the cessation of the endlessly proliferating engagements of mental activity, a reference to the *citta vṛtti* that Patañjali critiques in the second sloka of his *Yogasūtra*, and in both discussions the same Sanskrit terms are employed. The aforementioned *Yoga Vaśiṣṭha*, which is attributed to Valmiki, reads very much like Mādhayamaka Buddhist philosophy with only a few transformations, and is considered to have emerged out of a period of scholarship when the Mādhayamaka perspective held sway in the classical Indian monastic universities. Śaṅkara, the great exponent of Advaita, engaged in so many debates with Mādhayamaka Buddhists that it is difficult to sort out what in his thinking came from Buddhist and what from Hindu sources. It is the nature of any dialectics[14] that one's opponent comes to unwittingly adopt the perspective being opposed even as she or he puts forward arguments against it. As Derrida (1994: 156) has described, the proponent in an argument inevitably operates with a "countersophistics that at every moment runs the risk of replicating the *reply*: reproducing in a mirror the logic of the adversary at the moment of the retort." Surely, the endless public philosophical debates that took place in classical times between Advaitins and Mādhayamaka scholars had the result that they shared the same discursive practices, if not similar epistemologies. Hence, we can conclude that the yoga of classical times was not entirely free from Buddhist influences either. Of course, the ontological debates between the Sāṃkhya and Buddhists were real ones, but many of the most important epistemological insights were developed together; that is, they participated in the same philosophical culture. Neither Sāṃkhya thought nor Buddhist thought would be thinkable without the other.

The yoga of Patañjali, now considered "Classical,"[15] offers an epistemology that is basically Sāṃkhyan and includes features that are compatible with Indian Brahminical culture. The basic practices outlined there are theoretical or "purely psychological" (Dasgupta 1962: 244) and involve refined contemplative disciplines and emotional asceticism that offer considerable scope for spiritual inspiration, but they refer more to controlling sexual energies than to techniques for actively using sexuality to animate and energize spiritual evolution. It was the *haṭha* yogin who developed this within the context of yoga. As mentioned, these *haṭha* yogin opposed the caste system and attracted most of their followers from the *śūdra* caste, whereas the philosophical orientation of the Sāṃkhya was shepherded by priests from the brahmin caste, who act as custodians for the Vedas and the principal Upaniṣads. Because of these differences about caste, brahmins have always had contentious relations with the Kānphaṭas. On the days of worship of the anola tree, which was once associated with Buddhism and is now connected with Śiva, offerings are made to yogis; whereas the offerings are welcomed by Kānphaṭa yogis, they are refused by brahmins (Briggs 1938: 131).

The "Classical" yoga formulated by brahmins in the nineteenth to twentieth century is what the Europeans who first studied yoga learned, as their interests were primarily philosophical and they were most likely to meet Indians who were brahmin intellectuals. The physical aspects of postures and breath control were not taught systematically in the West until after World War I, and they did not become widespread until the late 1950's (Varenne 1976: 190). These tensions within yoga between traditions that were themselves amalgams of different traditions makes it very difficult to locate a yoga that is definitively authentic.

Syncretic Practices in Contemporary Yoga

Our analysis of the origins of yoga elides the question of whether the lack of a pure, consistent "origin" entails that we today have a warrant for reinventing a Western yoga, one based on our own idiosyncrasies, and still call it "yoga." Varenne (1976: 191) emphasized the importance of a course of ascetic practice learned during a long apprenticeship under a yoga master, and adds, "To refuse such adherence, to sort through the practices and theories of yoga, picking and choosing what we feel suits us, is an attitude we undoubtedly have the right to adopt, but it is one that places us outside yoga itself." So what are the important signs that can indicate what is "outside" of yoga? Many contemporary Hindus observe Western hippies traveling in India to learn about yoga and fail to witness anything identifiably "yogic" about what they are doing. Of what does their failure consist? Most Hindus would not permit a foreigner to enter a *sanctum sanctorum* or even to recite the Gayatri mantra, yet more than a few of the Western yogic practitioners who visit temples and recite the Gayatri freely are unaware that what they are doing may be offensive or profane. Are these Hindus (more of them are Vaiṣṇavite than Śaivite) defending a truly "traditional" yoga or have they themselves resynthesized some idea of "original" that is itself a reflection of Western (Christian and Islamic) ideals of religious practice and belief that have found their way into contemporary Indian Hinduism? It is known that brahmin religious sentiments hardened somewhat after the introduction of Islam. What Hindus are defending today is a spiritual practice that has absorbed many Western ideas derived from Islam, colonial Christianity, modern science, and now even some New Age notions. That is, their practice is syncretic as well.

Varenne (1976: 189–90) highlights other ironies that are in play in contemporary times:

> The sadhu, like the hippy, has rejected worldly values, renounced the social structure of his country, and is leading the life of a wandering beggar in which the use of drugs occasionally plays a part. In both cases the long hair, the conspicuously different clothing, and the spiritual thirst serve as identifying badges.

If the beatniks of the 1950s and early 1960s, such as Allen Ginsburg, popularized a yoga that they crafted as a synthesis of Buddhism and yoga that suited the exigencies of their own spiritual needs, how are we to know definitively that they operated "outside" of a tradition, when that tradition itself evolved as an amalgam of Buddhism and tantric yoga, and especially when the founding Kānphaṭas also sported long hair and occasionally used cannabis?[16] The hippies did not adopt the long hair because of the yogis, but they did discover some justification among the yogis' practices for their own appearance and counter-cultural critiques. Further, the distrust of intellectualism found among many contemporary *haṭha* yoga practitioners is consistent with the anti-intellectualism of the Kānphaṭas.

Of course, no one would argue that forms of culture should not be adapted to the local needs and contingencies of a society that comes to adopt them, but how much license can be taken? For instance, though since the earliest times nongrasping, and renunciation are mandated practices in yoga, in Western countries value is generally signified not by the absence of wealth but by how much something costs. Krishnmacharya, a Dravidian brahmin who learned his *haṭha* yoga in Tibet and is best known as the guru of B.K.S. Iyengar and Pattabhi Jois, had as his first Western disciple the Russian yogini Indra Devi, and Indra Devi taught her disciples to charge large sums for lessons in yoga, for the reason that she believed Americans were incapable of developing respect for anything that was free.[17] Yet in India, some Indian swamis steadfastly refuse to accept payment for spiritual instruction. Was the practice of Indra Devi, one of the pioneers of yoga in the West, non-yogic?

A few Western practitioners are able to devise a sense of authenticity that derives from the strangeness of the few Sanskrit terms they have learned. Even when mispronounced, the foreignness of the way they sound, along with the choreography of the occasion provided by an ambience of sandalwood incense, some taped sitar music in the background,[18] some short prayers, and a recitation of "Om," provides a veneer of sufficient authenticity to quell further investigation into what the authentic might actually be. The situation is comparable to the semiotics of the Western film as analyzed by Will Wright (1975) in which he discovered that certain narrative practices and features of the setting of the story, all provided by the filmmakers and all of them historically inaccurate, was what established the authenticity of any film as a believable Western. These semiotic features included the typeface of the title's graphics and of any signs that appear in the set, the use of a particular music (emphasizing the guitar and harmonica), the inclusion of stage coach and railway robberies (there were very few of these in the real West), and the populace (black people were much more in evidence in the actual West); the presence of these features were essential for public acceptance of any claim to be an authentic Western. That is, one was required to transgress the historical record to stand in conformity with the popular semiotics of authenticity. Yoga in the contemporary West similarly involves a choreography whose semiotic elements are widespread yet whose connections with an actually existing Indian yoga, past or present, are tenuous. However, we want to retain enough of a relativist position that we always feel obliged to offer sufficient respect for the creative diligence of others, knowing that the likelihood is that our own preferred criteria will be found wanting. It is disrespectful of other practitioners of yoga to simply impose one's personal criteria on them without first witnessing their life-world. However, how do we keep this relativism from paralyzing us, as it is capable of excusing everything?

The specific features of the occasions during which yoga is transmitted to a non-Indian audience are inevitably local social productions that owe as much to Christian, New Age, and modern gym-culture as they do to traditional contexts of yoga practice. One private gym in Madison, Wisconsin, placed a poster for their yoga class in their foyer, which read, "Experience the Zen of Yoga." This did not strike clients as dissonant, since it conformed to the smorgasbord of cultural play that is a normal part of the contemporary European-American appropriation of the world's traditions in this era of "globalization." In fact, such a cafeteria-like approach to spiritual experimentation is packaged in the globalized popular culture and sold in India as one more of the spiritual options, where "reiki" vies with yoga itself in bookstores and workshops. A segment of the Indian middle class is willing, if not eager, to assimilate American trends, and New Age forms have a currency that make them other than spiritual practices; in the case of reiki, an American interpretation of a Japanese idea is a widely available spiritual commodity in India. Another recently developed Western physical culture, "Pilates," derives a degree of its inspiration from vinyasa yoga and is not incompatible with it; accordingly, it has become a component of yoga workshops worldwide. How are such innovations to be evaluated? The innovative spirit of yoga itself, especially that of *haṭha* yoga, makes a severe dismissal of genuinely innovative explorations unsuitable; but then what becomes of yoga? Or is it even necessary that it retain its identity?

The problem for India is that India does not always know itself and has sometimes learned about its own traditions from the colonial other, which is now Western media. The greatness of a swami, from Vivekananda onward, is often reckoned by the size and wealth of his American, British, French, and other affiliated ashrams. Indians who propound a traditional yoga seek to justify it in terms of scientific validity. Though scientific research into yoga practices is most welcome and informative, when the validation of the worth of yogic practices is derived *more* from Western methodologies than on methods of traditional insight, then is yoga to be considered an Indian or European phenomenon, or an amalgam? The ironies here run thick and deep, as no one would aspire to freeze Indians inside of a caricature of what is traditionally Indian that itself is devised by the imagination of Orientalism. The point is that Indians must be free to develop in any direction they choose—as my original yoga guru, Swami Gitananda Giri, explained to me on several occasions, "The purpose of life, and therefore of yoga, is to evolve." However, his concern was with spiritual and not cultural evolution. Certainly the *haṭha yogis* who developed the system were bold about their practice; and it would be heterodox to confine contemporary yoga, which includes the yoga in India, within ideals constructed from ancient and medieval texts that are read in the modern fashion as disengaged from the context of their development. One popular innovation in Indian yoga during the last century is *yoga nidrā* (literally, yogic sleep), a set of nerve relaxation techniques that are valuable for letting the autonomic nervous system prevail and reduce the adrenaline output that inhibits immune function. *Yoga nidrā* has evolved quickly into an internationally adopted body of practices that are used to conclude many *āsana* lessons, and its instruction continues to be elaborated. Despite its recent introduction, it is taken to be a part of traditional yoga.

Authenticity as a Reflexive Practice

So where is the authentic yoga to be found? India does have an indigenous method that guides practitioners about what is authentic, and that is the importance that is placed on the lineage of teachers. In all of the Indian systems—Hindu, Sikh, Buddhist, Jain, Muslim—there is a lineage of gurus, each of whom has taken a personal responsibility for teaching their students, face to face and heart to heart, what is genuine. And one's personal teacher has learned what is most central to the practice from his or her teacher, who learned it from the teacher's teacher. In this way, the names of actual teachers of the lineage can be enumerated for many generations but, more important, something of the actual taste of the spiritual insight that is to be derived from a yogic practice can be transmitted. This is not to value orality over printed media for its own sake: It is to value the presence of a spiritual teacher who has retained a connection with the motives of his or her own teacher.[19] In all of these systems (except perhaps Islam), the *core* of the practice rests *not in docile texts* but in what has been transmitted in person. The modern practice of constructing a model of yoga from reading through the shelves of texts at Borders or other bookstores is contrary to the accepted traditional practice in yoga. However, the situation is more complicated than this, as the majority of the modern lineages of yoga are more recent in origin than the Nāths and others who compiled the texts that are "foundational" for *haṭha* yoga. Though the Nāth *sādhus* and recent yoga lineages do emphasize the continuity of guru and disciple more than they prioritize textual study, the teachers of these two eras do not form an unbroken lineage, hence compromising this lineage as a standard for what is authentic. In the contemporary period, reliance on foundational texts is as much a deliberate reconstruction of "authentic" *haṭha* yoga as it is the perpetuation of a genuine continuity of tradition. Joseph Alter (2004: 23) summarizes the situation:

> By the late 1920s and early 1930s, various people who were engaged in practice used the *Haṭhayogapradīpikā*, the *Śivasaṃhitā*, and the *Gheraṇḍasaṃhitā* to authenticate a broad spectrum of modern techniques and styles. Thus the texts tend to be used to authenticate the tradition as a whole by virtue of being 'ancient' and authored by semi-divine sages—and to connect modern, medieval, and ancient practice into homogenized historical continuity—but their currency as practical reference books is not very great.

Though some aspects of lineage and the foundational character of texts are the consequences of a degree of social artifice, the policy of relying on a living teacher who accepts responsibility for the student is preferable to an exclusive reliance on a neophyte's idiosyncratic interpretation of his or her collection of books and magazines about yoga. A large inventory of Western books on yoga is now available at Indian stores modeled on Borders and appears ready to overwhelm the small press-based inventory of yoga books indigenous to India.[20] In India and the West, spiritual yearning is vulnerable to commodity fetishism. Though lineages can be commodified as can books, within the face-to-face relationship of a teacher and student it is possible that commodification can be overcome.

Fidelity to a lineage is difficult for many Westerners as it entails the ideal of guru-devotion, which is used to animate the spiritual energies of a student. Devotion to a guru is unseemly for the critical traditions of postmodern culture, which has inherited a philosophical orientation that offers more scope for the abstracted exploration of ideas that are kept entirely divorced from any motives that involve personal evolution. An interest in personal evolution is taken to be subjective bias, if not homely, and must be kept separate from intellectual inquiry, a notion that many Indian spiritual practitioners consider to be sterile. Yet Western philosophical ideas generally, and postmodern criticism in particular, are welcomed by a large segment of contemporary Indian intellectuals, and in some places this critical attitude has even been grafted somehow onto guru devotion, as the lineage of gurus is still vital for the traditional aspect of yoga. Though it may be observed that the most genuine varieties of yoga in the West have arrived accompanied by a guru lineage, it should be stated that it is not very difficult for a yoga teacher to construct, as part of the packaging, a lineage that can be marketed with the yoga.[21] Initiations are even sold, and the process of accreditation with a legitimate lineage can be expensive; moreover, accreditation contains a paralegal element that may not always fit well with the spiritual wellsprings of yoga. Both the best and worst aspects of these two cultures are available for the syntheses that are emerging.

Yoga in contemporary India is considerably influenced by the validation of yoga that has emerged in the West during the last century. As Western nations dominate the publication of books, videos, and other media, the yoga studied and contemplated by many Indians is a Western adaptation of Indian yoga; indeed, much of its present status—not to mention its financial supports—are derived from the popularity of yoga in the West, and that inevitably influences the definition of yoga itself. Indians celebrate Western trends in the field and study Western texts on yoga, so in much of India yoga exists as the reflection of a reflection: It is as if two mirrors are staring at each other. However, there is a more vital point here than even this: In such a situation, what is "authentic" yoga is what people come to locate and admire, which makes the standards practically tautological. Such self-produced standards are used reflexively to justify the very practices that led to the establishing of the standards.

When Westerners come to India to learn about a yoga that is now partly a response to, and an appropriation of, Western reductions of yoga, the very reflexivity of the authenticity here can lead to vertigo. The reflexive nature of understanding permits *whatever* one comes on as what seems most relevant to be made the standard for authenticity. Instead of what is authentic offering some guidance about what one should accept, what one has accepted provides grounding that can authorize itself. After all, one sees best what one already knows, whereas learning what one does *not* know is what is difficult, and unlikely, even when that is what can lead one to what one most needs to learn. This takes us to the more general question of cultural hermeneutics: How do we keep our understanding open to what is *other* than ourselves? The problem is that the more ethnocentric one is, the more easily the slightest accent of otherness looms as sufficient difference to offer enough authenticity for the purposes at hand, even when it is mostly made from the cloth of one's own culture.

Highly commodified popular adaptations provide a sizable financial base for the growth of yoga in modern times. However, even more important than this, if yoga were not commodified, it is quite possible that it could not even be communicated in the modern world, for nothing that is incapable of being marketed can survive for long. The trends that have led to yoga magazines being placed on the checkout counters of American groceries have little to do with *aṣṭāṅgayoga* and are more about celebrity, fitness, and attractiveness. In fact, in some social circles and popular songs, yoga is derided for being the shallow, artificial trend that in some places it is. What is to be done? How is yoga to be adapted? It may be that one solution is to not exclude what is valid from Western traditions but to exclude what, in both Indian and Western traditions, is damaging to yoga while sustaining anything that is of genuine value for yoga. In this project, guidance may be provided by what has been time-tested in yogic cultures. However, we still face the hermeneutic task of sorting out just what that is, so we have not gained much ground.

As a contribution to the task of making commitments in spite of the aporia introduced by a frank admission of the reflexivity of authenticity, I conclude these reflections by making a brief tour of some of the candidate resources in yoga that might be retained as guidelines for what can be authentic in yoga today. These guidelines should not be erected as rigid rules meant in an absolute sense, for truth is rarely to be found in proscriptions; only cowardice is found there. Nevertheless, the sentiments that underlie these guidelines should be respected and considered. First among them must be the resolve, which is evident in all of yoga, to overcome egoism. This especially conflicts with contemporary Western culture and its individualism and its idolatry of celebrity; but anything that results in inflating the ego *cannot* be considered a yoga practice. It is the considered opinion of two millennia of yoga practice that egocentrism leads to ruin, so techniques for reducing the obsessiveness with which a student pursues his or her self-image and interests need to be preserved. Here guru devotion can be a counterpoise to these contemporary sensibilities, and it has a potential for altering self-centered habits. The difficulties that many Western students have regarding this can itself be an advantage, since self-centeredness will not subside without some trials. Even a practice as improbable as prostration can become a tool for learning humility. When a practice of yoga pushes one beyond the commonly accepted boundaries of life, his or her own agenda can be witnessed as the minute phenomenon it truly is, and some humility may follow from that. The most important part of guru devotion, however, is having a teacher who knows one well enough to know how to keep pushing one beyond the customary boundaries of one's imagination. This requires that both the student and the teacher assume responsibility for each other, a connection that is not provided for in capitalism nor in the ideals of professionalism that capitalism fosters. However, without the *emotional* bond between the student and guru, there will not be enough energy or understanding to cause a student to surrender his or her self-obsession. This needs to be an essential part of yoga instruction.

Postmodern criticisms of authenticity, such as have been presented above and elsewhere in this volume, should not be permitted to lead us into a radical relativism that paralyzes moral resolve. The system of yoga of Patañjali and of all yogis since have included the *yamas* and *niyamas* or something similar that refers to basic moral practices such as honesty, good will, selflessness, and the like, without which a daily practice cannot be considered to be "authentic" yoga. Accordingly, these need to be made a part of the regular and daily instruction in yoga classes worldwide. The situation today is that less than a small percentage of yoga students in the world can correctly identify the *yamas* and *niyamas*, let alone practice them. This is a scandal. I am speaking here of only the basic elements of what is traditional in yoga.

Here we face another conundrum: In most places in the West where yoga is taught, the discussion of spiritual matters is not permitted or is considered proselytizing, and yet a yoga without spirituality (here intended in a broad sense) is not yoga. Whether in a gym, educational setting, civic recreation center, or whatever, practices that have a spiritual nature are not allowed. The Religious Studies Department head at my university instructed me to remove the teaching of *āsana* in my course "Yoga in Theory and Practice," which I had been teaching for a decade, because she did not want to give evangelical Christians an argument for permitting prayer in university classes. I told her that *āsana* was not about spirituality but about the nervous system, but that was a falsehood if I were to teach yoga in a genuine way: The point of teaching *āsana* is to lead students to a pacification of nervous energy so that the spiritual rewards of simpler ways of being can be experienced for oneself. So my department head's instincts were correct. I was obliged to transfer my class to the Folklore Program. Similar difficulties occur when yoga is taught at the YMCA, and even in private studios, teachers are reluctant to risk cultivating spirituality as a motivating force; instead, they preserve a downgraded cultural ambience of Vedic chants and prayers so brief they are more theater than practice. Can there be an authentic yoga that is not oriented toward cultivating spiritual motives? Doing yoga is not like doing chin-ups, and the thoughtful cultivation of one's nerves and energies has a spiritual purpose. This does not mean it has to be worded or clothed in Hinduism, but it is to be felt along with "the exercise" and within each part of the exercise. And in this regard, the teacher of *āsana* and *prāṇāyāma* must provide skillful guidance, for only confusion will result without it.

Traditional orders of *haṭha* yoga provided food, shelter, or other social service (Postans 1838) to the needy. I have visited the ashrams of dozens of swamis who have built large institutions that care for the needy, for widows, or orphans. *Karma yoga* involves social service, which itself can contribute in a powerful way to the reduction of egoism. In the modern fitness marketplace, where the disciples are motivated primarily by the desire for an attractive body, social service can be employed as a radical method to redirect consciousness.

Finally, there is the large region of yoga that involves *tapas* or self-control that may involve "forceful repression" (i.e., *haṭha* yoga). In the era of channel surfing, cell phones, Internet exploration, video games, and the like, any practice that teaches the mind to be *less* distracted is salutary. Removing the home television can be *tapas* enough to generate some spiritual evolution. Simplicity should be taught and practiced, for it is the very heart of traditional yoga. We do not live in an ascetic age, but the asceticism of yoga can be instructive; somehow, its practice must be introduced into the modern studio instead of lines of yoga wardrobe. A fundamental yoga practice that is given short shrift even in the classic texts and commentaries is *pratyāhāra*—the withdrawal of one's natural, circumspective inquiry from the pursuit of external sources for happiness and the simultaneous cultivation of internal resources for enduring satisfaction. Contentment itself is a *niyama* that always seems to follow from simplicity, and its importance should be emphasized. One does not need a new yoga mat so much as one needs to learn how to tap into what is already residing within. That is yoga. Teaching such life practice is the responsibility of those who take on the task of transmitting yoga in the contemporary world, and yet one rarely hears of *pratyāhāra* in the modern yoga studio. Of course, there is no "program" for contentment, as it depends entirely on what the *sādhaka* (the serious student) can identify as effective—in some circumstances even watching television could be made an effective practice. It is not like following a prescription: One must continuously reevaluate the efficacy of each practice. Here again, a guru, or at least a spiritual community, can be helpful.

So these are a few of the classical ideas that can be made components of what is the measure of what is authentic in yoga: a full frontal attack on egoism, the mindful reduction of nervous tension, simplicity, the growth of ethical sensibility, and a practical and daily responsibility for one's own contentment. In brief, the cultivation of one's vital energies must be harnessed to the task of evolving, which can amount to being responsible for leaving this world more tamed than one found it.

Notes

1 Sensual pleasure.
2 Again, we should recognize that a term such as "medieval" is a European category that may or may not be applicable to South and Central Asia.
3 Tibetan tangkas depicting Matsyendranāth display him surrounded by fish ("*matsya*" means "fish"), a reference to the legend about his once being swallowed by a fish (Mallik 1954: 15).
4 Females take the surname "Nāthinī." The name "Kānphaṭa" was actually a term of disrespect applied to these yogis by Muslims. It means, literally, "split-eared" and refers to their practice of elongating their ears, a style that is common in the iconography of *bodhisattvas*.
5 *Nāth-sampraday*, Varanasi: Naivedya Niketan, 1966; cited and translated by Bandopadhyay (1992: 45).
6 This practice is connected with *kecharī mudrā*, described by most *haṭha* yoga texts but rarely practiced in modern times. The practice involves sealing off the upper *cakra* by inserting a retroflexed tongue into the palatal cavity. According to Goraknāth, the tongue and penis are joined in a single channel (from *Gorakh Bar*; cited by White 1996: 255). This tenth door is explained in Buddhist tantra as *vairocana-dvāra*, the most supreme gate; if this door is not closed, the *amṛta* will not be retained.
7 *Sūnyāśūnya*, literally "emptiness-nonemptiness," is itself a syncretic notion of the ultimate that combines both Mahāyāna Buddhist and *Sāṃkhya* ideas.
8 For example, see Tsong Khapa: 2002, composed in 1408.
9 A secondary explanation describes "*ha*" and "*ṭha*" as the sun and moon, respectively, a reference to the right and left, male and female, channels of energy in the body.
10 The 1901 census for India enumerated 45,463 Nāths (Briggs: 1938: 5).
11 Some humility regarding historical speculations such as these can be gained by recalling that neither "Buddhism" nor "Hinduism" were ever terms that Buddhists or Hindus used to refer to themselves.
12 During my extensive treks into the interior of northeastern Nepal, I discovered valleys where the shrines were Buddhist yet the people called themselves "Hindu," and other valleys where the shrines were Śaivite yet the people called themselves "Buddhist." Should they be dismissed as hotchpotch?
13 One of my early teachers, Swami Venkatesananda, was an academic and swami who was a disciple of Swami Sivananda. He emphasized self-experience as the sole source of authenticity in a practice of yoga; however, Venkatesananda himself is best known for his brilliant translation into English of the famously lengthy and profound *Yoga Vaśiṣṭha*. Despite his scholarly discipline, when I asked him about the probable dates of Patañjali, he replied to me, "The date of Patañjali is useless for you. If you find in your own practice that the *Yogasūtra* has some utility, then the date of its composition is irrelevant. And if you discover that the *Yogasūtra* is not helpful at all, then knowing a date is an insignificant piece of information that will not provide you anything." Swami Venkatesananda's instructions were faithful to the customary emphasis of the *haṭha* yoga tradition to rely on practice and not theoretical knowledge.
14 The term "dialectics" here is being used in two ways. Dialectics can be the process of the mutual negation and mutual transformation of competing philosophical notions that are considered together; on other occasions, dialectics can refer more specifically to any local, live face-to-face discursive confrontation between opposing philosophers. More precisely, I am speaking here of a dialectics (first sense) of dialectics (second sense), that is, of the synthesis-within-tension that resulted from the confrontation of ideas during the actual occasions that Indian philosophers engaged in live philosophical debating (See Liberman 2004a).
15 For a more elaborate account of how Patañjali became the 'Classical' yoga, see the contribution in this volume by Mark Singleton.

16 While traveling in the rural parts of northeastern Karnataka, I came on the Mudalahalli yoga ashram, which displayed a 250-year-old portrait of the swami who founded the ashram. He was depicted sitting and smoking ganja. When I asked the 102-year-old resident swami whether smoking ganja was presently endorsed by the ashram, he replied, "Assuredly not, our swami was already an accomplished master." Relying on one's own practical investigations, one might conclude that the use of cannabis can lead to insights regarding bodily senses but also that it is conducive to the cultivation of *citta vṛitti* or distracting mental engagements, the principal nemesis of a yogic practice. Just how the *haṭha*-yogis used ganja in a yogic practice is not a part of the historical record, but the fact that it was used by sādhus is undeniable. Similarly, a British military officer (Postans 1838: 269), visiting a group of Kānphaṭas who trace their origins to the Kānphaṭa saint Dharamnāth five centuries earlier, describes a sect of yogis who have for centuries been providing charity to any needy person regardless of sect or creed; these Kānphaṭas engage in a regular practice of taking opium along with their yogic *tapas*.

17 Personal observation—Indra Devi was a teacher of mine in the early 1970s.

18 Music of any kind is considered a distraction to any serious practice of yoga *āsana*, which must include a form of *dhāraṇā* or concentration before it is considered legitimate. However, could it be that in the interest of cultural adaptation, distraction can be made a component of *pratyāhāra*? The answer may be yes, if the result is an actual calming of the mind.

19 A metaphysics of presence is not required for placing value on being touched by one's teacher.

20 There can be no doubt that more Indians now read English than are literate in Sanskrit.

21 Though the relationship with one's guru is key for developing an effective practice of yoga, even in Indian society guru devotion can be practiced as merely a semiotic structure that is acted out by the participants without any serious responsibility for each other being assumed.

Bibliography

Abhayadatt (1979) *Buddha's Lions*, trans. James B. Robinson, Berkeley: Dharma Publishing.

Alter, J.S. (2004) *Yoga in Modern India: The Body Between Science and Philosophy*, Princeton: Princeton University Press.

Bandyopadhyay, P.K. (1992) *Nāth a Cult and Mahanand*, Delhi: B.R. Publishing Corp.

Bhattacharya, J N. (1968) *Hindu Castes and Sects*, Calcutta: Editions India.

Briggs, W. (1938) *Goraknāth and the Kānphaṭa Yogis*, Calcutta: YMCA Publications.

Dasgupta, S. (1962) *Obscure Religious Cults*, Calcutta: Forma K.L. Mukhopadhyay.

Derrida, Jacques (1974) *Of Grammatology*, Baltimore: John Hopkins University Press.

——(1994) *Spectres of Marx*. London: Routledge.

Dwivedi, H.P. (1950) *Nāthasampradaya*, Allahabad: Publisher unknown

Fuller, C.J., (1999) Review of *Asctès et Rois: Un monastère de Kānphaṭa Yogis au Nepal* (Paris: CNRS Editions, 1997), *The Journal of the Royal Anthropological Institute*, 5: 634–35.

Gold, D., and A.G. Gold (1984) The Fate of the Householder Nāth, *History of Religions* 24 (2): 113–32.

Iyengar, S. (trans) (1933) *Hathayogapradipika*, Madras: Theosophical Publishing House.

Khakhar, P. (1878) History of the Kānphaṭas of Kachh, *Indian Antiquity* 7: 47–53.

Liberman, K. (2004a) *Dialectical Practice in Tibetan Philosophical Culture*, Baltimore: Rowman & Littlefield.

—(2004b) Yoga Tourism, *Yoga Life* 35 (7): 23–32.
Lorenzen, D.N. (2002) Early Evidence for Tantric Religion, in K.A. Harper and L.R. Brown (eds) *The Roots of Tantra*, Albany: SUNY Press, 25–36.
—(1987a) Goraknāth, in M. Eliade (ed) *The Encyclopedia of Religion*, New York: Macmillan, 6: 77–8.
—(1987b) Hatha yoga, in M. Eliade (ed) *The Encyclopedia of Religion*, New York: Macmillan, 6: 213–14.
Majumdar, K. (1964) *Introduction to Yoga Principles and Practice*, New York: University Books.
Mallik, K. (1954) *Siddha-Siddhanta-Paddhati and Other Works of the Nātha Yogis*, Poona: Oriental Book House.
Postans, T. (1838) An Account of the Kānphaṭas of Danodhar, in *Journal of the Royal Asiatic Society* 5: 268–71.
Tsong, Khapa. (2002) *Rigs pa'i rgya mtso* (Ocean of Explanatory Reasonings), Karwar: Drepung Gomang Monastery.
Varenne, J. (1976) *Yoga and the Hindu Tradition*, Chicago: University of Chicago Press.
Vasu, S.C. (trans) (1933) *The Gheraṇḍasaṃhitā*, Madras: Theosophical Publishing House.
Weber, M (1958) *The Religion of India: The sociology of Hinduism and Buddhism*, Glencoe, IL: The Free Press.
White, D.G, (1996) *The Alchemical Body*, Chicago: University of Chicago Press.
—(2003) *Kiss of the Yogini*, Chicago: University of Chicago Press.
Wright, W. (1975) *Six Guns and Society: a Structural Study of the Western*, Berkeley: University of California Press.
Zvelebel, K.V. (1973) *The Poets of the Powers*, London: Rider & Co.

Part III

Spirituality, Sexuality, and Authority

Understanding the Experience of Contemporary Yoga Practice

6 Empowerment and Using the Body in Modern Postural Yoga

Klas Nevrin

In this chapter, I examine a few of the ways in which the body is used and experienced in Modern Postural Yoga (hereafter MPY).[1] Particularly, I argue that taking bodily experience into account is essential to the study of contemporary yoga, especially when attempting to understand the effects of yoga practice and to explain its increasing popularity. Moreover, a requirement for fully understanding bodily experience is a problematization of the relationships between body techniques and the contexts within which these are performed and interpreted. To that end, I highlight the importance of the practice environment in an individual's experience and understanding of yoga. Finally, in light of this analysis, my suggestion is that MPY very often works to empower the practitioner, even if in a variety of ways and for a diverse range of purposes.

In the first section, I give a brief presentation of some uses of the body in MPY and then proceed to mention a few of the challenges that have to be met if we are to understand what these do and mean to the people using them. The second section analyzes the ways in which yoga may be seen as involving processes of rehabituation (i.e., how experience is *changed* when practitioners learn new ways of making sense of and using their bodies). The effectiveness of these techniques, however, also depends on intersubjective relations and on a host of context-specific circumstances that need to be considered as well. The relationships between these various aspects are analyzed by acknowledging both the so-called lived body and the importance of the environment. In the third section, I critically discuss the notion of empowerment, which offers one way of summarizing how many practitioners experience and interpret their yoga practice.

It should be stated at the outset that the position adopted here takes a critical stand against the ways in which many explanations of yoga rely on psychologized models of the human being. In my understanding, these models will tend to see the individual (and the psyche) as somehow *apart* from the environment (and the body), whereas ecologically oriented models emphasize the *interdependence* between individual and environment in ways that differ from the former (Ingold 2000). Even though psychologized models may have a strong explanatory power for the yoga practitioner—a fact that, of course, needs to be respected and taken into account—I consider them limited when attempting a more comprehensive understanding of yoga. For example, I argue that empowerment depends on social situations and shared discursive practices in ways that typically remain unacknowledged from a psychologized viewpoint. Given these limitations, I attempt to further our understanding of experience in MPY through analytically including the practice environment in ways that go beyond individualistic models. However, this should not prevent us from taking a closer look at the role played by individual experience. We do not have to throw the baby out with the bathwater. Indeed, it seems that without taking embodied experience into consideration, one cannot do full justice to the nature and significance of contemporary yoga (Coney 1999). Another issue concerns the assumptions that psychologization often rely on, particularly when the person is assumed to be a "distinct unit" or "isolated self," in effect offering an ideology of separation (Carrette & King 2005: 57, 80). In such cases, psychologization not only serves pragmatic and purportedly "private" purposes but works to reproduce views that involve highly questionable normative claims. I mention and discuss a few of these assumptions in the final section.

Using the Body in MPY

My research has mainly been conducted with people doing yoga in practice environments inspired by Tirumalai Krishnamacharya (1888–1989). His followers have played a huge role in popularizing yoga in the West, the most famous being Pattabhi Jois (b. 1915), teaching in the style of Ashtanga (Vinyasa) Yoga; B.K.S. Iyengar (b. 1918), who developed what is known as Iyengar Yoga, and T.K.V. Desikachar (b. 1938), teaching in the style of Viniyoga.[2] Many contemporary MPY teachers have trained in the Iyengar, Ashtanga, or Viniyoga styles before developing their own method or have simply borrowed from them. Krishnamacharya's influence can be seen, among other things, in the emphasis on and development of postures (*āsana*), particularly by sequencing them and ascribing them specific therapeutic values.[3] My research material consists of interviews, participant observation, and publications from these schools, primarily in Sweden but also in India.

Postures (*āsana*), attentive breathing (*prāṇāyāma*), and chant (*svādhyāya, japa*) are generally the most important practices and are typically combined in different ways. Most often the novice will begin with learning breathing techniques as an aspect of sequenced postures, but they can also be taught separately. The physical training is usually experienced as arduous and challenging for most beginners. It consists of learning sets of postures (whether sequenced or not) in which the body is stretched, softened, relaxed, and strengthened to different degrees and in various ways. Most important, however, is that the postures are performed with a particular quality of attention and precision. Postural training can thus be seen as a form of meditation in action because the many details that the practitioner has to focus on—such as tempo; aligning the breath with postures; extensions and directions; the order of sequences; names of the postures; where to fix one's gaze; precise muscle use; and so on—often keep the practitioner particularly focused and attentive.[4] Postural training ends with a relaxation practice, in which the practitioner lies on the back, usually taking directions from the teacher how to relax the body completely (see Singleton 2005).

Over time, the practitioner will sometimes be encouraged to practice chanting. For example, in Viniyoga, an integrated sequence might consist of a flow of postures wherein the breath is aligned both with the body's movement and with the chanting of a mantra. In Iyengar and Ashtanga Yoga, by contrast, chanting is more often limited to reciting dedication mantras at the beginning or ending of a practice session (or both). Quite often, however, devoted practitioners tend to become increasingly interested in learning to chant also other texts or mantras (or both). Examples include the *Gāyatrī* mantra and the *Yogasūtra* text, the latter generally considered highly important to most MPY practitioners (see Mark Singleton's contribution to this volume), being employed both as a reference for practical and intellectual guidance and being chanted.[5]

When attempting to understand the experiential effects of these practices, I think it is helpful to distinguish between various styles of MPY because similar practices may be interpreted and experienced differently, depending on the context in which they are performed. As I attempt to show, stylistic differences are not only a matter of holding different beliefs but include the way in which a practitioner will *feel* in a particular practice environment. Many practitioners will, for example, emphasize the ways in which a particular practice environment might induce a sense of stillness or calm; a sense of belonging; an energized motivation; or a "spiritual atmosphere." Sometimes practitioners will prefer a style that is explicitly connected to what is perceived as "traditional Indian yoga," for example, through the use of Sanskrit names, recitation of mantras, the presence of icons, the use of incense, and the study of yoga texts. By contrast, in other practice environments, these features will be more or less absent. The stylistic differences will be important for whether the practitioner feels at home, for whether he or she has a sense of the atmosphere being right for him or her.

When we enter a Yogashala (a place for yoga classes), we encounter a number of things to which we have to respond (Lingis 1998). We are not simply entering a neutral space but a situation filled with meanings. We will, of course, carry with us ideas about what to expect, what yoga is "about," why we are there, and so on. However, the moment we enter we will also have to respond in some way to everything we meet. Thus, if we are to encounter, say, a symmetrically arranged row of nightlights that are placed in holders made of glass and shaped like lotus flowers; a smell of sweet incense; the sound of soft, melodious Sanskrit chant from the stereo; a group of smiling, pregnant women sitting on cushions around an antique, wooden table; and, on the wall, a large picture of a Yogi meditating in full lotus—how will all this make us feel? Will we feel comfortable and calm? Perhaps we will feel solemnity? Or curiosity? Or perhaps the situation will evoke memories from past travels in India?

Any reactions will probably be mediated in terms of socioculturally acquired habits. That is to say, nightlights and lotuses will mean something because of past experiences involving similar images, situations, and objects. We will also respond to the environment in terms of felt qualities that provide us with some prereflective sense of ourselves and the atmosphere in which we find ourselves. My point is that both reflective and prereflective responses are crucially important for how a practitioner will understand the nature and effects of yoga practice.

It should, then, be helpful to thematize the various elements that are involved in a person's experience of yoga. First, artefacts and social atmospheres are likely to initiate certain responses. This will include any conversations taking place between people being present—perhaps people from an earlier session exchanging and sharing experiences of their practice. The environment will function as a setting that shapes and contextualizes experiences that will arise in the practice session proper. Thus, prior to actually performing any specific yoga techniques, there are a host of things that provide an interpretive context. Second, "the practice" itself—as it is called by most practitioners—is a highly structured routine consisting of a variety of body techniques. These uses of the body, too, will create certain reactions, both physiological and emotional, which are then contextualized by being related to pre- and post-session contexts, to previous experience, and to any acquired knowledge about yoga. In other words, contextualization will involve adapting to a practice environment that supplies both articulate concepts and vaguely felt meanings that will influence the ways in which a particular individual will interpret the experiences that arise owing to performing certain body techniques. The precise elements that constitute these processes of contextualization will differ between practice environments, even depending on the pedagogical style of a specific teacher. As we have seen, some teachers will encourage what they consider to be a more "spiritual" atmosphere (then adopting culturally relevant artifacts, forms of sociality, and discourses to that intention), which might, say, induce a sense of solemnity, or encourage a behavior that is understood to be "yogic." Other practice environments will, by contrast, emphasize a more "athletic" style of practice, perhaps by encouraging more sports-like attitudes and by avoiding specific uses of music, chant, and imagery associated with Hinduism or India.

Yoga and Embodied Experience

How are we to understand uses of the body in MPY and the experiences that they may involve? To fully understand embodiment, as Merleau-Ponty (1962) argued, it is necessary to include the "lived body." This means not only looking at the body from the outside—as an object being talked about in discourse or as behaviorally conducted in social and material spaces—but understanding the body itself as a locus of experience. In the following, I focus on a few of the ways in which the body is experientially involved, thereby pointing out the more common forms of experiencing that seem to be central to the motivations of many practitioners. This is an attempt to understand why yoga is considered to be a meaningful and rewarding activity by those involved with it. We might say that the challenge lies in understanding why yoga is claimed to work against a depersonalization of the body, involving the practitioner in "modes of refined self-presencing" that make it possible to "(re)negotiate the terms and quality of engagement of the lived bodymind in its encounter with itself in the world" (Zarrilli 2004: 661). In an attempt to shed some light on this, I will distinguish between three overlapping aspects: (1) attending to movement, (2) heightened sensitivity, and (3) emotion.

Attending to Movement

A highly important aspect of contemporary yoga practice is learning *to feel the body move* and *to move the body differently.* MPY in particular enhances a direct involvement with and focused attention toward movement, thus being related to other movement studies such as the Alexander Technique, the Feldenkrais Method, Authentic Movement, or Body-Mind Centering. It is also, perhaps, related to various forms of sport, dance, and martial arts that involve a restructuring of movement. In my view, differences between these various types of activities consist not only in the learning of diverse movement patterns but in the dissimilar contexts within which they are performed, thus implying experiential variations as well. For example, the *purposes* for learning new behavioral routines are crucially important for the ways in which individuals will be affected, especially in their everyday life. Moreover, the fact that MPY involves the training of specific attentional techniques can hardly be overstated when comparing it to other movement studies.

One aspect of attending to movement is learning to intensify the experience of proprioception in general and kinesthesia in particular.[6] This may be compared to rituals that direct the focus toward the phenomenality of the body itself, thus "targeting the sensorium of the participant," as Judith Kovach (2002) puts it. In this function of ritual, the "natural attitudes" of the human body—its everyday postures, bearings, gestures and movements—are changed to produce different modalities of awareness, intensifying what is sometimes referred to as "the bodily felt sense" (Levin 2003: 180–1). *These modalities of body-awareness are then different as compared to the everyday.* Indeed, immersing oneself in movement can under certain circumstances, not least through diligent training, take the form of a sustained dynamic flow that is normally not experienced in everyday forms of body performance: "Experienced as an elongated or ongoing present, it is a world in which there are no befores or hereafters, no sooner-or-laters, no definitively expected endings or places of arrival" (Sheets-Johnstone 1999a: 490–1). Attending to movement in this way is to immerse oneself in kinetic experiences that are felt to have no goal or purpose beyond themselves, in which "the meaning of the kinetic experience is in the movement itself" (Sheets-Johnstone 1999a: 151). Modes of deeper and sustained flow will typically be achieved only by those who practice regularly and for a long time. Nevertheless, many practitioners will approximate such experiences in nondramatic ways, and as such they seem to constitute an important motivational factor for continuing to practice yoga.[7]

Maxine Sheets-Johnstone's work (1999a; 1999b; 1998) on kinesthesia and its relation to affectivity is particularly helpful for our purposes. She emphasizes that kinesthesia is, strictly speaking, not an object of consciousness or perception (cf. Gallagher 2002) but more accurately "a felt unfolding dynamic and, in virtue of that dynamic, a felt overall kinetic quality" (1999a: 152). Kinesthesia is fundamentally a nonverbal experience because movement has a distinctive spatiotemporal dynamic coincident with the manner or style in which we are moving and not primarily with the way we reflect on it. Moreover, intensely attending to movement for some people seems to offer more "plural self-identities" by producing heightened forms of multisensory awareness and a less stressed sense of identity (Smith 2002; Ness 1992)—a less rigid sense of oneself and the body, as it were. To learn how to move in ways that are not intended to accomplish something in "the outer world" will have the effect that movement has a less literal or tangible quality, not so much associated with "action" as with affect or mood (Bartenieff 1980: 59). This means that attending to movement may be a "liberating" experience. Whether this is articulated in terms of a "profound selfhood" or an "existentially absolute self" (Kovach 2002) seems to depend primarily on the practice environment and on the individual practitioner's background and interests.

Learning new styles of moving can also bring about transformed affectivities, depending on the particular qualitative, kinetic dynamic involved (Sheets-Johnstone 1999a: 158–9; 1999b). Approaching movement in this way is consistent with *Laban Movement Analysis*, a system devised for observing and analyzing movement that draws on theories originally innovated by Rudolf Laban (see e.g., Hankin 1984) and that offers important ways of understanding the interrelation between body performance and affectivity. That is to say, changing one's way of using the body can have a significant impact on how we feel about ourselves and the environment. In certain cases of depressed patients, for example, physiotherapist Irmgard Bartenieff (1980: 157–8) argues that when body performance is changed, it may have a considerable effect on the person involved:

> A person in a deep depression often has a quality of great heaviness resulting from an almost total—a passive—giving into body weight. When the slightest attitude toward the use of that body weight can be activated, a move that may lead out of the depression has been initiated. [...] What is important is its indication of participation rather than passivity and the diminution of heaviness and immobility in the experience of the depressed person (Bartenieff 1980: 56).

This is not, of course, to say that depression or similar conditions are reducible to body performance. Nevertheless, it seems important to acknowledge that there are complex links between movement and affectivity that can be influenced by sustained involvement with MPY practices—though certainly in various ways and to different degrees.[8] In summary, then, postural practice in MPY may allow the practitioner to change his or her qualitative use of movement: weight distribution, effort, temporality, the coordinated use of parts, and so on. This also includes a heightened attention to feeling movement itself, which will typically alter the practitioner's sense of self and body and invite for a variety of reflections regarding the nature and significance of this change.

Finally, it must also be mentioned, yoga training will generally boost the individual's health, for example by increasing the ability to pursue daily activities without feeling fatigued and with reduced risk for disease or pain. Beneficial effects due to yoga are often claimed to range from increased relaxation to enhanced muscular strength, from cardiorespiratory fitness to changed body composition, all of which will typically have considerable consequences for anxiety levels, stress resistance, and so on. Though I do not deal with this aspect here—and there are literally hundreds of research projects being conducted in this area—it is certainly important to how yoga practice is perceived and explained by most practitioners. Indeed, it is probably the most frequently voiced reason for attending yoga classes in the first place, and for many people fitness and health are what yoga is all about.

Though transformed body performance and heightened attention to movement will occur in highly individual combinations and with a great variety of results, not least depending on the practitioner's level of commitment and motivation, it is nevertheless very common that even novice practitioners will experience these changes as being highly positive. Moreover, the transformations might even be interpreted as being of a "spiritual" character. To give an example, one of the very common ways that practitioners have of describing the effects of a yoga session, especially in the relaxation phase at the end, is to talk about being immersed in "a whole different world." The experience of attending to movement will thus be understood as highly significant, compared to what one is used to, and the step toward talking about this as being of a "spiritual" nature—not least because interpreted as a more "authentic" way of being—is not a big one to take. Though this is, of course, only one way in which talk about spirituality might occur in specific MPY practice environments, it is nevertheless an important one.

Heightened Sensitivity

The results of yoga practice are often claimed to involve a "heightened sensitivity" of the body and a "heightened richness" of sensory experience. For example, many long-time practitioners will feel that they have become more sensitive to their surroundings and to their own bodies. To make sense of these claims, I draw on the work of Drew Leder (1990). Leder explains that there is a general from-to structure and a figure-ground configuration that characterizes all forms of experience. In other words, various elements of experience will be relatively tacit in different ways and to different degrees; as when something is only marginally present to us in experience, or when we have an awareness of something in a more obscure or vague fashion. This is so because when we direct our attention somewhere, we simultaneously direct it away from something else. And attentional skills are essentially habit-dependent. Moreover, says Leder, most everyday actions will be directed *away from the body* in that one "acts from the here-and-now body to spatially or temporally noncoincident objects" (Leder 1990: 18). This means that one's body is normally rendered subsidiary, not only as a physical means to an end but within the structure of attention as well. Most of the time, then, entire corporeal regions and powers are "absenced" by being part of the from-structure of experience, being directed toward some or other object in the outer world, which effectively relegates the body to the status of neutral background. In addition, relatively unused sensory capacities will have the effect that perceptual detail may recede from apprehension altogether, not being "actualized" or "differentiated" as it were. In other words, we under-exploit the potential for sensory experience to the extent that we narrow our perceptual skills to a relatively restricted range. This might happen owing to habitual (culturally conditioned) over-reliance on vision and thought and owing to inattentiveness to kinesthesia, smell, taste, and sound (Classen 1997). The overall result is that everyday uses of the body will tend to involve a form of "surface awareness" in which one is typically more dimly aware of certain sights, sounds, movements, and so on.

Arguably, experience will take on something of a continuous character owing to habit and, as such, will involve more or less persistent qualities being afforded to the world, to other people, and to oneself. Thus, for example, when the body is habitually used as a neutral background to goal-oriented thoughts and actions, the body is not experienced as "alive" in itself. This may even produce an excessive disconnection of ourselves (i.e., our bodies) from the environment in which one might feel alienated and emotionally disconnected from "the world." And, as Matthew Ratcliffe argues, "if one's sense of the world is tainted by a 'feeling of unreality,' this will affect how all objects of perception appear. They are distant, removed, not quite 'there'" (Ratcliffe 2005: 45; cf. Mazis 1993). In these hyper-detached forms of experience, we might say, perceptual and imaginative skills are habitually set on producing an affectively neutral and nondynamic experience of ourselves and the world.

However, habits can be changed. If we can learn how to utilize bodily capacities and powers differently, this may result in a form of heightened sensitivity in which additional sensory detail is differentiated. Moreover, as Phillip Zarrilli shows (2004), experiential skills can be acquired that involve a heightened awareness of the body (e.g., movement, breathing, and the like) even when our attention is directed toward something other than the body itself. Significantly, Zarrilli claims that this "allows for a shift in one's experience of the body and mind aspects from their gross separation, marked by the body's constant disappearance, to a much more subtle, dialectical engagement of body-in-mind and mind-in-body" (Zarrilli 2004: 661). Seen from another perspective, richness of sensory detail and a heightened sense of bodily involvement may also work to disrupt the experience of the environment ("the world") as consisting of static objects and discrete events. When compared to situations in which we relate to things and events in a relatively detached way, certain experiential skills may enable us to experience our surroundings and our bodies in a more dynamic, animated, and relational mode.

Experiential skills that involve a higher degree of perceptual differentiation also seem to overlap with how we feel, think, and imagine. Indeed, the yoga practitioner learns to attend to movement, breath, and sound in ways that depend not only on body usage and heightened forms of awareness but, for example, on learning a specific language of the body (such as distinguishing between different kinds of pain or different body parts) and the acquiring of a historical sense of bodily movements (Leigh Foster 1997), both of which entail the implementation of specific imaginative-discursive registers.

Zarrilli especially emphasizes "attentiveness to the breath" (2004: 661) as a technique for moving away from detached modes of experience and toward more relational modes. Similarly, Sundar Sarukkai views breathing primarily in terms of an engagement with the "inner body" that makes possible the "experience of the dimensionality that 'fills' our body" (Sarukkai 2002: 471). James Morley also argues that experience of breath control "is the concrete experience of the body as a *relation* between inside and outside" (Morley 2001: 76; emphasis in original). According to these authors, the cultivation of attentive breathing make possible modes of experiencing in which "inner" and "outer" are not as dualistically opposed. However, attentive breathing, too, will depend on the adoption of various nomenclatures and forms of imagination within a particular practice environment. This means that any "dimensionality" or "relation" will be experienced somewhat differently, depending on the precise nature of the breathing technique and on the purpose for which it is used. Differences may consist in whether attentive breathing is accomplished simultaneously with movement and in a variety of elements, places, or moments of breathing that can be accentuated differently. Also relevant are the precise ways in which particular breathing techniques are related to dealing with emotions and thoughts and how or to what extent they are utilized in everyday situations. Breathing techniques may also include the making of sound (such as *ujjāyī prāṇāyāma*). In fact, the use of sound and chant has often been claimed a central place within the history of yoga (Beck 1993) and has sometimes been explicitly connected to attentive breathing (Carpenter 2003).

Postural training and attentive breathing may also enhance the practitioner's sensitivity toward the body by improving awareness of particular bodily states and feelings. Richard Shusterman proposes that certain somatic practices can, besides making "the quality of our experience more satisfyingly rich," work to "improve the acuity, health, and control of our senses by cultivating heightened attention to and mastery of their somatic functioning, while also freeing us from bodily habits and defects that impair sensory performance" (Shusterman 1999: 305). As such, certain body techniques may "reveal and improve somatic malfunctionings that normally go undetected even though they impair our well-being and performance," thus providing for a "psychosomatic management of pain" (1999: 302–3). Shusterman gives us two examples of how this may work:

> We rarely notice our breathing, but its rhythm and depth provide rapid, reliable evidence of our emotional state. Consciousness of breathing can therefore make us aware that we are angry, tense, or anxious when we might otherwise remain unaware of these feelings and thus vulnerable to their misdirection. Similarly, a chronic muscular contraction that not only constrains movement but results in tension and pain may nonetheless go unnoticed because it has become habitual. As unnoticed, this chronic contraction cannot be relieved, nor can its resultant disability and discomfort. Yet, once such somatic functioning is brought to clear attention, there is a chance to modify it and avoid its unhealthy consequences, which include not only pain but a dulling of the senses, a diminution of aesthetic sensitivity and pleasure (Shusterman 1999: 302–3).

Emotion

MPY will also involve a spectrum of emotionalities, even if this fact is typically ignored in many accounts of yoga. Indeed, emotion is generally mentioned only in passing, often with a pejorative undertone (e.g., as "passions" to be overcome). However, I argue that emotionality is involved in a variety of ways, for example, through identification and belonging; through the sharing of experiences between practitioners, what we might view as the production of "emotional histories"; through the use of artifacts (e.g., particular lighting, icons of Hindu deities, incense, music, and so on, which invite for certain emotional responses); or through specific affective-imaginative engagements in yoga practice. In the following paragraphs, I give a few examples.

Ben Malbon (1999: 72–4) argues that group activities will typically involve a "collective sensibility" or "being-togetherness" that can, temporarily at least and given the right circumstances, unload the burden of individuality. Thus, by moving among and being in proximity to others ands identifying with others in a group and with a collective focus (such as a particular music, yoga practice, and so on), one can slip between consciousness of self and consciousness of being part of something larger, between anonymizing and individualizing. Moreover, sensations of belonging can be prolonged, as when one identifies with certain sites, times, memories, paraphernalia or others not physically present. These are forms of emotional involvement that seem to be quite common in many MPY environments.

Take, for example, the use of music and sound. Arguably, music will instill certain responses, as a bodily sense of participation, a patterning of lived time and space (Etlin 1998). Through the use of sound people are "moved," they become emotionally and imaginatively engaged. Indeed, as Malbon recognizes, music often plays a central role in the constitution of a community, allowing people to situate themselves historically, culturally, politically, and stylistically. As such, it can transform or create social spaces, providing both aural backdrops and foci for many aspects of social interaction, not least by articulating identities and developing a sense of belonging. Music can also intensify shared experiences by evoking similar emotional and physical responses among a group of people (Malbon 1999: 77–80). Indeed, within many MPY practice environments, music is a highly important resource for identification, extending far beyond the actual yoga practice. Examples range from yoga teacher Shiva Rea's use of "trance dance" and music, to the popularity enjoyed by the so-called "chant masters" Krishna Das, Jai Uttal, and Deva Premal, among many MPY practitioners. The chanting of mantras and texts may also serve simultaneous purposes of identification, contemplation, and demonstration of expertise (see Nevrin forthcoming).

Yoga practices may also be accompanied by a particular emotional and imaginative poise, performatively enacted and felt by the person involved (Crouch 2003). This means that yoga practitioners not only learn new ways of moving and sensing with the body but they will be emotionally involved in and through the particular action. One source for emotion is the bodily techniques themselves, as certain bodily performances, such as kneeling, slow breathing, and so on, will involve affective associations (Holloway 2003), *qua* "emotionally marked actions" (Leavitt 1996). Affective associations depend, of course, on cultural stereotyping but also to a certain degree on kinetic qualities involved in the action itself because our "bodily feelings of movement have a certain dynamic. We feel, for example, the swiftness or slowness of our movement, its constrictedness or openness, its tensional tightness or looseness, and more" (Sheets-Johnstone 1998: 272). As such, bodily actions entail structures of experience that invite for affective and imaginative elaboration in certain directions, even if never mandating these elaborations as invariants.[9]

An example is that sun salutations are sometimes performed in a devotional style, directed toward an imagined other, such as "the sun" or "God."[10] These styles of performance will draw on the prostration-like form of the sun salutation, directing the emotionally marked character toward something or someone beyond the individual, perhaps as a form of dedication. This can be compared to when sun salutations are performed in practice environments where the emphasis lies on, say, correct physical execution, and when the quality of attention is oriented more directly toward experiencing the body itself. Simply put, the affective-imaginative engagement will be quite different between these various styles of performing, though the body techniques themselves are roughly similar. This difference is not peripheral to the practice but rather quite fundamental. In fact, many practitioners have repeatedly informed me how they actively seek out a particular practice environment that "fits them," where the style of performance and the atmosphere were experienced as conducive to their own personality, taste, and aspirations. Quite often, people will indeed comment on such things as the atmosphere of a school or the style of a practice. Moreover, differences in emotional and imaginative involvement will have considerable consequences for how a practitioner might change his or her attitudes toward various issues in everyday life.

Empowerment: A Critical Analysis

MPY practices of attending to and with the body can be said to *existentially* empower the practitioner by making him or her feel more "whole," "alive," and so on. This empowering effect is achieved through the learning of a variety of skills and techniques and by taking part in an emotionally invigorating social space. MPY practice environments also offer ways of increasing self-confidence by *socially* empowering the individual, which serves to establish attitudes and choices vis-à-vis some issue that is of concern to the individual. For example, life style changes are typically initiated by the ways in which a particular practice environment may offer emotional support and encourage specific forms of behavior understood to be "yogic" (as opposed to, say, "egoistic," "weak," "addicted," or "unhealthy"). In the following, I discuss these two forms of empowerment in more detail, showing both how they are intimately related to each other and how they involve problematic issues.

Existential Empowerment

The attentional skills and the nonordinary uses of the body that one acquires through yoga practice can be said to counteract detached and inflexible modes of experiencing. However, it is often taken for granted that these skills are also fully transposable to other situations, thus ignoring the fact that they are rather purpose-specific and therefore limited. Though many practitioners may recognize this, they rarely discuss it openly, and some yoga discourses do in fact insinuate that mastering yoga means having achieved authentic access to "reality" or "the realization of one's true nature" (Jois 2002: 5), regardless of specific situational circumstances. However, such an assumption may give rise to arrogance when denying the infinitely many ways in which one might attend differently to the world. It also suggests that the individual (whether as "worldly" or "pure" consciousness) is (or can be) a more or less independent entity, disconnected from the environment. The question then arises whether this assumption is not evidence of a utopian dream. Indeed, many yoga discourses do seem to support a concept of self-realization that emphasizes "the complete freedom of the mind" (Strauss 1997: 36), thus propagating a highly individualistic view of the human being that, in my opinion, disregards the many ways in which we are dependent on one another and on the environment. Indeed, such a view will also tend to dichotomize "inward freedom" over and against "outward conformity" (Gendlin 1987).

Acquired skills may of course be transposable to some degree and extent. For example, skills of concentration learned in one context may be useful in other situations, and having some acquaintance with the experience of movement flow may prove valuable as well. Having achieved a certain level of health and fitness will surely have repercussions in many situations in everyday life. And to the extent that yoga makes it possible to achieve relatively relaxed and maturized forms of body performance, this will most certainly have ramifications for daily life.

However, as I have argued throughout this chapter, we need also to take into account the importance of social, discursive, and material environments. This means that experiential freedom and authenticity, say, cannot depend solely on the individual's skills and abilities but always already involves constantly changing circumstances. For example, in some situations, detached modes of experience may arise because of circumstances that to some extent lie beyond the individual's intentional powers, including the following: how we are expected to emotionally relate to one another in a given social situation (e.g., many social contexts establish the priority of ideational knowledge over and against emotional, or hierarchically value the visual over the tactile-kinesthetic); the emphasis on individualistic self-narratives within many forms of media and education; regulation and commodification of the body in modern consumer-oriented settings, including "emotional control" and "experiential consuming"; stressful living-conditions, not least an achievement-related production of anxiety and stress; the influence of technologies and architectures on social interactions and on individual experience of space and time (e.g., increased social isolation and "disembodied" life styles); and many other things.[11] So long as we are involved in social interactions with other human beings, circumstances such as these are bound to influence us to some degree, not least by restricting our ways of feeling, thinking, and acting.

There is thus a limit to how yoga can change a person, because he or she is highly dependent on environmental circumstances, including the presence of fulfilling relationships and beneficial living conditions. The neglect to address this limit often results in a rhetoric claim that yoga has a dimension of truth and authenticity supposedly lacking in other activities. This rhetoric is closely tied to the notion of "spiritual insight," which is often used to claim status and legitimize authority. Another purpose is to establish motivational incentives. Thus, when something (e.g., a behavior or an experience) is termed "spiritual," it often means that the person in question wants to claim its importance to his or her own life and in relation to others' lives. Though these purposes may seem innocent enough, "spirituality talk" typically establishes and reinforces a status struggle in which yoga is claimed to be a more correct way of accessing reality. This of course underestimates the many alternative ways in which a person can transform habits of experience (e.g., through artistic or communicative skills). Besides relying on problematic ontologies (Ingold 2000), the overemphasis on sensory experience within an individualistic and psychologized interpretive framework downplays the need for communication and dialogue. Moreover, if experiential freedom is dependent on social situations, one would also have to take into account such things as power structures and living conditions. Though there are exceptions, recognition of the social, not only ethically but ontologically (Anton 2001), is conspicuously missing in many yoga discourses.

A final issue concerns the fact that reflection and thought are often seen as being opposed to yogic practice. However, this seems counterproductive to some of the professed aims of yoga, such as enhancing experiential freedom and authenticity. The emphasis on "practice" approaches yoga as a form of *de*-habituation and *de*-identification, and polarizes the alleged authority of "personal experience" over and against "language" or "theory," as if the latter were somehow outside the field of experience (and despite the fact that they are, in my view, heavily involved in yoga practice). This polarization makes it very difficult to critically assess the ways in which particular discourses might involve naïve attitudes toward society's influence on the individual. It also acts as a defense for a lack of training one's ability to reflect, which in turn might result in inflexible action. Indeed, it may well be argued that freedom is dependent also on our capacity to break out of and carry forward the language we inherit and find ourselves already using, which requires that one learns how to think more creatively with words (Levin 1997). There are many examples of innovation within yoga, for example, the conception of new vocabularies of the body and of emotions. Yet, these instances of reflection typically remain unacknowledged. Finally, developing self-reflexivity, as in exposing prejudgments, is of course a highly important point of departure for communicating with others and for making possible mutual understanding and respect. When neglected, this means one runs the risk of adopting chauvinistic or naïve attitudes toward others. A depreciation of reflection and thought may thus serve to cement, and even veil, highly questionable and disconcerting stereotypes (such as racism, sexism, beautism, and healthism). In summary, then, psychologized and individualistic models, accompanied by a rhetoric of truth, make difficult the recognition that yoga is also a social practice. In the following section, I attempt to show how MPY creates social spaces in which people engage with one another in various ways.

Social Empowerment

MPY practice environments also provide for trust and solidarity, as a form of social empowerment. Through various social interactions, the practitioner might be encouraged to "be oneself," to avoid drugs and other bad habits, such as unhealthy diets or relationships, even to resist consumerist attitudes. Moreover, to relax into an emotionally supportive atmosphere may enable the person to more openly express emotion and to feel "at home" with others.

A common example is the overcoming of resistance, pain, and fear when pursuing challenging postures. This works to empower the practitioner, by enhancing his or her willpower and self-confidence. He or she thus gets acquainted with the feeling of overcoming difficulties, which may of course affect daily life as well. However, all this happens not least because of social support and teacher guidance. Many practitioners will indeed attest to the importance of having been in a practice environment that inspired and challenged them in various ways.

As Randall Collins (2004) has argued, when individuals gather together and participate in a collective action—what he calls interaction rituals—this may produce a powerful emotional stimulus. This is because we are prereflectively sensitive to each other's bodily presence; we affect and respond to others' bodily expressions, entering into shared rhythms, being caught by each other's movements and emotions. Collins's point is that the more participants focus on a common activity and the more they attune to each other, to what everyone else is doing and feeling, the more intense the experience. This is a form of emotional energy, which will typically take the form of exhilaration, confidence, trust, enthusiasm, and a strengthened sense of initiative. Individuals who are full of emotional energy feel "good" and "valuable." These empowering experiences can then also be evoked in situations when one is "alone."

I argue that this form of emotionality is an important aspect of social empowerment, particularly in those MPY practice environments in which collectivity is accentuated. Indeed, in Malbon's analysis, empowerment—or playful vitality, as he calls it—is largely emotional in constitution and arises partly through the flux between self and collectivity and through the prioritizing of the affectual, of proximity and tactility, and of the "here and now." As such, it is "partly a celebration of the energy and euphoria that can be generated through being together, playing together and experiencing 'others' together. Yet vitality is also partly an escape attempt, a temporary relief from other facets and identifications" of an individual's own life: from work, from the past or the future, from worries, and so on. In situations wherein playful vitality is cultivated, it is primarily a construction in which "the everyday is disrupted, the mundane is forgotten and the ecstatic becomes possible" (Malbon 1999: 164). For my part, I would not want to view this in terms of an "escape," as that seems to value the everyday and the mundane as somehow being more true or real. Nevertheless, Collin's and Malbon's analyses of interaction rituals and playful vitality are pertinent to an understanding of the social aspects of MPY practice environments. Indeed, social empowerment seems both necessary and desirable, perhaps even an unavoidable aspect of situations in which people get together and do something.

Moreover, social empowerment in MPY is probably to some extent related to sociopolitical changes in late modernity. For example, lack of power in areas where one is dependent on security and trust will likely produce reactions such as shame and feelings of defeat, failure, insufficiency, alienation, and abandonment. These are symptoms of threatened or insecure social ties and the effects of lack of control, increasingly common in many modern settings. Therefore, as Michel Maffesoli (1996) argues, the establishment of "emotional communities" is essential for the vitalization of social interactions and for satisfying a need for emotional intimacy and nearness. Mellor and Shilling (1997) similarly claim that contemporary forms of social bonding are often based on emotional, bodily, and sensual interactions that differ from older, traditional forms. Indeed, I would argue that MPY can be seen as offering discourses and practices that open up new spaces in which alternative ideologies and practices of the body can be explored, simultaneously offering opportunities for social empowerment and the formation of alternative social interactions (Turner 1994; Burkitt 1999: 145)—a resistance against conventional forms of sociality, as it were. Paradoxically, however, many MPY practitioners are playing on both sides: on the one hand constructing social alternatives, yet on the other hand reinforcing an ideology of separation, at least to the extent that the importance of the social is underrated.

Also relevant is the fact that social situations consist of micro-political dimensions such as struggles for authority and symbolic capital (Bourdieu 1977); that is, the accumulation of status or recognition that constrain or make possible a person's actions within a specific social context. An important variant is physical capital, a notion coined by Chris Shilling (1993) to analyze the increasing commodification of the body and the important links between identities and the social values accorded to bodies. However, these facets of the social are typically unrecognized in many yoga communities. For example, in MPY, accumulation of symbolic and physical capital often involves the use of the designations "spiritual" and "healthy." More overtly political uses might include the construction of emotional identities that provide for confrontational attitudes (McKean 1996), mobilized against competing schools by proclaiming a lineage-holder's higher degree of "spiritual authenticity," or by declaring a teacher's legitimacy in terms of his or her adherence to a "spiritual tradition." The epithet "spiritual" also tends to conflate the difference between, on the one hand, the sense of self-ease that can arise due to certain bodily practices and, on the other hand, the self-confidence that arises due to accumulation of symbolic capital.

Collins (2004) shows that individuals will typically acquire or lose emotional energy in interactions that are characterized by power and status. For example, the feeling of belonging to a group will significantly increase a person's emotional energy. Moreover, the "sociometric star" will tend to receive the most emotional energy and affection, whereas the outsider or novice receives much less (Freund 1990). In other words, a teacher or advanced practitioner—stated bluntly, those who belong to the elite of the in-group—will feel confident, strong, and successful not only because he or she has acquired "yogic skills" but owing to being at the center of attention and having acquired symbolic capital. This will even have repercussions on the ability to be attentively involved because achieving flow is much easier when a person feels confident, enthusiastic, and emotionally energized. Indeed, many practitioners have attested to the inspirational and motivational significance of being in an "energized" environment, often openly discussing the differences between teachers in terms of the level of "energy" that they "radiate" or "inspire."

These aspects of a group dynamic, even if unrecognized by its participants, raise important questions concerning the norms and ideals that are involved. In MPY, for example, the use of "healthiness" to indicate status and achievement is particularly prevalent. Health is then often used as an all-inclusive and vague catchword, ranging in meaning from fitness to self-realization (Nevrin

2004). Many practitioners also tend to assume that everything that has to do with health is somehow good. In MPY, however, this will sometimes involve the naturalization of an idealized, aestheticized body (Glassner 1989)—the so-called "body beautiful"—which involves highly questionable norms. This becomes even more problematic when "healthiness" and "spiritual insight" are associated. The problem is not necessarily that someone feels or looks strong, healthy and confident, say, but when associated with "spiritual progress" this may consolidate an unquestionable status and legitimacy to certain normative ideals.

There are, of course, MPY practice environments that constitute clear exceptions. For example, some teachers will explicitly emphasize the uniqueness of a person's body. However, the general tendency is for practitioners to be influenced by largely unconscious ideals concerning the individual's possibility of living a healthy life without addressing sociopolitical issues. Moreover, because the precise meaning of being healthy is rarely discussed explicitly by MPY practitioners, its meaning is simply assumed. This will then have the consequence that normative ideals are reproduced and presented in ways that effectively hinder their reflexive assessment.

In my view, it is important to recognize the ways in which MPY address alternatives to mainstream medical care. This recognition includes identifying the employment of attentional techniques that prove useful for a variety of purposes, not least for counteracting a detachment that negatively affects people's lives. We have also seen how yoga communities may meet a particular individual's need for alternative forms of emotional solidarity by creating an arena for vitalized social interactions. Yet, many MPY practice environments are uncritically involved in a development that attempts to "locate meaning within the individual according to a selective valuing of intense experiences within the self and a closed system of cognition" (Carrette & King 2005: 82). The challenge, it seems to me, lies in being able to recognize both the beneficial and empowering effects of yoga practice and the limitations and any questionable norms that may be involved.

Acknowledgements

I thank all participants at the Modern Yoga Postgraduate Workshop in Cambridge in April 2006 and all participant-informants involved in my fieldwork over the years. Fieldwork was made possible through funding by *Helge Ax:son Johnsons Stiftelse*. Thanks are due also to Erik af Edholm, Per Drougge, Göran Ståhle, and Aspasia Leledaki.

Notes

1 The term *Modern Postural Yoga* is used by Elizabeth De Michelis (2004). MPY stresses the orthoperformative aspects of yoga, thus resorting "to very basic and polyvalent suggestions concerning the religio-philosophical underpinnings" of its practices

(De Michelis 2004: 187). Though Modern Yoga stems from classical Hindu traditions, it is only very selectively related to historical forms, especially by concerning itself to a large extent with personal health and well-being (see Alter 2004 and Nevrin 2004).

2 Though the epithet "Viniyoga" has recently been abandoned by Desikachar, it is still in use by some of his students. Suffice it to say that I take it to be an appropriate name for a family of teachings and practices descending from Krishnamacharya and Desikachar. Other examples within the Krishnamacharya-inspired branch of MPY are Flow Yoga, Process Yoga, Power Yoga, Yin Yoga, and Dynamic Yoga. Most often these are attempts to synthesize yoga practices and discourses that have their origin in Krishnamacharya's, Desikachar's, Jois's, and Iyengar's teachings (occasionally including elements also from other forms of Modern Yoga), though more often than not grounded in the highly popular Ashtanga Yoga.

3 Though he has not, of course, been alone in this development (Alter 2004). In another article, I discuss Krishnamacharya's influence and the importance of his Śrī Vaiṣṇava heritage (Nevrin 2005).

4 See Iyengar (1995), Desikachar (1995), and Jois (2002) for descriptions of Yoga practices by leading MPY teachers.

5 When the *Yogasūtra* is chanted, this is typically done by using techniques of Vedic chant common in South India, which considerably elevates the status of the text by treating it as if it were a Vedic or Tantric text with mantras to be chanted and not sūtras to be memorized (see Nevrin forthcoming).

6 "Proprioception refers generally to a sense of movement and position. It thus includes an awareness of movement and position through tactility as well as kinesthesia, that is, through surface as well as internal events, including also a sense of gravitational orientation through vestibular sensory organs. Kinesthesia refers specifically to a sense of movement through muscular effort" (Sheets-Johnstone 1998: 272, n. 13).

7 The term *flow* has been popularized by Csíkszentmihályi (1990). In my reading, however, his understanding of flow does not include an adequate account of embodiment. As such, it focuses on "consciousness flow" or "altered states of consciousness," thus underemphasizing the role played by emotionality, sociality and, indeed, the body.

8 See my forthcoming Ph.D dissertation for a more detailed movement analysis of the many forms of postural training that abound. In my view, a decisive factor for cultivating responsivity and sensibility is the ability to improvise, a skill that is typically downplayed in many MPY practice environments. This is not to say, of course, that some practitioners cannot or do not improvise. However, in some cases, the specific character of postural training involves relatively restricted and self-controlled forms of body-awareness that may inhibit emotional flexibility and intensify self-assertive attitudes.

9 Here I have benefited from Leder's notion of "phenomenological vectors" (1990: 150).

10 "Sun salutations" are a sequence of postures that have become centrally important to MPY. Their origin is controversial (see Alter 2004). Also see Nevrin (2005) for examples on devotional interpretations and styles of practice in Viniyoga that are derived to a significant degree from Śrī Vaiṣṇavism.

11 See, among others, Burkitt 1999; Thrift 2000, 2004; Shilling 1993; Featherstone 1982; Leder 1990; and Anton 2001.

Bibliography

Alter, J. (2004) Yoga *in Modern India: The Body Between Philosophy and Science*, Princeton: Princeton University Press.

Anton, C. (2001) *Selfhood and Authenticity*, Albany: SUNY Press.

Bartenieff, I. (1980) *Body movement: coping with the environment*, Langhorne: Gordon & Breach.

Beck, G. (1993) *Sonic Theology: Hinduism and Sacred Sound*, Columbia, SC: University of South Carolina Press.

Bourdieu, P. (1977) *Outline of a Theory of Practice*, trans R. Nice, Cambridge: Cambridge University Press.

Burkitt, I. (1999) *Bodies of Thought: Embodiment, Identity and Modernity*, London: Sage Publications.

Carpenter, D. (2003) Practice Makes Perfect, in I. Whicher and D. Carpenter (eds) *Yoga: The Indian Tradition*, London: Routledge/Curzon.

Carrette, J. and R. King (2005) *Selling Spirituality. The Silent Takeover of Religion*, London: Routledge.

Classen, C. (1997) Foundations for an anthropology of the senses, *UNESCO* 153: 401–12.

Coney, J. (1999) *Sahaja Yoga: socializing processes in a South Asian new religious movement*, Richmond: Curzon.

Collins, R. (2004) *Interaction Ritual Chains*, Princeton: Princeton University Press.

Crouch, D. (2003) Spacing, performing, and becoming: Tangles in the mundane, *Environment and Planning A*, 35: 1945–60.

Csikszentmihalyi, M. (1990) *Flow: The Psychology of Optimal Experience*, New York: Harper & Row.

De Michelis, E. (2004) *A History of Modern Yoga: Patañjali and Western Esotericism*, London: Continuum.

Desikachar, T.K.V. (1995) *Heart of Yoga: Developing a Personal Practice*, Bombay: Inner Traditions India.

Etlin, R. (1998) Aesthetics and the spatial sense of self, *The Journal of Aesthetics and Art Criticism*, 56 (1): 1–19

Featherstone, M. (1982) The body in consumer culture, *Theory, Culture and Society*, 1: 18–33.

Freund, P. (1990) The expressive body: A common ground for the sociology of emotions and health and illness, *Sociology of Health & Illness*, 12 (4): 452–77.

Gallagher, S. (2002) Bodily self-awareness and object-perception, *Theoria et Historia Scientiarum: International Journal for Interdisciplinary Studies*, 7 (1): 53–68 [special issue: Embodiment and awareness. Perspectives from phenomenology and cognitive science].

Gendlin, E. (1987) A Philosophical Critique of the Concept of Narcissism: The Significance of the Awareness Movement, in D.M. Levin (ed) *Pathologies of the Modern Self*, New York: New York University Press, 251–304.

Glassner, B. (1989) Fitness and the postmodern self, *Journal of Health and Social Behavior*, 30: 180–91.

Hankin, T. (1984) Laban Movement Analysis in dance education, *Journal of Physical Education, Recreation & Dance*, 55 (9): 65–6.

Holloway, J. (2003) Make-believe: Spiritual practice, embodiment, and sacred space, *Environment and Planning*, 35: 1961–74.

Ingold, T. (2000) *The Perception of the Environment*, London: Routledge.

Iyengar, B.K.S. (1995) *Light on Yoga*, New York: Schocken Books.
Jois, P. (2002) *Yoga Mala*, New York: North Point Press.
Kovach, J. (2002) The body as the ground of religion, science, and self, *Zygon*, 37 (4): 941–61.
Leavitt, J. (1996) Meaning and feeling in the anthropology of the emotions, *American Ethnologist*, 23: 514–39.
Leder, D. (1990) *The Absent Body*, Chicago: University of Chicago Press.
Leigh Foster, S. (1997) Dancing Bodies, in J. Desmond (ed.) *Meaning in Motion*, Durham, NC: Duke University Press.
Levin, D.M. (ed.) (1997) *Language Beyond Postmodernism: Saying and Thinking in Gendlin's Philosophy*, Evanston, IL: Northwestern University Press.
—(2003) *The Body's Recollection of Being: Phenomenological Psychology and the Deconstruction of Nihilism*, London: Routledge & Kegan Paul.
Lingis, A. (1998) *The Imperative*, Bloomington: Indiana University Press.
Maffesoli, M. (1996) *The Time of the Tribes: The Decline of Individualism in Mass Society*, London: Sage.
Malbon, B. (1999) *Clubbing: Dancing, Ecstasy and Vitality*, London: Routledge.
Mazis, G. (1993) *Emotion and Embodiment: Fragile Ontology*, New York: Peter Lang.
McKean, L. (1996) *Divine Enterprise: Gurus and the Hindu Nationalisit Movement*, Chicago: University of Chicago Press.
Mellor, P. and C. Shilling (1997) *Re-forming the Body: Religion, Community, and Modernity*, London: Sage Publications.
Merleau-Ponty, M. (1962) *Phenomenology of Perception*, trans C. Smith, London: Routledge & Kegan Paul.
Morley, J. (2001) Inspiration and expiration: Yoga practice through Merleau-Ponty's phenomenology of the body, *Philosophy East & West*, 51 (1): 73–82.
Ness, S.A. (1992) *Body, Movement, and Culture: Kinesthetic and Visual Symbolism in a Philippine Community*, Philadelphia: University of Pennsylvania Press.
Nevrin, K. (2004) Från frälsning till kroppsligt välbefinnande, *Chakra*, 2: 70–84.
—(2005) Krishnamacharya's Viniyoga: On modern yoga and Sri Vaisnavism, *Journal of Vaisnava Studies*, 14: 65–94.
—(forthcoming) Performing the Yogasutra: Toward a methodology for studying recitation in modern Hatha Yoga, *Chakra*.
Ratcliffe, M. (2005) The feeling of being, *Journal of Consciousness Studies*, 12 (8–10): 43–60.
Sarukkai, S. (2002) Inside/outside: Merleau-Ponty/yoga, *Philosophy East & West*, 52 (4): 459–78.
Shilling, C. (1993) *The Body and Social Theory*, London: Sage Publications.
Sheets-Johnstone, M. (1999a) *The Primacy of Movement*, Amsterdam: John Benjamins.
—(1999b) Emotion and movement, *Journal of Consciousness Studies*, 6 (11–12): 259–77.
—(1998) Consciousness: A natural history, *Journal of Consciousness Studies*, 5 (3): 260–94.
Shusterman, R. (1999) Somaesthetics: A disciplinary proposal, *The Journal of Aesthetics and Art Criticism*, 57 (3): 299–313.
Singleton, M. (2005) Salvation through relaxation: Proprioceptive therapy and its relationship to yoga, *Journal of Contemporary Religion*, 20 (3): 289–304
Smith, M.L. (2002) Moving self: The thread which bridges dance and theatre, in *Research in Dance Education*, 3 (2).
Strauss, S. (1997) *Re-orienting Yoga: Transnational Flows from an Indian Center* [unpublished thesis], University of Pennsylvania.

Thrift, N. (2000) Still life in nearly present time: The object of nature, *Body & Society*, 6 (3–4): 34–57.

—(2004) Bare life, in H. Thomas and J. Ahmed (eds) *Cultural Bodies*, Malden, MA: Blackwell.

Turner, T. (1994) Bodies and antibodies, in T. Csordas (ed) *Embodiment and Experience*, Cambridge: Cambridge University Press.

Zarrilli, P. (2004) Toward a phenomenological model of the actor's embodied modes of experience, *Theatre Journal* 56: 653–66.

7 "With Heat Even Iron Will Bend"

Discipline and Authority in Ashtanga Yoga

Benjamin Richard Smith

Discipline and authority lie at the heart of the Indian yoga tradition, but their relevance to contemporary transnational yoga is less clear. In most cases, the forms of control and asceticism central to that tradition, in particular the *guru-śisya*[1] ("teacher-disciple") relationship, are clearly absent. However, Pattabhi Jois's Ashtanga Yoga,[2] a form of contemporary or modern yoga practice, is marked by an orientation toward both discipline and authority. This chapter examines this orientation, simultaneously exploring the manner in which the contemporary practice of Ashtanga Yoga is constituted within a late-modern transnational field rather than marking a simple continuation of earlier forms of yoga practice.

My particular focus here is the emphasis teachers and dedicated practitioners of Ashtanga Yoga place on *tapas*, the "heated effort" of ascetic practice, and the ways in which *tapas* is linked to sweating and bodily heat. Among practitioners, this link is commonly taken to exemplify a relationship between the physical ardor of the Ashtanga Yoga method and this method's "correct"[3] relationship to canonical textual sources. Practitioners understand the discipline and effort required for Ashtanga Yoga practice to be indicative of both its authority and its potency compared to other forms of modern yoga. Further, the validation of Ashtanga Yoga by reference to canonical sources reinforces practitioners' sense of the authority of these sources and of Ashtanga Yoga itself. In aligning a modern practice to a selective reading of textual sources—including those that discuss *tapas*—constructions of authority in Ashtanga Yoga are markedly circular (Singleton, this volume). This circular construction of authority is apparent both in Pattabhi Jois's written and oral accounts of yoga and in other teachers' and practitioners' accounts of Pattabhi Jois's method, even as these latter accounts depart from Pattabhi Jois's teaching.

A circular relationship is also apparent between the experience of yoga practice and supposedly authoritative accounts of Ashtanga Yoga. The practice of Ashtanga Yoga is not only shaped by teachers' interpretations of Pattabhi Jois's method; practitioners' embodied experiences of yoga are also made meaningful through such interpretations. As a result, practitioners' received understandings of yoga both shape and are confirmed by their practice, reinforcing the authority of teachers' interpretations. However, this relationship between practice and text can also be innovative. Many senior practitioners' accounts of Ashtanga Yoga depart from the teaching they have received from Pattabhi Jois. Notably, such departures appear to draw on their experience of yoga practice and on their own readings of various texts.

This chapter's analysis of discipline, authority, and *tapas* in Ashtanga Yoga is not intended as authoritative in any simple sense. Likewise, the intention of the analysis is not to determine the authority or "correctness" of differing interpretations. Rather, this chapter approaches Ashtanga Yoga as a shared but heterogeneous social and cultural field, constituted by particular forms of knowledge and practice and within which forms of authority are substantiated and contested.[4] To develop this analysis, I begin by outlining the Ashtanga Yoga method and the emphasis on *tapas* in Pattabhi Jois's teaching and the accounts of senior Western teacher-practitioners. I then turn to the relationship between discipline and authority in Ashtanga Yoga schools in India and the West, exploring the ways in which authority is produced through the teaching and practice of yoga. These two aspects of discipline and authority shed light on one of Pattabhi Jois's most commonly cited aphorisms—"with heat, even iron will bend." This aphorism indicates the importance of *tapas* within Ashtanga Yoga but also points toward the assertion of Pattabhi Jois's authority in his own teaching and in the schools run by those senior practitioners he has authorized or certified to teach.

Pattabhi Jois's Ashtanga Yoga

Ashtanga Yoga is a method of Modern Postural Yoga (De Michelis 2004), the principal *guru* of which is Śrī K. Pattabhi Jois of Mysore, India. This method is said to originate from a text called the *Yoga Korunta*,[5] which Pattabhi Jois apparently received from his own *guru* Śrī T. Krishnamacharya (Stern 2006: 85; Miele n.d.). The Ashtanga Yoga method includes the practice of several series of *āsana* (yoga "poses" or "postures"), individual *āsana* being linked by *vinyāsa*, a "movement breathing system" involving a particular kind of breathing (*ujjayī prāṇāyāma*). In addition to these, a number of other *prāṇāyāma* (breathing practices for the control of bodily energy) are taught to advanced practitioners (Miele n.d.: 156–60; Smith 2007).

Pattabhi Jois's Ashtanga Yoga began its transnational spread in earnest in the 1970s, though a number of foreigners had studied with him in Mysore previously. These foreigners included the Belgian Andre Van Lysbeth, whose listing of Pattabhi Jois's address in his book on *prāṇāyāma* (Van Lysbeth 1979) led other Western practitioners to Pattabhi Jois's school. In 1973, two Americans, David Williams and Norman Allen, studied with Pattabhi Jois after meeting his son Manju at Swami Gitananda's *āśram* (residential school) in Pondicherry. In 1974, Pattabhi Jois traveled to lecture in South America and, in 1975, Williams, along with Nancy Gilgoff, organized for Pattabhi Jois and Manju to travel to Encinitas, California, where Williams was already teaching the Ashtanga Yoga method (Stern 2002; Williams n.d.).[6] Since that time, Ashtanga Yoga has grown in popularity, particularly from the mid-1990s onward. Pattabhi Jois and his family now travel yearly to the United States, the United Kingdom, and other parts of the globe. Hundreds of (predominantly Western) students also travel to Mysore each month to study with Pattabhi Jois and his grandson Sharath Rangaswamy at their Ashtanga Yoga Research Institute (AYRI) (Burger 2006; Liberman n.d.).

Like other varieties of modern yoga (see Strauss 2004), Ashtanga Yoga is now markedly transnational. Practitioners and teachers are situated across a variety of mostly urban, cosmopolitan milieus, including relatively large contingents in East and Southeast Asia. The majority of these practitioners practice *āsana* on an occasional basis for the purposes of keeping fit and flexible and managing stress.

Nonetheless, this practice is also commonly marked by vaguely "spiritual" associations. A smaller number of practitioners have a more serious engagement with yoga, typically based around daily practice of *āsana* and perhaps also including *prāṇāyāma*, the chanting of *mantras*, or the study of Patañjali's *Yogasūtra* and other translated Sanskrit texts.[7]

Interestingly, this more serious engagement may be particularly common among those practicing Ashtanga Yoga in comparison with other forms of transnational yoga. This more serious orientation of a number of Ashtanga practitioners seems to be related to the physically demanding style of *āsana* that forms the basis of Pattabhi Jois's method, the programmatic form of the Ashtanga Yoga *āsana* series, and a strong pedagogic emphasis on daily practice. This serious orientation also reflects the type of "driven" personality drawn to Ashtanga Yoga and the resonance of this form of yoga with the late-modern cosmopolitan milieu in which it has become popular (Smith 2004).

A marked emphasis on discipline and authority is apparent among these more dedicated practitioners both "at home" and during visits to study in Mysore. This emphasis is apparent in their strong commitment to daily practice, a clear orientation toward "progress," strong deference to their *guru*, and a stress on maintaining received styles of teaching and practice. Doubtless this stress stems partly from Pattabhi Jois's own teaching, which emphasizes the need for students' commitment to the physically, mentally, and spiritually transformative powers of his yoga method when it is "correctly" taught and practiced.

Pattabhi Jois often links this transformative power of yoga to "heat," a theme closely tied to the (post-)Vedic concept of *tapas*, which variously refers to asceticism, discipline, and the generation of "internal heat." For Pattabhi Jois, it is the heat of *tapas* that leads toward the perfection of the body and the sense organs and onward toward the final goal of yoga—the attainment of *samādhi*, the blissful state of realization of the true Self that is the final limb and pinnacle of Patañjali's eight-limbed (*aṣṭāṅga*) "yogic path of self-transformation" (Whicher 1998: 181). However, while Pattabhi Jois asserts that his yoga is based on Patañjali's eight-limbed path (Jois 2002 [1999]), Ashtanga Yoga—as it is taught by senior Western practitioners and by Pattabhi Jois himself—represents a particular approach to the practice of yoga based on a synthesis of *haṭha* yoga and Patañjali's *Yogasūtra* and on a profound syncretism of "Indian" and "Western" understandings of personhood and bodily techniques.

Tapas in Ashtanga Yoga

The concept of *tapas* has played an important role in Indian philosophy and religious practice since the Vedic period. In his examination of *tapas* in Vedic thought, Kaelber notes the complexity of this concept as it occurs in Vedic literature. Deriving from the Sanskrit root *tap*, "to give out heat," "to make hot," or "to be hot," *tapas* variously refers to a process and a product, including the "heated effort" of ascetic practice and the sacred or magical heat that that effort produces (Kaelber 1989: 2–3; see also Eliade 1969 [1958]: 106–8). In the Vedic tradition and in later developments in Indic thought, this ritual heat—when produced in a practitioner's body—is linked to personal transformation and spiritual refinement. "The ascetic's path to liberating knowledge is made possible essentially and conspicuously by *tapas*," and this path is itself a *tapta-mārga*, a "heated passage" (Kaebler 1989: 6).

In his discussion of the Vedic notion of *tapas*, Kaebler notes the ability of internal heat to be either generative or degenerative. Its generative aspect is exemplified by the production of "heated power or potency" through ascetic effort (Kaebler 1989: 144—5). Through such effort, the sweat-inducing *tapas* of the ascetic—homologous to the monsoonal heat that leads to generative rains and to the boiling milk of the sacrificial cauldron (itself equated with semen) [8]—leads to spiritual rebirth. This heat is also seen as purifying, "burning out" the impurities of the ascetic (Kaebler 1989: 145). Last, the heat of *tapas*, linked to the figure of Agni, the god of fire who was also a seer,

> provides the devotee with a "head heat," turning him into a seer as well. Relatedly, the heated effort of ascetic practice kindles an "inner fire" of illumination, yielding ecstatic insight. Like the paradigmatic *ṛṣi*s ["seers" or "sages"], the earthly ascetic is able to "see" or behold through his *tapas*, though his self-imposed austerity. In this context his *tapas* takes the form of a "cognitive brooding," or "intense meditation." The power which is *tapas* is clearly here a "contemplative power" (Kaebler 1989: 145–6).[9]

Beyond the Upaniṣads, *tapas* is a recurring theme in the Hindu canon. In the *Manusmṛti*, techniques for internalizing heat (*tapasyā*) are prescribed for priests, students, and servants as a means of minimizing their outer attachments (Marriott 2004: 362). And *tapas* also features both in the *Māhābhārata* (particularly in its themes of: heat, fire and pain," Fitzgerald 2004: 59–61) and the *Rāmāyaṇa* (e.g., *Bālakāṇḍa* 22, 34, 36; *Āraṇyakāṇḍa* 4, 5; *Uttarakāṇḍa* 74–6). The *Bhagavadgītā* (17.14–17) outlines three aspects of *tapas*, relating to austerities of body, speech, and mind. In the *Gītā*, various observances, including bodily purity, the reciting of scared lore, and self-restraint are combined in the practice of *tapas*, which properly combines the three aspects without attachment, aspiring for praise or causing pain to oneself or others.

Though most, if not all, of these sources are cited in Pattabhi Jois's writings and oral teaching, perhaps the text most relevant to his emphasis on *tapas* is Patañjali's *Yogasūtra*, which explicitly mentions *tapas* several times. *Tapas* is part of the definition of Kriyā Yoga (the "yoga of action") in the second chapter (2.1), where it is described as essential to the achievement or perfection of yoga alongside "self-study" (*svādhyāya*) and "the worship of God" (*īśvara-praṇidhāna*) (Carpenter 2003; Feuerstein 2003: 37; Whicher 1998: 186). *Tapas* is also listed as the third of the five *niyama* or "observances"(*Yogasūtra* 2.32). These *niyamas* are "particular activities that are conducive to the quest for spiritual liberation" (Whicher 1998: 191; see also Feuerstein 2003: 291–3), and they provide the foundation for the higher limbs (*aṅga*) of Patañjali's exposition of yoga. Later in the same chapter (2.43), *tapas* is noted as a means for perfection of the body and the organs through the lessening of impurities, a necessary foundation for the perfection of yoga. And *tapas* reappears at the start of the fourth chapter (4.1), where it is again described as a foundation for the *yogin*'s development of extraordinary capabilities or achievement of perfection.

A connection between Vedic and post-Vedic accounts of *tapas* and the Ashtanga Yoga method is evident in texts published by Pattabhi Jois and several of his pupils. These texts include Pattabhi Jois's own account of Ashtanga Yoga in the book *Yoga Mālā*, which was published in the Kannada language in 1962 by one of Pattabhi Jois's Indian students, and in English translation in 1999 (Jois 2002 [1999]). Pattabhi Jois's method is also outlined in the authorized account of Ashtanga Yoga by his Italian pupil Lino Miele (Miele n.d.) and in a "tribute" to Pattabhi Jois, published in 2002 by Eddie Stern and Deirdre Summerbell on the occasion of the opening of the new Ashtanga Yoga Research Institute (AYRI) in the Mysore suburb of Gokulam.[10]

In his articulation of the meaning and purpose of yoga, Pattabhi Jois draws on a number of texts from the Hindu canon, many of which deal explicitly or implicitly with *tapas*. Patañjali's *Yogasūtra*, in particular, provides Pattabhi Jois with the traditional authority for his emphasis on *tapas*, though his method is clearly also inflected by *haṭha* yoga's emphasis on bodily energies. The centrality of *tapas* in Pattabhi Jois's Ashtanga Yoga method is first flagged in *Yoga Mālā*,'s initial outline of yoga, which combines Patañjali's (1.2) definition, glossed in the English version of *Yoga Mālā*,, as "Yoga is the process of ending the definitions of the field of consciousness" (Jois 2002 [1999]: 5). Here, *Yoga Mālā*, further emphasizes "the strength gained through practise" by means of which "we can come to know the method for bringing the mind and sense organs under control" and "achieve yoga" (Jois 2002 [1999]: 5).

Pattabhi Jois also cites the *Yogasūtra* (2.43) to define this process of developing strength, which in turn leads to knowledge via the control of the mind and sense organs, in terms of *tapas*. This process is glossed in the English version of *Yoga Mālā*, as "[t]he perfection of the body and the sense organs...due to intensity in spiritual practice [*tapas*], being the elimination of impurities" (Jois

Figure 7.1 Ashtanga Yoga Research Institute, Gokulam

2002 [1999]: 15). Here *tapas* "means observances performed to discipline the body and sense organs" (Jois 2002 [1999]: 15). By means of the prescribed forms of *tapas*, "impurities are destroyed, the *antah karana* [*antaḥkaraṇa*] (the 'inner instrument,' made up of mind, intellect, ego, and the faculty of discrimination)[11] becomes purified, and the body and sense organs are perfected" (Jois 2002 [1999]: 14–5).

For Pattabhi Jois, this process of purification is (at least in the first instance) a *physiological* one—though it involves both the "gross" physical body and the "subtle" or "energetic" body.[12] The "inner instrument" that is purified through *tapas* has a physiological form and location. It is the junction of all the *sira*, "thin and nervous" tubes that "bring all messages from the mind here, to this message box" (Stern and Summerbell 2002). The *sira* are conventionally identified as one kind of *nāḍī*, tubes or pathways of which three forms—*dhamini*, *nāḍī*, and *sira*—comprise the gross, subtle, and very subtle channels of the body. *Sira* are those *nāḍī* that carry messages from the *antaḥkaraṇa*, a "message center" located in the region of the heart, throughout the body, and also provide a "vital link in the functioning of the sense organs" (Jois 2002 [1999]: 10, fn. 11). In this account of the physiological basis of purification through yoga, Pattabhi Jois draws on Patañjali's *Yogasūtra* and Svātmarāma's *Haṭhayogapradīpikā* to present a physiospiritual topography of the aspects of body upon which the techniques of Ashtanga Yoga operate.

In *Yoga Mālā*'s section on *prāṇāyāma*, Pattabhi Jois provides perhaps the most clearly articulated account of the connection between disciplined practice, "strength," and the path to the achievement of yoga:

> Body and mind are inseparably related, one to the other. ... If the mind is in pain, the body loses weight, becomes weak and lustreless; if the mind is happy and at peace, the body thrives and develops a strength and luster [sic] beyond compare. Hence the body and sense organs are linked to, and depend on, the strength of the mind. It is for this reason that the method of concentrating the mind should be known. To learn how to achieve such concentration, the body must first be purified, and then mental strength developed. The method for purifying and strengthening the body is called *asana*. When the body is purified, the breath also becomes purified, and the diseases of the body are eliminated (Jois 2002 [1999]: 22).

The practice of *āsana* is thus a form of *tapas* that should be undertaken to "purify and strengthen" the body as a preliminary stage in the practice of yoga. If the *Yogasūtra* emphasizes the role of *tapas* in purifying the body and the senses (2:43; see also Carpenter 2003: 28–9), Pattabhi Jois emphasizes the necessarily corporeal focus of this purification, at least in the early stages of yoga practice.

The account of Ashtanga Yoga's operation on the practitioner's body is also outlined in Lino Miele's book *Aṣṭāṅga Yoga*, which is authorized by Pattabhi Jois. Miele (n.d.) presents accounts both of the toxin-eliminating qualities of *vinyāsa* and the role of heat in a parallel form of internal cleansing, purification, and transformation. *Vinyāsa* is said to employ the synchronized relationship of breath and bodily movement, alongside the practice of energetic "locks" (*bandha*), to produce "an intense internal heat" that:

> purifies muscles and organs, expelling unwanted toxins as well as releasing beneficial hormones and minerals, which can nourish the body when the sweat is massaged back into the skin. The breath regulates the vinyasa and ensures efficient circulation of blood. The result is a light, strong body (Miele n.d.: 2).[13]

Later in Miele's book, however, a somewhat different account of heat and transformation is offered. Following his detailed account of the sequences of *āsana* that comprise the Ashtanga Yoga practice, Miele provides the following account of the benefits of the practice:

> These āsana make the outer fat of the body firm and strong. They work to purify the entire body. According to the "Shastras" [*śāstras*],[14] the regular and continued practice of these āsana purify the blood. It is written that after taking food, the blood absorbs the nutrients and after 32 days 1 drop of new blood is made. It takes 32 drops of this new blood to make one single drop of Viria (Vital life force) or Amṛtabindu ["drop of nectar"]. This Amṛtabindu is stored in the Sahasrāra Chakra (Crown). When we live badly, eat badly, think negative thoughts, perform negative deeds (Tamasic life) the store of Amṛtabindu is depleted. It begins to travel downwards and is

consumed by the upward flow of Agni (Digestive Fire). When Amṛtabindu is lost, life itself is lost.

The practice of inverted āsana [which "finish" the various *āsana* series of Ashtanga Yoga]...are the method for storing Amṛtabindu. When we are inverted the Amṛtabindu remains safely in Sahasrāra Chakra, its downward flow is prevented. The Agni (Digestive Fire) always travels in an upward direction, in the inverted āsanas it travels towards the anus cleansing and purifying the organs of digestion and the rectum/anus (Miele n.d.: 130).

What Miele presents here is a truncated account of a key aspect of *haṭha* yoga. David Gordon White (1996: 36–47) provides a detailed scholarly treatment of this aspect of *haṭha* yoga, revealing the ties between semen (interestingly replaced by "blood" in Miele's account), breath, and the ascetic heat of *tapas*. In brief, the aim of this yogic practice is to reduce the influence of the heat of the lower half of the "subtle" body (in particular the lower abdomen), associated with mundane existence, and to increase the "lunar nectar" stored in the cranial vault. This is accomplished "by raising the yogin's semen from his lower abdomen along the length of the medial channel" (*suṣumṇā nāḍī*). As it rises, the semen is transformed into the divine nectar of immortality (*amṛta*), which replenishes the store in the cranium.

White writes that this transformation, which lies at the heart of *haṭha* yoga, involves "the forceful channelling and control of the vital breaths (*prāṇas*) and of the thermal energy (*tapas, yogāgni*) of the subtle body" (White 1996: 39). Through "heroic efforts of mental concentration and physical exertion, the yogin...initiates a controlled raising of his seed, the heat of his solar fires, and his breath along the medial channel" (White 1996: 39). The heat of the medial channel "effects the gradual transformation of 'raw' semen into 'cooked' and even perfected nectar, *amṛta* ... This transformation of semen into nectar [then stored in the cranial vault] wholly transforms the body, rendering it immortal" (White 1996: 41).

If Pattabhi Jois's teaching is marked by both connections with and transformations of Patañjali and also *haṭha* yoga[15]—for example, in the emphasis on the transformational power of *tapas* and the shift from semen to "blood" in the production of *amṛta* in the *yogin*'s body—many teachers and practitioners seem to have further transformed the character and understanding of the practice of yoga, not least in relation to the role of heat and sweat. For example, it is relatively common for Ashtanga Yoga schools to maintain relatively high temperatures in practice rooms to promote greater flexibility and deeper twists and to assist practitioners in "wringing the impurities out" from their bodies. Other teachers explicitly oppose this use of external heat. In a recent treatment of Pattabhi Jois's Ashtanga Yoga method, for instance, the Australia-based teacher Gregor Maehle cautions against the obsession with external heat:

[c]are needs to be taken not to overheat if one is engaging in strenuous practice is a hot environment. ... Sweating is healthy, but if sweat drips

> from the body it is a sign that it is no longer able to cool itself adequately. Sweating to this degree on a daily basis literally drains life force from the body. ...Heating the yoga room to above 25° may produce more flexibility, but it decreases strength, stamina and concentration (Maehle 2006: 21).

Maehle's observations about the obsession of many Western Ashtanga Yoga practitioners with external heat are undoubtedly correct, but his use of the *Haṭhayogapradīpikā* to substantiate his argument does not simply mark a return to canonical wisdom.[16] Instead, Maehle's claims number among many divergent claims about the "correct" practice of Ashtanga Yoga, many of which seek to authorize themselves through reference to various Sanskrit texts, Pattabhi Jois's teaching, or through an understanding of yoga developed through personal practice. Similarly divergent forms of practice are apparent with regard to the teaching of the various sequences of *āsana* taught as part of the Ashtanga Yoga method. Some teachers stress the need to adjust the practice of *āsana*s and *vinyāsa* in relation to general personal capability, tiredness, "levels of bodily energy," or the temperature of the practice space. Other teachers remain committed to what they understand to be the correct form of Ashtanga Yoga as taught by Pattabhi Jois. For the latter group—as with Pattabhi Jois's own teaching (see Jois 2002 [1999]: 30)—the only acceptable adaptation is to not complete the entire sequence; the *vinyāsas* and *āsanas* should remain as Jois teaches them.[17] Thus, while some teachers suggest varying the numbers of *sūrya namaskāra* or kinds of *vinyāsa* practised depending on the temperature of the practice room, many practitioners insist on maintaining the "prescribed" number of *sūrya namaskāra* or the same form of *vinyāsa* regardless of the conditions. Further, this adherence to received forms of teaching is reinforced by Pattabhi Jois's insistence that authorized teachers should return regularly to AYRI in Mysore, where practitioners are reminded of the "correct" form of Ashtanga Yoga practice.

The increasing emphasis on external heat and the achievement of flexibility—in which sweat is seen as indicative of the successful generation of bodily heat as a *means* for achievement in the performance of *āsanas*—is one of many areas in which Ashtanga Yoga, as a transnational field of practice, is constituted through complex articulations of authority and interpretation. Like the other methods of Modern Postural Yoga within the Mysore Palace yoga tradition (including the yoga methods of T. Krishnamacharya, his son T.K.V. Desikachar, B.K.S. Iyengar, and K. Pattabhi Jois), Ashtanga Yoga has been profoundly influenced by the interplay of "Western" and "Indian" philosophies and practices since the late nineteenth century (see Alter 2004; Sjoman 1999[1996]). This is not to say that such yoga has simply been "Westernized." Rather, the intercultural history of Pattabhi Jois's Ashtanga Yoga, like the other methods of yoga shaped by the influence of Krishnamacharya, consists of a complex series of historical continuities and changes and an ongoing syncretic interplay between "Indian yoga" and the "West."

Though such syncretism is apparent in Pattabhi Jois's teaching, care needs to be taken in reading English accounts of this teaching as evidence of "Western influence," whether in translation or via the publications of his students. The quality and accuracy of these accounts is uncertain even where they are authorized by Pattabhi Jois himself. Though Pattabhi Jois now speaks more English than the handful of words he apparently spoke in the early 1970s, his command of the English language remains limited. This fact, alongside the difficulty of translating many of the concepts that underlie Pattabhi Jois's teaching, has doubtless affected the transnational understanding of his yoga method. As a result, these English-language accounts have led to misunderstandings or reinterpretations of Pattabhi Jois's approach to yoga and have consequently allowed for further transformations in the practice of Ashtanga Yoga beyond AYRI.

Pattabhi Jois's ideas about sweat stand as one example of this. Though he and his authorized teachers certainly emphasize the production of sweat through the practice of *vinyāsa* and *āsana*, the emphasis is on a light sheen of sweat rather than profuse sweating. It may well be that the notion of expulsion of toxins through sweat, which is common among teachers and practitioners of Ashtanga Yoga, is physiologically incorrect,[18] but Pattabhi Jois links these to the *Haṭhayogapradīpikā*'s (2.13) emphasis on the practice of rubbing sweat back into the body to make the body "strong and light," rather than departing from the textual authority of *haṭha* yoga. And it seems clear that this emphasis on sweat is only part of the work of heat in Pattabhi Jois's teaching. More generally, the emphasis on sweat is more complex—and more deeply connected to the canonical emphasis on *tapas*—than the approach taken by many Ashtanga practitioners suggests. Elsewhere in Pattabhi Jois's teaching, the heat generated by *tapas*—in the form of the practice of *vinyāsa* and *āsana*—is linked to earlier accounts of internal cleansing and refinement. The idea that the practice of yoga purifies the various subtle channels of the body, for example, is drawn from medieval *haṭha* yoga. However, many Western "Ashtangis" seem unaware of or disinterested in this complex approach to *tapas*, though a smaller number of teachers and practitioners are aware of these complexities and seek to take account of them in their approach to yoga.

White's account of medieval *haṭha* yoga reveals further links between *haṭha* yoga and Pattabhi Jois's yoga method. As White notes, the preliminary stage of the practice of *haṭha* yoga is a cleansing (*śodhana*) of the body, "flush[ing] out the body's physical impurities" to let the vital breaths (*prāṇas*) freely circulate in the subtle body (White 1996: 271–2). After the cleansing of the body, the practitioner "begins to truly transform his body—by sweating, which is viewed as the first stage in the process of yogic transformation" (White 1996: 273). In particular, the practices of *prāṇāyāma*—especially the retention of the breath (*kumbhaka*)—produce sweat that, though "voided through the pores...has in fact been forced out through the seventy-two thousand *nāḍīs*, thereby purging them of all impurity" (White 1996: 273, after *Haṭhayogapradīpikā* 2.12, 19). It is after this process that the *yogin* is instructed to rub (*mardana*) the body with the perspiration produced to make the body firm and light (White 1996: 273, after *Haṭhayogapradīpikā* 2.13).

White's work also indicates that the notions of purification present in Pattabhi Jois's yoga system are similar to (and likely drawn from) those found in *haṭha* yoga texts. On this basis, a common claim among practitioners of other methods of yoga—that Pattabhi Jois's method is simply or overwhelmingly concerned with the practice of *āsanas*—seems problematic. A closer reading of Pattabhi Jois's English texts and his students' publications makes it clear, rather, that Jois emphasizes the importance of *āsana*—and the *yama*s and *niyama*s (the first two limbs of Patañjali's *āṣṭāṅgayoga*)—along with *prāṇāyāma* for more accomplished students—as forms of preliminary cleansing and transformation that prepare the body for the attainment of yoga's higher limbs.

This is not to say that Pattabhi Jois's teaching is not without either contradictions or intercultural influences. In the sections I have cited from the authorized Ashtanga Yoga literature, there seem to be several different processes associated with the *tapas* generated by the Ashtanga Yoga practice. These include a notion of elimination of toxins through the skin, another of the internal purification of the gross and subtle aspects of the body, and finally an idea of the purification of the blood into the vital essence of *amṛtabindu* (the latter apparently a version of *haṭha* yoga's ideas on the transubstantiation of semen into *amṛta*, the nectar of immortality). However, these processes are not necessarily incompatible, and all of them are closely tied to *tapas*.

Though it is impossible to discount the idea that these notions mark a flawed attempt at syncretism within Pattabhi Jois's system, to presume this would probably be a mistake. Rather, they seem to represent a synthesis of different aspects of yogic practices *within* his system. As Miele notes, the purpose of the Ashtanga Yoga practice is to employ "[s]trength, stamina and sweat," a combination that requires "considerable effort" to "'urify the nervous system" (Miele n.d.: 3).[19] In this regard, it is also important to note Pattabhi Jois's own differentiation—repeated in the texts produced by his pupils—between the purpose of the first or Primary Series (*yoga cikitsa*) of *āsana*, which "detoxifies and aligns the body"; the second or Intermediary Series (*nāḍī śodhana*), which "purifies the nervous system by opening and clearing the energy channels" (see also White 1996: 271 on *śodhana*, cited above); and the later or Advanced Series (typically divided into two or four parts) (*sthira bhāgah samāpta*), whose *āsanas* "integrate the strength and grace of the practice, requiring higher levels of flexibility and humility" (Miele n.d. 2–3).[20] Pattabhi Jois clearly perceives different aspects within the practice of *āsana* and other aspects of the practice of yoga, which can be used to achieve different but not incompatible results. Further, some of these aspects of yogic practice are necessary to provide the foundations for other "higher" aspects. Perhaps unsurprisingly, the most widespread aspects of Pattabhi Jois's teachings are the most basic, intended to prepare those few students who pursue them seriously to perhaps move on to greater achievements. Though many transnational practitioners have chosen to limit themselves to the physical benefits of his Ashtanga Yoga, it seems that Pattabhi Jois sees these benefits as simply a foundation for the later achievement of yoga's higher aims, whether in this life or a later one.

Achievement, Discipline and Authority in Practice

An emphasis on *tapas* lies at the heart of Pattabhi Jois's Ashtanga Yoga. However, this emphasis is not only philosophical. Pattabhi Jois also stresses discipline and authority in the practice of yoga, particularly—though not solely—as it is practiced at his Ashtanga Yoga Research Institute in Mysore. This stress is often replicated in the method of teaching adopted by those who have received their yoga teacher's certification or authorization from AYRI. In the schools or *śālās* of these teachers, the "heated discipline" of *tapas* and the authority of the *guru* are also apparent, and this stress on discipline and authority is commonly internalized by those practicing at these schools. This transnational emphasis on discipline and authority means that a common character is apparent in the approach of Ashtanga Yoga teachers, and the "feel" of their schools, across the globe, despite other differences between their teaching styles.

This common feel—and the particular character of different schools—is part of what Nevrin (this collection) calls the "performance of spirituality" in modern postural yoga. Nevrin notes the ways in which the atmosphere of yoga schools or *śālās* shapes both particular practitioners' experience of yoga practice and the more general "character" students associate with yoga. The spatial layout of the practice room or rooms, the iconographic and other visual aspects of the space, and the sounds and smells in the room (recorded Indian or "new age" music and the smell of incense, for example) are all aspects of this performance. And the feel of the floorboards or carpet and the lighting—whether artificial or natural—also contribute to the "poeticization" of these spaces as places conducive to the practice of yoga. Styles of interaction that predominate in these spaces—for example, the kind of greeting offered by receptionists, teachers, and other practitioners and the ways in which teachers interact with students during practice—further shape practitioners' experiences of yoga. Beyond the general feel of the room, the character that yoga seems to possess is due to the collective nature of practice in yoga schools, which involves a shared "emotional energy" among practitioners (Nevrin, this collection), and—on occasion—between students and teachers.[21]

Practitioners of Ashtanga Yoga often refer to this kind of shared affective experience, which is taken to be the result both of the efficacy of the practice of yoga and the "energy" that inheres in practice spaces.[22] John Scott, in his authorized account of the Primary Series, writes that the "group dynamics" of Ashtanga Yoga and its *vinyāsa* system mean that "[t]he heat, the combined Victorious Breath [*ujjayī prāṇāyāma*], and the intense focus of the students produce a high-energy atmosphere" (Scott 2000: 36).

The poeticization of two key pedagogic forms at AYRI—"practice" (of *āsana* with the "correct" *vinyāsa*) and "conference"—both notably emphasize the authority of Pattabhi Jois as the *guru* of Ashtanga Yoga. On arriving at AYRI, students are assigned a time to attend for their daily *āsana* practice. Early each morning, students arrive at or close to this time to wait in the anteroom of the main *śālā*. To begin their practice, they must both negotiate the baroque politics of "who goes next"[23] while waiting for a call for "one more" student to enter to occupy a vacated space in the crowded room.

Once they have entered the room, the empty space is quickly taken, the student rolling out their yoga mat with a minimum of fuss. There is a marked atmosphere in the room, apparently the result of the heat, focus, and breathing noted by Scott. While the student begins his or her practice, Pattabhi Jois and his family move around the room, physically intervening in their students' practices by "adjusting" their poses. These interventions are strikingly authoritative, often wordless or accompanied by minimal and brusque instructions, manifesting a "no-nonsense" style of teaching. This no-nonsense approach also extends to interventions where a student is seen to be practicing "incorrectly"—that is, in a style that differs from the orthodox AYRI method. "Adjustments" at AYRI are also commonly physically strong—even overwhelming—again marking the teachers' control over the students' bodies and practice (see also Smith 2004, 2006, 2007).

Pattabhi Jois's authority as a teacher—now often exercised through his grandson R. Sharath—is also made evident in his control over the development of each student's own practice. Initially, students at AYRI are allowed to run through the practice they do "at home." However, after a few days, the student

Figure 7.2 *Āsana* practice, AYRI, Mysore, April 2004

will be "stopped" at a certain point in the set sequence of *āsana*s and sent off to the "finishing room" for the closing sequence of postures. Over time, and as Pattabhi Jois and Sharath see fit, the student will be "given" further poses to add to the sequence until the complete sequence is being practiced.

This control over progression through the series is the subject of constant obsession by many students away from the *śālā*, evident in complaints made to fellow students about where in the sequence they are being stopped, how long it has been since they were allowed to "go on," and a lack of recognition of their own abilities. Similarly, the rule that even students who practice the "Intermediate" or "Advanced" series of poses at home must practice the "Primary" series on their first visit to AYRI is a cause for protest among students, many of whom feel the effort and time they have invested in "their practice" is not being properly recognized.[24] Other students take these impediments to be part of Pattabhi Jois's pedagogy, pointing out to those complaining that their frustrations provide them with a means of showing "how much ego is invested in the practice" and an opportunity to "break down" this investment, thus pursuing the "goal of yoga" further.

In addition to the daily practice of *āsana*s, students at AYRI attend a weekly "conference" with Pattabhi Jois. Even more than the morning *āsana* sessions, conference articulates Pattabhi Jois's status as the principal *guru* of Ashtanga Yoga, and identifies "correct" and "incorrect" approaches to yoga. Seated on a chair on a raised dais in front of the assembled students (who sit on rugs on the floor of the *śālā*), Pattabhi Jois expounds on the practice and philosophy of yoga, drawing on his command of Sanskrit literature, often in response to questions from the students. However, perhaps the most striking embodiment of the *guru*'s authority in this markedly transnational setting—AYRI has only a handful of Indian students, who attend separate classes later in the day (see also Burger 2006: 88)—is the line of students who wait after the end of conference to bow down in front of their *guru*, touching his feet three times in a traditional gesture of devotion.[25]

Topics covered in a conference session may include the purpose and proper method of practicing *sūrya namaskāra*, *ujjayī* breathing and other *prāṇāyāma*, what yoga students should eat and the like. These questions are answered in Pattabhi Jois's limited English, often built around Sanskrit quotations from various texts which he then glosses in English. A similar structure of citation appears in Pattabhi Jois's English answers, in which a series of well-established phrases—most of which are familiar to any student of Ashtanga Yoga, and which are cited in Pattabhi Jois's students' books are repeatedly drawn upon to orient students to the 'correct' approach. 'Ninety-nine percent practice, one percent theory', 'practice and all is coming', for example, are commonly heard in these sessions. So too is another common Pattabhi Jois aphorism: 'with heat, even iron will bend'.

The latter phrase again highlights both the 'heated discipline' and often-fiercely imposed authority that characterize Pattabhi Jois's teaching of Ashtanga Yoga. Even in jest, this authority is striking, sometimes literally as

Jois administers an impatient or irritable slap to an offending student, loudly admonishing the 'bad man' or 'bad lady' concerned: 'Why like this? Twenty dollar fine!' Sometimes the interventions are less amusing. 'Adjustments' can be overwhelming, producing fear and extreme discomfort in students as they are pushed beyond their physical and psychological comfort zones in often-difficult, even dangerous *āsana*. At the same time, Pattabhi Jois's aphorism refers to the way in which the heat of the practitioner's body and the ascetic heat of focused practice can leave a practitioner stunned by the way his or her body opens up, or moves deeper and deeper into the poses, often guided or driven by the teacher's interventions. Doubtless an inheritance from his guru Krishnamācārya's own renowned fierceness - 'When that man looked at you, you were afraid' (Pattabhi Jois, cited in Stern and Sommerbell 2002)—Pattabhi Jois's 'fierce' approach pushes many of his students to achieve far more than they considered possible.

The authority and discipline which shape the practice of Ashtanga Yoga in Mysore are often internalized by Pattabhi Jois's students, and they are apparent in various ways in their ongoing practice and teaching of yoga away from AYRI. Further, the authoritative presence of Pattabhi Jois—and, by implication, the 'correctness' of the yoga being taught and practiced—is also made manifest through photographs or pictures of Pattabhi Jois that are commonly displayed on a shrine or on the wall of Ashtanga Yoga schools across the world (Figure 7.3).

The transnational teaching of Ashtanga Yoga is often marked by attempts to reproduce the challenging 'adjustments' experienced at AYRI at local yoga schools, with mixed results. The more accomplished teachers—whose knowledge and personalities allow them to approach their students' bodies with a degree of insight and sensitivity—often successfully embody the challenging but often eventually nurturing atmosphere at AYRI. Others, often seemingly intent on succeeding in getting students into poses, leaving a trail of injured bodies in their wake. Likewise, a number of students not only obsess about the limitations imposed on their practice at AYRI, but push themselves to achieve various poses in their practices 'at home'. Rather than a form of *tapas* pursued without expectation and without inflicting harm to the self or others, these approaches typically lead to more or less serious injuries from which some practitioners may learn (Smith 2004), but which dishearten others who may abandon the practice of yoga as a result.

Pattabhi Jois's emphasis on the correctness or incorrectness of approaches to yoga also affects the approach of Ashtanga Yoga students and teachers across the globe. The set sequences of *āsanas*—which are fairly rigidly policed in Mysore—are often regarded as unchangeable both by those practitioners who have studied at AYRI and those who have not (Others, however, may mark their distance from Pattabhi Jois by formulating their own version of the Ashtanga Yoga practice). It is not uncommon to see Ashtangis of various degrees of accomplishment comment or intervene in others' practice during or after a class when they perceive other students to be 'doing it wrong'. Likewise, the

Figure 7.3 Painted portrait of K. Pattabhi Jois, Ashtanga Yoga Shala, New York City

sequences of the various *āsana* series are widely regarded amongst Ashtangis as unalterable, despite the fact—obvious to the few students who have visited AYRI across a longer period of time, but not widely recognized amongst the majority of practitioners—that Pattabhi Jois has himself changed the sequence and content of the various series since the 1970s. Here, as often seems to be the case in transnational Ashtanga Yoga, interpretation of the ways that yoga is taught and explained in Mysore allows for various interpretations—and sometimes profound misinterpretations—by students and teachers.

Conclusion

Although the majority of modern yoga practitioners have little or no interest in the forms of discipline and authority that inhere in the Indian yoga tradition, contemporary forms of discipline and authority remain apparent amongst many serious or dedicated practitioners of Ashtanga Yoga. A number of factors —including the challenging character of this style of yoga, and the potential for the development of a teleological orientation to its practice, mean that a number of serious practitioners dedicate themselves to the daily practice of a physically strenuous and challenging sequence of *āsanas*. Many also immerse themselves in the practice of *prāṇāyāma*, or learn to read Sanskrit and to chant mantra. These dedicated practitioners are also likely to undertake repeated visits to Mysore to study with Pattabhi Jois, the principal guru of Ashtanga Yoga. These visits are one aspect of these practitioners' deference to their chosen guru. On the basis of these visits, many dedicated practitioners also undertake to maintain received styles of teaching and practice, styles that mark continuities with the forms of deference and authority that have long characterized the teaching of yoga in India. Others later depart from these received styles, seeking to develop a 'better' or 'more suitable' approach to yoga.

An emphasis on tapas, ascetic heat and effort is usually maintained in both of these approaches Ashtanga Yoga. In his teaching, Pattabhi Jois draws on many of the canonical textual sources of modern postural yoga—including Patañjali's *Yoga Sūtra* and the *Haṭhayogapradīpikā*—to emphasize the transformative heat of *tapas*. Despite the sometimes unclear articulation of Pattabhi Jois's method in English translation, and in the books written by his senior students, it seems that the heat of *tapas* is associated with the elimination of toxins through the skin, the internal purification of the gross and subtle aspects of the body, and the transubstantiation of bodily fluids into the vital essence of amṛta. All of these understandings of tapas draw on the philosophy of *haṭha yoga*, which outlines the efficacy of the transformative heat and sweat generated through yoga practice. Even where transnational teachers depart from Pattabhi Jois's method and authority, they commonly maintain this emphasis on the transformative power of *tapas*.

But whilst the practice of Pattabhi Jois's Ashtanga Yoga maintains forms of ardour and authority reminiscent of the Indian yoga tradition, the post-Vedic understanding of *tapas* as transformative ascetic heat, and the idea that yoga should be practised dispassionately without hope of reward and without harm to oneself or others, is often replaced by a drive to 'achieve' an accomplished yoga practice amongst many contemporary practitioners. Likewise, the notion that āsana is merely a means of creating the foundation for the higher practices of yoga, which is emphasized in Pattabhi Jois's teaching, is often replaced by an emphasis on the achievement or perfection of *āsana* practice. According to the traditional Indian approach to yoga, the heat of *tapas* can eventually destroy all the barriers that limit the incomprehension of the true Self and the attainment of *samādhi*. In the transnational spread of Ashtanga Yoga, however, this ascetic heat can be obscured by a more mundane emphasis on the heated body's ability to stay fit and flexible and to progressively achieve greater heights in the performance of yoga poses.

Acknowledgments

I am grateful to Jean Byrne, Elliott Goldberg, Klas Nevrin, Mark Singleton, and the anonymous reader at Routledge for their comments and suggestions, which have helped me in bringing this chapter to fruition. I should also thank Inez Baranay, Elizabeth De Michelis, Ken Liberman, Makarand Paranjape, and Norman Sjoman for their encouragement of my research on the topic of yoga. My greatest debt is to the teachers with whom I have practiced: Śrī K. Pattabhi Jois and Sharath Rangaswamy of the Ashtanga Yoga Research Institute; M.S. Viswanath of FPYK (Bangalore); Gail Robertson, Paul Frechtling, Oliver Bacchus, and Iain Clark, all of whom have provided ongoing inspiration and helped me to keep returning to my yoga practice.

Notes

1 Throughout this text, I have used diacritical markings for Sanskrit terms and names except where these are absent in directly cited texts. I have also italicized my own uses of Sanskrit words and phrases, except personal names.

2 In this chapter I write of "(Pattabhi Jois's) Ashtanga Yoga" and "(Patañjali's) *aṣṭāṅga*" to distinguish between them.

3 Pattabhi Jois often reiterates the distinction between the "correct" or "right" teaching and practice of yoga. This is often distinguished from yoga that is "only exercise" or "circus acts." See Stern and Summerbell 2002, for example.

4 The analytic account of Ashtanga Yoga presented here draws on a combination of personal experience and critical reading. It is based on my own participation and observation in Ashtanga Yoga classes in India, Australia,and the United Kingdom and on accounts of the Ashtanga Yoga method produced by Pattabhi Jois and by several senior Western teacher-practitioners. I use these observations and accounts to develop a sociocultural analysis of Ashtanga Yoga. Though the chapter is written from a practitioner's perspective, my intention is nonetheless to produce a critical account of Ashtanga Yoga as a contemporary field of knowledge and practice (see also Smith 2007: 31-33).

5 Lino Miele (n.d.) identifies the *Yoga Korunta* as an "ancient text written in Sanskrit." Norman Sjoman (personal communication, April 2007) suggests that the "Korunta" of the title is *kuruṇṭa*, "doll or puppet," noting that Gita Iyengar (daughter and student of B.K.S Iyengar) has mentioned the name. Indeed, an online article by Gita Iyengar notes that:

> though the book is not available, Guruji [i.e. B.K.S. Iyengar] has seen a handwritten book with his own Guruji Shri Krishnamacharya, in Mysore, a book called *Yoga Kurunta*. Kuranti in Sanskrit means a puppet. You are familiar with the puppet show where threads are tied to the puppet. The puppet moves or dances according to the movement of the thread. Guruji [B.K.S. Iyengar] saw his Guruji [Krishnamacharya] perform certain movements and actions with the ropes: a yoga puppet show. Yoga Kurunta means yoga puppet show. The textbook says that in the olden days when the yogis were living in the forests they would put ropes on the branches of the trees and perform different sorts of movements or positions. All the details are not available as to what they were doing, but still this clue was enough. We can perform certain things with the ropes (Iyengar, n.d.).

Stern (2006: 87) notes that "Pattabhi Jois says that this Korunta [i.e., the *Yoga Korunta* referred to by Pattabhi Jois] holds all the teachings that he follows concerning *Aṣṭāṅga* Yoga, though he has never seen the text, but received the teachings verbally from his guru, Krishnamacharya" (see also Stern 2002 [1999]: xv–vi). It seems possible that the *Yoga Korunta* represents a modern version of a customary device for introducing innovation within a tradition that insists on received authority. This device often depended on supernatural agency (compare, for example, Krishnamacharya's own receipt of the "lost" *Yoga Rahasya* from the spirit of his forbear, the sage Nāthamuni (see Desikachar 2003[1998]: 13–14; Stern 2006: 87). I intend to discuss these customary and modern forms of innovation in yoga traditions elsewhere.

6 Several of these early students later moved to Maui, one of the Hawaiian Islands. A number of these students continue to live on Maui, several of them (including David Williams and Nancy Gilgoff) traveling worldwide to conduct workshops.

7 A smaller number of Ashtanga Yoga practitioners are able to read and understand Sanskrit written in *devanāgarī* script, with many students undertaking at least some study of Sanskrit while studying in Mysore. By contrast, very few students demonstrate any interest in learning even rudimentary Kannada, the main language of Karnataka (see also Liberman n.d.).

8 White (1996: 20) notes that the metaphor of cooking is common in Vedic and post-Vedic thought, referring to various transformative processes, including yogic austerities (*tapas*). By means of yogic *tapas*, an internalization of sacrifice, "the body is to be 'cooked to a turn' (*paripakvā*)." Note also that the ***haṭha*** yoga tradition, which has deeply influenced Pattabhi Jois's system and teaching, involves internalized transactions in sexual fluids "incorporated into the so called subtle body (*sūkṣma śarīra*)" (White 1996: 4). Semen, in particular, "is the raw material and fuel of every psychochemical transformation the yogin...undergoes" (White 1996:27). See below on the "purification of the blood" to produce *amṛtabindu* in Jois's teaching.

9 Feuerstein, in his commentary on *tapas*, instead identifies the heat of *tapas* and yoga to the figure of the Sun, which he links with the Vedic figure Hiraṇyagarbha ("Golden Germ/Womb") and the Sun-figure Vivasvat in the *Bhagavadgītā*, who is "referred to as the primordial teacher of ancient Yoga" and "the first teacher of *tapas*, since *tapas* is at the heart of all yogic disciplines" (Feuerstein 2003: 143; see also Eliade 1969[1958]: 154). Pattabhi Jois also links his Ashtanga Yoga to the Sun God, noting that "[t]here is no Aṣṭāṅga yoga without Sūrya Namaskāra (the 'salute to the sun' [which students practise at the start of each Ashtanga Vinyasa *āsana* session]), which is the ultimate salutation to the Sun God" (Jois 2005: 38). Elliott Goldberg is currently conducting research on *sūrya namaskāra* and the uptake of this practice within the Krishnamacharya yoga lineage, which includes Pattabhi Jois's Ashtanga Yoga.

10 This building replaced Pattabhi Jois's earlier *śālā* (and family home) in the nearby suburb of Laxmipuram (Stern and Summerbell 2002).

11 *Antaḥkaraṇa* or "inner instrument" is a term drawn primarily from *Sāṃkhya*—and in particular, from the *Sāṃkhyakārikā*. *Sāṃkhya* philosophy is, of course, closely related to Patañjali's articulation of yoga. Whicher (1998: 92) suggests that *antaḥkaraṇa* is a synonym for the latter's *citta*. Pattabhi Jois uses both terms, indicating the multiple textual sources that underpin his own approach to yoga.

12 See also Alter (2006: 764), who notes that *haṭha* yoga "[is] inherently physiological rather than metaphysical, even in its most philosophical articulation."

13 Sjoman (1999 [1996]: 65, fn. 55) presents a critical discussion of the origin of the term *vinyāsa* and its apparent use in the context of Ashtanga Yoga "to imply some kind of vedic [i.e., canonical] sanction to yoga practices."

14 "Treatises," authoritative textual sources or "scriptures" (Jois 2002 [1999]: 15, fn. 15). Elsewhere, Pattabhi Jois notes that his *guru* Krishnamacharya "knew many *shastras* ... *Sankhya* [*Sāṃkhya*], *Yoga, Vedanta, Mimamsa, Nyaya*—he knew all the *shastras*" (Stern and Summerbell 2002), here using the term *śāstra* to identify five of the six orthodox systems of Indian philosophy more commonly referred to as *darśana*.

15 A further question here, with regard to Pattabhi Jois's references to Patañjali, is the extent to which even the principal *gurus* of modern postural yoga in India have (and have been able to) engage with the yoga of the *Yogasūtra*. Sjoman (1999[1996]: 37) suggests that even if there was a yoga tradition within which Patañjali was situated, it is a dead textual tradition with no discernable continuity in the recent history of yoga. Sjoman (1999[1996]: 38) also suggests that the *haṭha* yoga tradition "is equally enigmatic." As Singleton (this collection) notes, in its modern revival, the *Yogasūtra* is commonly used to legitimize various contemporary forms of yoga by appeal to the "yoga tradition" which it is held to represent.

16 Mark Singleton (personal communication, July 2007) notes that the emphasis on moderation that underpins Maehle's argument is at odds with the sometimes extreme character of *haṭha* yoga.

17 I am indebted to Jean Byrne (personal communication, July 2007), whose comments assisted greatly in writing this section.

18 Elliott Goldberg, personal communication, April 2006.

19 The mention of "nervous system" here—clearly a gloss of the *nāḍī* that comprise the "subtle body" on which the techniques of *yogāsana* and *prāṇāyāma* operate—

suggests that though the syncretism between various influences within Pattabhi Jois's teaching may not be complete, it is nonetheless impossible to disentangle its "Western" or "modern" and "traditional" or "Indian" aspects. The "considerable effort" cited here is likely a reference to *haṭha* yoga.

20 Some practitioners also speak of the first part of the advanced series as having "nerve cleansing" effects. In relation to the difference in emphasis between both the English glosses of Sanskrit terms and the original Sanskrit, in accounts of Pattabhi Jois's teachings, and the ways in which English translations support particular Western interpretation or approaches, it is interesting to note that the gloss of "Primary, Intermediate and Advanced series" suggests a kind of hierarchy of achievement absent—at least explicitly—in the Sanskrit names that Pattabhi Jois uses for these "series."

21 Though students' direct interactions tend to be supportive, student-teacher interactions are commonly marked by an emotional reserve on the part of the teacher.

22 In some cases, this energy is also understood to result from the presence of the *guru*.

23 This politicking over turn taking is an inheritance from the "stair politics" of the old Laxmipuram *śālā*, where students waited their turn on the narrow staircase outside of the tiny practice room.

24 This sense of ownership or attachment to a "practice" calls to mind Sjoman and Dattatreya's comment that one might "consider the objectification that has taken place in yoga students' minds today where they utter that 'they have a practice' and consider themselves superior because of that. A practice is not an object" (Sjoman and Dattatreya 2007: 109).

25 An important question—not considered further here—is what meanings such acts of devotion and surrender have for Western students, most of whom have little familiarity or immersion in the cultural context from which such forms of devotion are drawn, outside of their practice of yoga.

Bibliography

Alter, J. (2004) *Yoga in Modern India: The Body Between Science and Philosophy*, Princeton: Princeton University Press.

——(2006) Yoga and fetishism: Reflections on Marxist social theory, *Journal of the Royal Anthropological Institute*, 12 (7): 63–783.

Burger, M. (2006) What price salvation? The exchange of salvation goods between India and the West, *Social Compass*, 53: 81–95, 52–74.

Carpenter, D. (2003) Practice makes perfect: The role of practice (*abhyāsa*) in Patañjala Yoga, D. Carpenter and I. Whicher (eds) *Yoga: The Indian Tradition*, London: Routledge Curzon, 25–50.

De Michelis, E (2004) *A History of Modern Yoga*, London: Continuum.

Desikachar, T.K.V. (2003 [1998]) *Nathamuni's Yoga Rahasya*, 2nd ed, Chennai: Krishnamacharya Yoga Mandiram.

Eliade, M. (1969 [1958]) *Yoga: Immortality and Freedom*, Princeton: Princeton University Press.

Feuerstein, G. (2003) *The Deeper Dimension of Yoga: Theory and Practice*, Boston: Shambala.

Fitzgerald, J.L. (2004) Mahābhārata, in S. Mittal and G. Thursby (eds) *The Hindu World*, New York: Routledge

Iyengar, G. (n.d.) *Geeta talks about props*. Available HTTP: <http://www.yarravilleyoga.com.au/writings/propsgeeta.html> (accessed May 7, 2007).

Jois, K. P. (2002 [1999]) *Yoga Mala*, New York: North Point Press.
——(2005) *Sūryanamaskāra*, Mysore: Astanga Yoga Research Institute.
Kaelber, W.O. (1989) *Tapta Mārga: Asceticism and Initiation in Vedic India*, Albany: State University of New York Press.
Liberman, K (n.d.) Yoga tourism in India [unpublished manuscript].
Marriott, M. (2004) Varṇa and jāti, in S. Mittal and G. Thursby (eds) *The Hindu World*, New York: Routledge, 357–82.
Maehle, G. (2006) *Ashtanga Yoga: Practice and Philosophy*, Innaloo City: Kaivalya Publications.
Miele, L. (n.d.) *Aṣṭāṅga Yoga Under the Guidance of Yogāsanavisharada Vidwan Director Śrī K. Pattabhi Jois*, 4th ed, Rome: Lino Miele.
Scott, J. C. (2000) *Ashtanga Yoga: The Essential Step-by-step Guide to Dynamic Yoga*. London: Gaia.
Sjoman, N. (1999 [1996]) *The Yoga Tradition of the Mysore Palace*, 2nd ed, New Delhi: Abhinav.
Sjoman, N., and H.V. Dattatreya (2007) *Dead Birds: The Commentary on* Yoga *Touchstone*, Calgary: Black Lotus Books.
Smith, B.R. (2004) Adjusting the quotidian: Ashtanga Yoga as everyday practice, *Online Proceedings of Cultural Studies Association of Australia Conference (CSAA) 2004*. Available HTTP: <http://wwwmcc.murdoch.edu.au/cfel/csaa_proceedings.htm> (accessed June 19, 2007).
——(2006) Community and inner experience amongst dedicated yoga practitioners [unpublished manuscript].
——(2007) Body, mind and spirit? Towards an analysis of the practice of yoga, *Body & Society*, 13 (2): 25–46.
Stern, E. (2002 [1999]) Foreword, in P. Jois, *Yoga Mala*, New York: North Point Press.
——(2006) The yoga of Krishnamacharya, *Nāmarūpa*, 5: 85–93.
Stern, E., and Summerbell, D. (2002) *K. Pattabhi Jois: A Tribute*, New York: Eddie Stern and Gwyneth Paltrow.
Strauss, S. (2004) *Positioning Yoga: Balancing Acts across Cultures*, Oxford: Berg.
Van Lysbeth, A. (1979) *Pranayama: The Yoga of Breathing*, London: Mandala Books.
Whicher, I. (1998) *The Integrity of the Yoga Darsana: A Reconsideration of Classical Yoga*, Albany: State University of New York Press.
White, D.G. (1996) *The Alchemical Body: Siddha Traditions in Medieval India*, Chicago: University of Chicago Press.
Williams, D. (n.d.) *Ashtanga yogi: biography*. Available HTTP: <www.ashtangayogi.com/HTML/biog.html > (accessed December 7, 2005).

8 The Numinous and Cessative in Modern Yoga

Stuart Ray Sarbacker

Transformation and Continuity in Modern Yoga

The recent scholarship of Norman Sjoman (1996), Joseph Alter (1992; 2000; 2006), and others has brought to light a number of issues relevant to the process of the formation of "modern" forms of yoga in the late nineteenth and early twentieth centuries.[1] These studies have demonstrated that the roots of the contemporary phenomena regarded in conventional usage collectively as "yoga" are deeply situated in the soil of Indian modernism, tied to emergent forms of cosmopolitan religiosity, Indian nationalism, and various types of bodily culture. It has become clear that many of the key formulators of modern yoga in twentieth-century India, such as the South Indian guru Tirumalai Krishnamacharya and Swami Sivananda of Rishikesh, consciously integrated native Hindu discourses on yoga from varying historical periods together with intellectual and bodily cultures of Indian and European origin, including wrestling, gymnastics, and the martial arts. Though the practice of yoga is often portrayed by its adherents and advocates as fundamentally nonsectarian and nondenominational, a degree of orthodoxy persists within contemporary traditions of yoga, rooted in part in the principles of the "Hindu Renaissance" and the formulation of Hinduism under the rubric of an all-embracing universalism. Questions regarding the authenticity of yoga and the authority of its proponents have developed as a subtext in the contemporary discourses that frame the practice of yoga. These questions are most pointed with regard to the distinctions between sectarian divisions or schools of yoga and between communities professing affiliation with particular Indian lineages versus those that do not. An important element of these discourses of authenticity and authority is the question of what the particular goals or teleology of a tradition and teacher are. These goals exist on a scale that ranges from mundane concerns such as beauty, health, strength, and so on to those that are founded on esteemed "spiritual" truths and realizations, the latter in the form of knowledge of the nature of reality and liberation from worldly attachments and afflictions.

What is argued here is that this spectrum of goals, extending from this-worldly to other-worldly teleologies, is not novel in modern yoga or its contemporary descendents but rather is consistent with traditional understandings of

Indian ascetic practice, literally "heat" (*tapas*) and the formal range of mental and physical disciplines referred to under the rubric of the term *yoga*. This understanding is that *tapas* and yoga can be said to lead alternately, given differing teleological orientations, to the attainment of what can be termed the "numinous" power of divinity, and to the "cessative" release from pain and affliction through the suppression or cessation (*nirodha*) of ignorance and attachment. Examining modern and contemporary forms of yoga in light of this understanding yields a number of insights into the phenomenological dynamics of yoga as a virtuoso practice and its operation as a paradigm for particular types of communities and organizations. These implications are demonstrated, among other ways, in the logic of "competition" among gurus, including "feats of mastery" that demonstrate the power of a given practice (and often a teacher or prominent disciple), the conjoining of yoga to other virtuoso modes of physical culture, the forming of alliances between gurus and the economic and cultural elite, and the status of yoga as an enterprise of "personal" empowerment that has an ambivalent or multivalent connection to metaphysical concerns and sectarian institutions.

Cessation and the Liberative Teleology in Yoga

Yoga is often framed within an ascetic paradigm that postulates a method of developing detachment from and control of one's physical and mental capacities for the sake of achieving an exalted spiritual or religious state of knowledge or being. This aspect of the practice of yoga reflects a larger and virtually universal dualism of materiality and mind or spirit that grounds ascetic practices of self-discipline and self-mortification as effecting the strengthening of one aspect (mind or spirit) of phenomenal life through establishing detachment from or control of the other (Flood 2004: 4-8). Through disciplining the body, one gains purity and freedom from affliction by desire and other unwholesome states of physical and mental existence and purifies and strengthens the will and other spiritual capacities. This logic is amply demonstrated by methods of self-denial and self-mortification as expressed in practices such as fasting and celibacy. The overarching goals of detachment, knowledge, and liberation provide a solid ideological foundation for the justification of the negation of phenomenal existence and the tolerance of great pain and misery in the pursuit of spiritual goods (Glucklich 2001: 40-62).

This mode of practice is demonstrated extensively in the renouncer or "striver" (*śramaṇa*) traditions of the first millennium B.C.E. that are at the foundation of the development of the practices of asceticism and yoga within Hinduism, Buddhism, and Jainism. In the literature of these traditions—such as the Pali Nikāya literature of Theravāda Buddhism, the Upaniṣad literature in Hinduism, and the Jaina Āgama literature—time and again, yogic methodologies are employed for the sake of developing detachment from all worldly phenomena, from gross sensory experience to metaphysical conceptions such as a permanent substantive self or a creator deity. The *Kaṭha Upaniṣad* verse VI.11, for example, provides one of the earliest literary sources for the definition and practice of yoga, postulating it as a means of controlling one's senses, the implication being that yoga is a practice or a process whereby one limits or controls the interface between oneself and the world. In the *Dhammapada*, in discussing the importance of restraint and tranquility for the spiritual life, the Buddha is presented as setting forth the idea that there is no wisdom without meditation and that the calming of the mind in meditation is a vehicle for achievement of peace and ultimately the deathless (Shaw 2006, 24). In *Dhammapada* verse 282, yoga is associated with the attainment of wisdom and the lack of yoga with the opposite, thereby indicating two paths representing increase and decline (Radhakrishnan 1999: 148). Yoga acts in such contexts as an instrumental mode of practice that restrains and controls psychophysical life to bring about the cessation of the processes that bind one to the world through attachment and ignorance. This ideology is exemplified in *Yogasūtra* (YS) I.2, *yogaścittavṛttinirodhaḥ*: "yoga is the cessation of the fluctuations of mind." Having brought the mind to a standstill through contemplation (*samādhi*), the culminating "limb" of yoga (*yogāṅga*), phenomenal reality gives way to dwelling in the peace of the "person" (*puruṣa*) or "seer" (*draṣṭṛ*), the eternally detached witness of phenomenal reality. This is stated in YS. I.3, *tadā draṣṭuḥ svarūpe'vasthānam*: "then the seer abides in its own form." This sense of withdrawal, or cessation (*nirodha*), of phenomenal form, whether physical or mental, is thus a culmination of this type of renouncer ideology. Likewise, the third "noble truth" of Buddhism is that of the cessation (*nirodha*) of suffering (*duḥkha*). There are significant differences among these sectarian traditions as to how cessation is accomplished, such as the severity of ascetic practice, the role of knowledge, and the nature of the metaphysical status of liberation. Liberation might be seen as union with an absolute reality such as *brahman*, the separation of the soul (*puruṣa* or *jīva*) from materiality, or an indescribable state (Bronkhorst, 1993).[2]

This cessative mode of practice, centered on the teleology of liberation, is closely tied into systems, including ethical prescriptions, that are viewed as foundational to the practice of contemplation. Two representative examples of this are the *aṣṭāṅgayoga* or "eight-limbed yoga" system as elucidated by Patañjali in the *Yogasūtra* and the *aṣṭāṅgikamārga* or *aṣṭāṅgamārga* (Pali *aṭṭhaṅgika magga*) or "eightfold path" elucidated in both Theravāda and Mahāyāna Buddhist traditions.[3] In the first case, the roots of yogic practice are ethical observances referred to as five types of *yama*, or "restriction." These five restrictions include nonharming (*ahiṃsā*), truthfulness (*satya*), nonstealing (*asteya*), celibacy (*brahmacarya*), and nongreediness (*aparigraha*) and are referred to as the *mahāvrata*, or "great vow."[4] The *mahāvrata*, in turn, is understood to be a universal ethos, one that is not restricted by birth (*jāti*), place (*deśa*), time (*kāla*), or condition (*samaya*), valid in all worlds (*sarvabhauma*). The *mahāvrata* is virtually identical in structure and usage to the *aṇuvrata* and *māhavrata* for laypersons and monastics in Jainism, and it is difficult to imagine that there is not a genetic relationship between the two traditions, rooted in the common *śramaṇa* heritage (Jaini 1990: 157–85, 241–73). The *aṣṭāṅgikamārga*, likewise, sets up a system whereby a greater perspective or wisdom (*prajñā*) regarding the religious life lays the foundation for a life rooted in ethics (*śīla*) and ultimately to the extirpation of afflictions and ignorance through meditative processes (*samādhi*). The component members include correct (*samyag*) view (*dṛṣṭi*), correct intention (*saṃkalpa*), correct speech (*vāc*), correct action (*karmānta*), correct livelihood (*ājīva*), correct effort (*vyāyāma*), correct mindfulness (*smṛti*), and correct contemplation (*samādhi*; Edgerton 1972b: 431).[5] Of particular importance here is the idea that ethics, *śīla*, hinges on the observance of precepts—and most notably a core grouping of them referred to as the "five precepts" (*pañcaśīla*). These five precepts include prescriptions against killing living creatures, stealing, sexual misconduct, lying, and consuming intoxicants, agreeing directly with four of five elements of the *mahāvrata*. The prohibition against consuming of intoxicants might be said to be comparable in some degree to *aparigraha*, if intoxication (especially through alcohol) is seen to be directly related to the problem of addiction (and thus greed). These conceptions of the ethical life develop into much more extensive systems, such as the hundreds of precepts of the Theravāda code of conduct (*pāṭimokkha*) for Buddhist monks and more elaborate systems of *yama* and *niyama* found in post-classical texts such as the *Haṭhayogapradīpikā* and the Yoga Upaniṣad literature (the *Yoga Darśana Upaniṣad*, for example) and in Hindu monasticism. In all of these cases, a particular lifestyle and ethos are seen as both conducive to and encouraged by the practice of yoga as a physical or mental discipline. This conception extends from the renouncer traditions into the householder traditions, which have and continue to exist in a dynamic relationship with one another in this context (Olivelle 1992: 19–57; Bronkhorst 1998, 11–42).[6]

The Cessative in Modern and Contemporary Yoga

It is not surprising, then, to see that figures of significant importance in the formation of modern yoga, such as B.K.S. Iyengar and K. Pattabhi Jois, frame their practice in terms of such traditional doctrinal and ethical systems—Jois, for example, refers to the system of yoga that he teaches as, literally, *aṣṭāṅgayoga* (Jois 2002: 3–31).[7] Similarly, Iyengar frames his perspective of yoga in his highly influential *Light on Yoga* within the authority of the rubric of *aṣṭāṅgayoga* and that of Patañjali, the author of the *Yogasūtra* (Iyengar 1994: 19–53). The ethical principles outlined in the *aṣṭāṅgayoga* rubric situate modern practice in light of an overarching authoritative structure of gradated but ultimate meaning. Within modern and contemporary yoga exist examples of communities that are rooted in the teaching of renouncers (such as Swami Sivananda and his disciples Swami Satyananda Saraswati and Swami Satchidananda) and of householders (such as Krishnamacharya and his disciples K. Pattabhi Jois and B.K.S. Iyengar), indicating variance in the degree to which the emphasis on monasticism and of the most strict interpretation of restraint prevails. In a number of exemplary cases, a "renouncer" guru tells a disciple to return to the world to share the teachings as a householder, as in the case of Krishnamacharya (Desikachar 1998:

44–5). This dynamic between renouncer and householder, more like a scale of possible alternatives than a dichotomy, was present in the Vedic context and early Buddhism, being a recurrent theme throughout Indian literature. A dynamic relationship exists between renouncer and householder societies, as in the case of the merit-exchange and support of monastic practice that exists in the Theravāda and other Buddhist sects (Harvey 2000: 60–4). The cessative aspect serves as a teleological object and as the foundation for a yogic "ethos" that is both contextually rooted (in the case of the *aṣṭāṅgayoga*, in the Hindu rubric) and at the same time easily argued as universal. These presentations are compelling, in part because they are rooted in attempts to mediate the shifting social, political, and economic situation of the *śramaṇa* era traditions. The development of the *śramaṇa* ethos was tied into the changing cultural landscape of an urbanizing Indian populace and the dynamic between city and forest in the early centuries B.C.E. (Olivelle 1998: 3–27; Nakamura 2000: 159–60; Bailey and Mabbett 2003: 13–36). This may well be one of the reasons why such cessative models appeal to many in the contemporary cosmopolitan audience—practitioners find resonance with the *śramaṇa* ethos, given their experience of alienation produced by rapid urbanization and the centrality of "productive" employment that characterizes the capitalist ethos.[8]

Models such as *aṣṭāṅgayoga* were also championed by figures in the Hindu Renaissance of the late nineteenth and early twentieth century, such as Vivekananda, as paradigmatic representations of "the royal yoga" (*rājayoga*), in contrast to many of the forms derived from *haṭha* yoga that would arguably have been more prevalent at that time but would have seemed extreme or strange to a cosmopolitan audience. This is likely because of an interest in representing yoga in a respectable form to a modern audience in a manner compatible with European and Christian mores, Theosophical and occult interests, and the philosophy of neo-Vedānta (De Michelis 2004: 149–80). It may well have also had to do with the discovery of and the focus on the *Yogasūtra* as a text by European scholars, thereby acting as a point of intersection between Indological and Orientialist representations of yoga and authoritative representations by high-profile Hindu reformers. What is clear, however, is that paradigms such as that of *aṣṭāṅgayoga* emerge in the twentieth century as important overarching structures of authority—scriptural and, by extension, institutional—that have framed the practice of yoga in the twentieth century and beyond.

The cessative in both historical and contemporary contexts is particularly important in that it situates the bodily and contemplative practices of yoga within a moral context. The logic of cessation is the logic of "removal"—of ignorance, affliction, desire, illness, and so forth—to achieve a state of being that is more satisfactory. The removal of either physical or metaphysical illness figures quite prominently, given the fact that it offers a spectrum of possibilities that range from physiologically rooted problems (such as diabetes) to ultimate questions of teleology (such as suffering and liberation from it). From a phenomenological perspective, one is undergoing a virtuoso practice through which the elimination of one's afflictions can be brought about, whether they be mundane or metaphysical in nature. From a more sociological perspective, however, we might compare this with another mode of religious practice—exorcist practices associated with the larger phenomenon of possession ritualism. Besides the many analogies that are possible between the repertoire of shamanic ritual techniques and those of the various yoga traditions, it is clear that an overarching theme associated with both is the removal of afflicting spirits or conditions that cause physical and mental malaise (Lewis 1989: 22-31). What is particularly interesting about this, however, is the manner in which removal of the foreign object or state constitutes a moral and a spiritual victory (29, 144). Just as with possession, it may well be that the cessative aspect of yoga is intimately connected with the movement from an antistructural or peripheral position relative to a moral and social "center" toward a more structured and central position within a community (Sarbacker 2005: 65–74). One finds that the more institutionalized, conservative, and "orthodox" a community of practitioners is, and thus the more thoroughly socialized, the greater emphasis there is on the cessative aspect of yoga and the moral principles such as the *yama* and *niyama* components of *aṣṭāṅgayoga* or a prescriptive lifestyle. This emphasis is characteristic of major institutional traditions founded in the modern period, including those of Sivananda and his disciples Satyananda Saraswati and Swami Satchidananda, and Krishnamacharya and his disciples K. Pattabhi Jois and B.K.S. Iyengar, among other prominent gurus and lineages. Likewise, there are possible analogues to be found on this topic between the prominence of women in exorcist possession cults and the prevalence of female practitioners within the context of European and American yoga traditions, if not their precursors as well. In this case, the removal of offending thoughts, emotions, and physical states could be argued to provide an outlet leading to a process of "normalization" or at least the apparent approximation of social expectations within the yoga community and perhaps the larger society. Likewise, the contextualizing of the experience of women's ecstasy or of self-absorption within a larger framework allows it to be "discharged" or expressed in a manner that ultimately supports and reifies the community within which the particular yoga or shamanic tradition exists (Lewis 1989: 26).[9]

The Numinous Paradigm in Indian Asceticism and Yoga

The logical counterpart to the cessative mode of ascetic and yogic practice can be referred to as the "numinous" dimension. This aspect of yoga does not map as clearly onto the spectrum of social values presented by narratives of liberation and soteriology. In some contexts, the numinous dimension coexists with or supports the liberative, and in other contexts it is arguably at odds with goals that are cessative in nature. The numinous in this context indicates that the practice of bodily and contemplative discipline yields powers of action and perception that are typically predicated of a divine being (*deva, devatā*) or set of beings.[10] Yoga and the associated *tapas* lead to a process of transformation of the mind or the body (or both) of the practitioner into that of divinity.

This may occur through states of meditation (such as *samādhi*), in which the mind of the practitioner becomes like a divine one, or through practices that effect the energetic channels and energies (*nāḍī, prāṇa*) of the subtle body and thereby divinize it, or some combination thereof.[11] Through these processes, it is understood that the boundary that separates human beings from the world of spirits becomes fluid, and the practitioner attains a liminal or liminoid state that challenges the existing order or power structure of the cosmos. In Indian literature, individuals obtain powers such as physical invulnerability, invisibility, flight, the ability to read others' minds, bodily perfection and beauty, and so on, through their ascetic and yogic practices. Likewise, in the narrative literature are numerous examples of Indian sages that have fought magical battles or engaged in magical contests to demonstrate the superiority of their attainments or teachings—including Gotama Buddha, Vardhamāna Mahāvīra, Śaṅkara, and many of their disciples and sectarian rivals (Strong 2001: 100–123; Jaini 1990: 21–5; Nakamura: 2000: 292–308; Granoff 1985). These powers are attested to in Indian philosophical literature, including the Upaniṣad narratives (see *Śvetāśvatara* II.1–17, for example), the *Yogasūtra*, which dedicates one of its four chapters to *vibhūti* or "powers," the so-called Yoga Upaniṣad literature, Buddhist *Abhidhamma* and *Abhidharma* discussions (including the *Visuddhimagga* and *Abhidharmakośabhāṣya*), and Hindu and Buddhist *haṭha* and Tantra literature (including *haṭha* yoga texts such as the *Haṭhayogapradīpikā*, Buddhist Tantras such as the seminal *Guhyasamājatantra* and the elaborate *Kālacakratantra*, and Hindu Tantras such as the *Kulārṇavatantra*). The various conceptions of the powers that are the result of ascetic and contemplative practice have yielded a number of paradigmatic lists of powers. One key example is that of the "eight *siddhi*" or "eight accomplishments," which include minuteness (*aṇimā*), lightness (*laghimā*), obtaining (*prāpti*), willfulness (*prākāmya*), greatness (*mahimā*), lordship (*īśitā*), mastery (*vaśitā*), and suppression of desire (*kāmāvasāyitā*), a list of powers that is referred to in the *Yogasūtra*, the Purāṇa literature, and in the Tantras.[12] Another, found in the Buddhist context, is the list of five or six *abhijñā* (Pali *abhiññā*) or forms of "higher knowledge," including the divine eye (*divyacakṣus*), divine hearing (*divyaśrotra*), knowledge of others' minds (*paracittajñāna*), the recollection of former lives (*pūrvanivāsānusmṛti*), accomplishments (Skt. *ṛddhi*, Pali *iddhi*), and (in lists of six members) the knowledge of the destruction of the outflows (*āśravakṣayajñāna*; Edgerton 1972b: 50).[13] Tantric texts in some cases refer to "six rites" and the powers that each offers, with one standard representation of the collection being appeasement (*śānti*), subjugation (*vaśya*), immobilization (*stambha*), enmity (*dveṣa*), eradication (*uccāta*), and liquidation (*māraṇa*; Bühnemann 2000).

What is important for our discussion here is that virtually every major Indian tradition, regardless of mode of practice, acknowledges that various powers result from the discipline of yoga. The underlying assumption is that the practices of asceticism and yoga and the related phenomenon of Tantra yield power, and the question is of how such powers fit (or do not fit) into the teleology of religious practice. It is interesting to note, however, that according to the

Yogasūtra and other presentations of yoga, powers or accomplishments (*vibhūti* or *siddhi*) are not the sole province of yoga but can result from other sources. YS IV.1 states *janmauṣadhimantratapaḥ samādhijāḥ siddhayaḥ*, "accomplishments arise via contemplation, asceticism, incantation, herbs, and birth." This suggests that the powers obtained by yogic means, such as contemplation (*samādhi*) and asceticism (*tapas*), also can be associated with one's nature at birth (*janma*) through consumption of medicinal herbs and potions (*oṣadhi*) and through verbal formulae or incantations (*mantra*). The powers obtained with yoga are thus coextensive with powers that are obtained through other human disciplines and through biological factors. Asceticism (*tapas*) as a category suggests a universality to the power of self-denial or self-mortification, one that is coextensive with other sources of magical power, such as potions or amulets. Along these lines, Gotama Buddha is presented in the *Kevatta Sutta* of the Dīgha Nikāya as admonishing his monks to not demonstrate their powers in front of laypeople, pointing out how the powers that result from meditation might be compared to those of legendary amulets and other magical devices.[14] Such a statement assumes the existence of such powers but situates them on the periphery of what is central to this particular vision of Buddhism (the cessative goal of *nirodha* or *nibbāna*). Gotama Buddha is also represented in the *Cullavagga* of the Vinaya Piṭaka as comparing the flaunting of the virtuoso powers that result from mental cultivation to laypeople by monks to a prostitute displaying herself for a cheap wooden coin.[15] From this perspective, powers are ambiguous in that they demonstrate virtuosity but are not necessarily indications of the realization of the cessative teleology. These issues are less of a problem in contexts in which powers are more readily embraced, such as in *haṭha* yoga and tantric traditions. In these contexts, the embodying of the powers of a divine being becomes much more central to practice, liberation being perceived as the foremost of all of the *siddhi*. Whether it is in the ideal of the *siddha* or "accomplished one," the powerful Mahāyāna *bodhisattva* and *buddha* figures, or the *jīvanmukti* ideal, the idea that liberation is coextensive with virtually unlimited power is another possibility that is offered on the spectrum between the liberatory cessation of worldly affliction and the numinous embrace of cosmological power (Sarbacker 2005: 35–9). In some cases, the powers augment the ability of such beings to help others, such as in the Mahāyāna and Vajrayāna soteriology; in others, the virtually amoral application of power seems to symbolize a soteriological vision of limitlessness.[16]

Context and Pretext of the Numinous

This seeming moral ambivalence, if not multivalence, of asceticism and yoga is also testified to by Hindu literary figures such as Rāvaṇa, Hiraṇyakaśipu, Tāraka, and others, who threaten the world order through conquests that are grounded in power and invulnerability resulting from their ascetic practices. Likewise, in narrative literatures of Jainism and Buddhism, figures such as Gośāla Maskarīputra and Pūraṇa Kāśyapa exhibit a mastery over supernormal powers and have to be dealt with through the vehicle of a battle or contest of magical mastery. In the *Mahābhārata*, yoga and ascetic discipline are tightly woven with narratives of warrior (*kṣatriya* or *rājanya*) discourse, with the tension between renouncer values of nonharming (*ahiṃsā*) in conversation with the embracing of violence that is integral to the warrior ethos. There is a distinct recognition of the manner in which asceticism and yoga are the source of power, and even suggestions that the gods obtained their sovereignty due to the practice of yoga (Brockington 2003: 17). This perspective alternates with the viewpoint that the pursuit and usage of such powers is a dangerous, if not a nefarious, enterprise (17–18). In one case, Bhīṣma, one of the foremost of warriors and the teacher of the protagonists (the Pāṇḍava brothers) of the Epic, acts as a guru figure with respect to the elaboration of the mental discipline of yoga, described in a fashion that is notably similar to Buddhist presentations of *dhyāna* and *samādhi* (Sarbacker 2005: 82). In the *Bhagavadgītā*, yoga is represented by Kṛṣṇa to Arjuna as not a means of avoiding the violence that warfare between his and his cousins' families portends but rather as a way of finding peace and liberation within the parameters of his duty (*dharma*) of fighting the battle. Yoga as represented in the *Bhagavadgītā* is not a mode of outer, but of inner renunciation, viewed as consistent with the embracing of a worldly ideology of social and cosmic order.

Likewise, an important literary narrative with respect to the attainment of yogic power is that of the "temptation" of the practitioner by divine agents or the powers themselves. In this paradigm, it is understood that as the fruit of meditative and bodily discipline manifests, the practitioner is "tempted" to embrace those fruits and thereby attenuate their ability to develop further insight into the nature of reality.[17] This logic is evidenced early in the *Kaṭha Upaniṣad* (I.23–5) where the teacher (Yama, the god of death) implores the protagonist to choose a range of worldly boons (wealth, a beautiful heavenly maiden, etc.) instead of knowledge of the highest order. It is also found in the drama of the Buddha's awakening, in which Māra, the deity that personifies death, sends his daughters to seduce Gotama, along with subsequent promises of worldly power and fortune for his willful submission (Nakamura 2000: 150–84). Narratives of ascetics that discharge their *tapas* through dalliance with heavenly *āpsara* maidens (often at the encouragement of Indra, fearing that he would be usurped as king of the heavens) and of male deities that covet the attention of female practitioners of *tapas* abound in both Hindu and Buddhist literature, perhaps the most famous examples being those of Ṛṣyaśṛṅga and Viśvāmitra (Doniger 1981: 42–68; Lanman 1917: 138–9). This logic can also be reversed, in that *tapas* can be a source of power whereby one can seduce another, as per the literary examples of Pārvatī and Mohinī and others that portray Indra himself as seduced by female ascetics (Doniger 1981: 64–5). These narratives arguably demonstrate the further logic of renunciation, how every accomplishment (*siddhi*) must ultimately give way to a greater accomplishment as one ascends the cosmic hierarchy of powers to reach an ultimate realization or accomplishment (Eliade 1990: 47–52, 85–90, 293–6, 333). However, this analysis does not capture the ambivalence or multivalence of the powers themselves, which can vary profoundly with respect to their placement within an overarching set of assumptions. From the normative viewpoint established by Hindu and Buddhist classical text and neo-orthodoxy, the powers are to be dealt with cautiously if not to be prohibited or avoided entirely. However, such positions of orthodoxy are relative to the practices, not constitutive of them. The ascetic act of *tapas* or yoga, such as the endurance of pain, may support a liberative teleology but not inherently so—as there are many other potential spiritual "goods" in the economy of the *śramaṇa* worldview and its descendents.[18]

The more complex "temptation" motif, that *siddhi* or *vibhūti* serve as impediments to reaching a state of cessation (*nirodha*), is exemplified in the *Yogasūtra* in verses III.37 and III.51, which respectively describe how such powers are an impediment to (*nirbīja*) *samādhi* and how the "spiritual goods" offered by *tapas* can prove a distraction to such a pursuit. The passage of verse III.37, *te samādhāvupasargāḥ vyutthāne siddhayaḥ*, "these powers are obstacles to *samādhi*, but perfections in manifestation," suggests that perfections such as the previously mentioned (III.36) *prātibha* (illuminated) modes of sense perception are masteries that are directed "outwards" toward worldly manifestation (*vyutthāna*) rather than cessation (*nirodha*).[19] The second passage, in light of Vyāsa's commentary, refers to the entreaties of the gods to enjoy the spiritual goods of practice. This passage (YS III.51), *sthānyupanimantraṇe saṅgasmayākaraṇaṃ punaraniṣṭaprasaṅgāt*—"Upon the entreaties of the established ones (gods), there is no cause for rejoicing, due to their association with further undesirable consequences,"—links the enjoyment of the fruits of yoga and *tapas* to future experiences of an undesirable sort. What is particularly notable, however, is Vyāsa's association of this passage with the so-called spiritual goods of Indian literature. These goods are mentioned tangentially in YS I.15, *dṛṣṭānuśravikaviṣayavitṛṣṇasya vaśīkārasaṃjñā vairāgyam*: "detachment is the consciousness of mastery of desire for both seen and heard conditions."[20] This distinguishes "seen" conditions, experienced objects within one's world such as beauty, material wealth, and power, from "heard" objects that are gleaned from narrative literature (such as *vibhūti* and *siddhi* but not exclusively). Thus, a different, and perhaps more subtle, form of desire is for those objects that are cultural, magical, or religious "goods" that can be obtained through yoga and *tapas* and perhaps more mundane means. In the commentary to III.51, Vyāsa notes the myriad spiritual goods offered by divine powers to the ascendant *yogī*: a heavenly maiden (*āpsara*), magical elixirs (*rasāyana*), the wish-fulfilling tree (*kalpadruma*), viewing of the illustrious *mandākinī* river, *siddha* and *mahāṛṣi*, and the attainment of the divine eye and ear (*divya śrotracakśus*) and an indestructible diamond (*vajra*) body (*kāya*). This reality, or perhaps virtual reality, in YS III.51 is filled with spiritual goods that are characterized by the archetypical or paradigmatic "ultimate" objects of the culture. Whether to interpret this as cosmological, the functioning of the unconscious, or both, it demonstrates the principle that yoga is a vehicle for wish fulfillment as much as it is a mode of world-transcendence. The framework of the YS clearly places the numinous as such in a subordinate, but still important, position underneath an overarching ideology of a cessative orientation. The degree of emphasis on cessation is by no means equal in all traditions, and it is dangerous on an interpretive level to hold the position of the YS and its primary *bhāṣya* as a measure for all yoga traditions.

Morphology of the Numinous

There are of course numerous interpretations possible with respect to literary representations of such powers and their execution. One would be to see them as a literary device, developed as a metaphor for the degree of esteem and authority attributed to a text, or to inspire a reader by setting apart a narrative from more mundane forms of discourse. Such narratives might be said to generate faith—much in the way that narrative representations of the use of such powers are situated in a didactic context, in which they attract individuals to, or intensify the power of, the teaching. The connection between magical acts and the interface with folk religion and grassroots tradition is likely an element that is at play with respect to such narratives as well.[21] The faith generated in a particular doctrine might be cultivated on the basis of the magical supremacy of one's own teacher (be it the Buddha, Mahāvīra, or another teacher) or the sheer rhetorical power of the force behind the teachings, with the former being a literary correlate of the discourse of debate (Granoff 1985). Another interpretation would be to look at the powers as metaphoric representations of human abilities that can be cultivated through the practice of yoga—a concentrated mind leading to heightened senses and rapid mastery over mental or physical life, or that of a strong and energetic body as the basis for beauty, health, and virtuoso physical performance. In this mode of interpretation, the power to read others' minds might be an elaborate ability to read faces and intuit emotion. Certain powers are, however, more easily interpreted in light of a metaphorical explanation than others (compare mind reading to flight, for example). Another approach would be to look at the powers as a disingenuous "hook" that attracts the cultivation of faith in the practice by tapping into the desire for magical power among those that perceive themselves as disempowered with respect to the ordinary channels of agency in their lives. A more psychological or psychoanalytic interpretation might situate the powers within the domain of the unconscious and its symbolism, either as a manner of activation for the sake of a positive reconciliation of inner and outer world or as a narcissistic withdrawal into an inner world of wish fulfillment as a flight of fantasy (Obeyesekere 1990: 51–68; Masson 1980: 121–141).

Texts and personages associated with such numinous powers are encoded with charismatic authority, which is established by the force of their reality-altering and -mastering ability. As Weber argued, a key part of what establishes charisma and its authority is the degree to which a figure embodies antistructural forces, and it might be added that this is notably the numinous power of the sacred reality that he or she is associated with (Dow 1978: 83). This power, as Weber notes, has moral ambiguity and, as such, can be said to be *elemental* or *daemonic* rather than *moral* (Dow 1978: 84). This point is excellent for explicating at least one aspect of the functioning of the numinous as an aspect of the practice of yoga. The *yogin* or *yoginī* that has achieved yogic mastery becomes like a deity; the boundary between the human and the divine becomes fluid, in body, mind, or both. As such, the practitioner can be said to exist in a liminal or even a liminoid state, where the authority of their power is equivalent to that of divine beings. This antistructural type of authority may well have been perceived in terms of its contrast to more structural forms of authority, say kingship. The Buddha, for example, is a sort of spiritual world emperor (*cakkavatti*), demonstrating first the charismatic authority of the king through his spiritual mastery and then ultimately transitioning to institutional authority as the head of the *saṅgha* and routinized through his speech (*buddhavacaṇa*) and bodily relics.[22] Likewise, through this lens, the threat that the ascetic (antistructure) poses to Indra (structure) through their *tapas* and yogic practices becomes clearer—as the ascetic becomes more powerful, the structural power of the cosmos (and metaphorically society) becomes weakened, and requires contestation or alignment. The metaphor is that of the alliance or contestation between ascetic and ruler, demonstrated amply in both literature and in history (including contemporary history) on the Indian subcontinent.[23] In Indian history, the two streams at times flow almost completely together, as in the case of medieval Tantra in Hinduism and Buddhism, where the inner yogic alignment of tantric deities in a symbolic abode (*maṇḍala*) is often linked to worldly governance and its hierarchy (White 2004; Davidson 2004). Numinous power is demonstrated in a number of ways, including through the sheer mental or emotive force of rhetorical presence (physical presence, speech, and embodiment of symbolism via clothing and other material culture), through the authority commanded over worldly disciples, and through ascetic or ritual virtuosity that inspires the experience of the numinous through performance. Such demonstrations are either impossible, or virtually so—and therefore appear to be on the threshold of human capacity, breaking down the boundaries of the human. As with the cessative, one can link this to the dynamic of possession ritualism—through adorcism (the logical opposite of exorcism), one cultivates a possession state within oneself that breaks down the boundary between the human and divine, creating an antistructural state. There are parallels with yogic possession (*āveśa*) and cultivation (*bhāvanā*) with respect to adorcism, and their social situation is likely extremely similar—on the periphery of a larger authoritarian structure or perhaps at the center of one among numerous competing sects or communities. To follow Weber's terminology, this is a representation of elemental (numinous) power and adorcistic logic, which stands in contradistinction to the ethical (cessative) power cultivated through the exorcist logic of removal.

The Numinous in Modern and Contemporary Yoga

An initial observation, perhaps obvious to anyone vaguely familiar with contemporary yoga, is that there are a range of motivations behind the practice of yoga and thus a range of environments within which yoga can be practiced. As Smith has noted, one of the communal tensions within contemporary yoga, especially in its transnational forms, is that between yoga in "studio" contexts and that of health clubs (Smith 2004). In the simplest analysis, the first would represent lineage-oriented traditions that often are viewed as tied through lineage (*paramparā*) to a guru-disciple relationship (*guru-śiṣya*) with an authoritative Indian teacher. In some cases, the *guru* of a particular lineage may state directly what the difference between the authentic practice of yoga and mere "calisthenics" or physical exercise is (Jois 2002: 40; Iyengar 1994: 40–1). The second would represent derivative forms that do not emphasize lineage or the rootedness of the tradition in the religious context, focusing instead on the physical benefits of the practice with respect to fitness, beautification, and the like. The fitness-oriented practices of the health club may be rooted in their own "lineages" of sorts, but typically these are not native to India, though in some cases practices (for example, the so-called "Power Yoga" of Beryl Bender Birch) are deliberate attempts to make Indian traditions (in this case Jois's *aṣṭāṅgayoga*) palatable and practically executable by non-Indians and those not as interested in the metaphysical trappings of traditional sources. One of the implicit assumptions that could be said to operate in this respect is the idea of the "authentic" yoga that is set apart from that of physical fitness and the assumption that there is a fundamental difference between the framework of the orthodox lineage and that of a more physically oriented yoga. Though there are clearly important distinctions to be made between these two inclinations, especially from the perspective of the history of yoga in its various forms, there are at least two key problems with such an assumption. The first is that, as we have seen, the attainment of worldly and other-worldly goods or conditions (*dṛṣṭānuśrāvakaviṣaya*) is clearly tied into the logic of asceticism and inextricably connected with the practice of yoga, whether or not a given text or tradition endorses the application of practice for the sake of reaching those ends. To postulate that yoga is "authentically" limited to a renunciatory mode of practice is highly problematic. In the traditions stretching from the earliest strata of literature to the "classical" era of the *Yogasūtra* and *Abhidharma* literature to the medieval *haṭha* and *tantra* literature, numerous examples of obtaining bodily perfection, beauty, and other "physical" goods through yoga are expressed. This is not to mention the more metaphysical elements of divine powers and attributes that are the logical extension of the perfection of human embodiment. A second point is that the history of modern yoga, as it is beginning to emerge in the light of academic study through the work of scholars such as Alter, Goldberg, and Sjoman, among others, is deeply connected with fitness culture (Alter 1992; 2000; 2006; Sjoman 2007; 2004; 1996; Goldberg 2006). Alter, for example, demonstrates the connections between the *sūrya namaskāra* exercise, a profoundly prominent element of modern yoga, and Indian wrestling, European physical culturalist traditions, and the overarching rubric of an early twentieth-century Indian nationalism that linked a healthy individual body to that of a healthy and strong nation. He also has demonstrated how the "scientific" study of yoga in twentieth-century India helped to strip yoga of metaphysical assumptions and thus prepare it for the interface with a cosmopolitan audience. Goldberg has extended such observations, through demonstrating the larger *zeitgeist* of physical culture and the prominence of fitness gurus, including one (K.V. Iyer) that shared a gymnasium in the Mysore palace with Krishnamacharya during a formative period in the development of yoga. Sjoman's work in this respect may perhaps be the most noteworthy in that he ties together several pieces of the puzzle with respect to the various physical disciplines and paraphernalia of the Mysore Palace (including wrestling, gymnastics, and exercise equipment) and one of the few *āsana* texts with illustrations that links modern practice with that of the early modern and perhaps medieval period. What these scholars and others have contributed to the discussion is an awareness of the contextuality of the formation of modern yoga and its derivatives. If modern yoga has conceptions of "physical fitness" woven into its very fabric, if not the fiber, of what constitutes yoga, it would seem to follow that it would be better to see physical fitness and yoga as intimately related to one another than as in opposition. The sheer physicality of many of the contemporary yoga lineages, with an extensive focus on *āsana* and often *vinyāsa* (linking a moving set of postures with breath), is telling with regards to the sensible linkages that one might make between such disciplines. Physical culture is thus a sort of *lingua franca* that translates yoga from one context to another and ultimately part of the force behind yoga's cosmopolitan impact. One might, for example, fruitfully link such emphasis on embodiment to the implications of modifying body structure and movement through the lens of Bourdieu's conception of bodily *hexis* and to theories of proprioceptive and kinesthetic transformation (Smith 2004; Singleton 2005; Bailey 1997). Within the spectrum of "callisthenic" to more idealized yoga forms, we might have some traditions that emphasize *guru-śiṣya* and *paraṃpara* such as that of Bikram Yoga, but yet emphasize greatly the physicality of the practice, even to the extent of viewing yoga as athletics, and others that though quite athletic, nevertheless could be said to frame their practice in an overarching value (if not metaphysical) structure such as Jois's *aṣṭāṅgayoga*. It should be noted as well that the role of charismatic figures in athletic enterprises, especially the "guru" that is a proponent of a particular virtuoso practice, provides significantly fertile ground for comparison with the field of data provided by the study of yoga.

Another fruitful way of looking at the connection between fitness and yoga in terms of practice is through the lens of *tapas*. In the context of YS II.1 and YS II.32, *tapas* is included within the categories of the "yoga of action" (*kriyāyoga*) and as a member of that of "observance" (*niyama*). It is explicated in YS II.43 as *kāyaindriyasiddhiḥ aśuddhikṣayāt tapasaḥ*, stating "*tapas* perfects the body and the senses, by means of destroying impurity." This is rooted, in part, in a very early conception emerging from the Vedic materials that the development of inner "heat" (*tapas*) can be a means of purifying oneself for ritual performance and can be a source of power. This logic, that the development of inner heat destroys impurities and thus brings perfections to mental and sensorial faculties, might be argued to be consistent with athleticism and physical fitness. In other words, physical fitness can arguably be subsumed under the rubric of *tapas*. Through a variety of physical disciplines—such as running, biking, swimming, team sports, and the like, one is physically creating heat in the body and through that process purifying one's body and senses. It is clear that exercise has a cathartic effect physically and emotionally and that cathartic effect can be analyzed in terms of the power that gives one over one's body and senses.[24] The athlete is comparable in this respect to the virtuoso *yogī* or *tapasvin* who is master of the "elemental" forces that are determinative of his or her psychophysical existence. This is not to say that athletes do not have moral associations made with them—this is a characteristic mistake of confusing numinous attainment with that of the cessative, as occurs in yoga. In this respect, exercise is understood to simply "work," much in the way that *tapas* operates or works in the Indian context, regardless of the overarching motivations of the agent.[25] Similarly, modern and contemporary yoga teachers often emphasize the transformative or purifying nature of developing heat—K. Pattabhi Jois, for example, speaking of the heat resulting from intense *vinyāsa* practice in his *aṣṭāṅgayoga* as "purifying the blood," sweating out impurity, and ultimately curing disease in a manner analogous to the operation of a fever (Jois 2002: 111–13). An interesting and ironic case in point as well is that of the so-called "hot yoga" of Bikram Choudhury. The use of heat in that particular system is tied into his appropriation of yoga as a therapeutic physical modality, one in which the use of external heat helps bring greater flexibility and thus a deeper and more healing practice. In this case, an athletic mode of practice, performed by a former bodybuilder, returns to *tapas* via the role of heat as a means of rapid progress and transformation (Choudhury 2007: 24–5, 73–6). Part of the success of this model, arguably, is the cathartic effect of such a practice, in which one effectively "purges" oneself through the process of sweating. As such, it at least bears a hint of relationship with the historical usage of *tapas* and other traditions of heat bearing.

The Krishnamacharya lineage of yoga provides ample ground to demonstrate the relationship between the traditional powers associated with yoga and the virtuosity that is crucial to understanding the development of modern yoga. The influential Krishnamacharya lineage (exemplified by the South Indian guru T. Krishnamacharya and his disciples B.K.S. Iyengar and K. Pattabhi Jois) is rooted to a great extent in the model of the "yoga demonstration" as a source both for popular dissemination of their teachings and for making high-profile alliances with royalty and celebrities. Krishnamacharya's charismatic authority, according to his biography, is rooted in his revelatory visions of his ancestral patriarch, Nāthamuni, in his excursions to Northern India (Banaras) and ultimately in his journey to and return from Tibet, where he is said to have studied under the renowned Himalayan master Rama Mohan Brahmachari

(Desikachar 1998: 27–48, 77–83).[26] On his return to South India, he pursued an arduous course of yoga demonstrations that ultimately helped him build a reputation as a virtuoso teacher and practitioner, augmented by his highly visible position as yoga teacher in the Mysore Palace (Desikachar 1998: 85–7). This alliance with Krishnaraja Wodeyar, the Maharaja of Mysore, demonstrates the power of alignment between the charisma of the ascetic and the institutional power of the king, in an environment where political and economic instability was prevalent. There are clear parallels between the Maharaja's Mysore and Bhavanrao Pant's Aundh, where Pant sought to embody the ideals of the emerging Indian nation, and perhaps Hindu nationalism, through physical virtuosity (Alter 2000: 83–112).[27] As the focus of yoga shifted in modern context to the body as a site of virtuosity, it makes sense that the expression of the numinous should be accomplished through mastery of increasingly more complex and challenging postures. The antistructural component of virtuosity is evident in modern yoga through pushing the limits of the body's flexibility, with sheer numbers of yogic postures demonstrating the range of mastery, and particularly complex postures—such as extreme variations of lotus posture (*padmāsana*) and various balancing postures—pushing the limits of human anatomy. This is also related to a larger range of yogic "feats" that have become paradigmatic, such as being "buried alive" for a period to demonstrate control over one's respiration and metabolism, or stopping and then restarting one's heart and thus at least metaphorically dying and returning to life.[28]

The competition for patronage and disciples through yoga demonstrations mirrors the literary "battles" between practitioners that were mentioned earlier and demonstrate the ongoing relevance in yoga of charismatic authority rooted in ascetic mastery. Within modern and contemporary yoga lineages, narratives that argue for the methodological purity or superiority of a given teaching are in fact often illustrated by stories of demonstrations and competitions where a "besting" of some sort occurs.[29] In the Krishnamacharya lineage, both K. Pattabhi Jois and B.K.S. Iyengar attracted Indian disciples and ultimately a profoundly cosmopolitan audience through their demonstrations and those of their key disciples (often their children, such as Manju Pattabhi Jois). It may well be that these efforts have been influenced by other performative arts and disciplines that would have been in competition for attention and patronage, such as the marital arts, wrestling, and perhaps even acrobatics and circus performances.[30]

An aesthetic dimension enters the picture as well through the vehicle of performance, with figures such as Krishnamacharya and Iyengar demonstrating their stunning physiques and physical virtuosity through photography and film (Iyengar 1987: 27). Photography, film, and video have clearly served this dimension of modern yoga and clearly have helped to solidify its cosmopolitan appeal and expand its potential audience, Iyengar's *Light on Yoga* being at the forefront of the celebrity-making appeal of the image.[31] Likewise, the explosion of yoga commodities, such as the image of a deity (*mūrti*), jewelry, apparel, yoga "props" such as mats, and the like, indicates the commodification and fetishization of the objects of yoga in the Krishnamacharya and other lineages.

The commodification process can be said to be one way in which the abstract "power" of yoga becomes concrete and is transformed from the abstract to the concrete and from cultural to economic capital. For the consumer of such goods, they serve a symbolic function as embodying the potential (if not the actual) numinous power that is latent within the practice of yoga. The deities of yoga are tangible representations of the numinous (and perhaps also the cessative) power of yoga, the symbolic representation of the power and "otherness" (antistructure) toward which the yoga practitioner is striving. More prominent examples are those of Śiva, Viṣṇu/Kṛṣṇa, and Śākyamuni Buddha (Gotama Buddha), along with a particularly interesting *mūrti* that is becoming more common of Patañjali himself, in a mythic form as *nāgarāja* (half human and half serpent). These contribute in creating an exoticized environment that symbolically represents the alternate or idealized reality that the practitioner hopes to enter into or become part of through the practice. The studio and the home become the abode of the divine, a numinous place that is closer to the ideal world that the *yogin* or *yoginī* is striving to create or inhabit. This is further augmented in some contexts by the self-selecting nature of participants in practice, who often have limber, lean, and strong physiques, providing an undercurrent of the space as being one inhabited by the beautiful and gifted (as would be characteristic of the celestial realms).

The implications of these elements in terms of class and gender (given the prevalence of middle-class female practitioners in European and American contexts) are numerous. They exemplify the connection between the power and authority of the numinous and the contestation or allegiance forged between the antistructural ascetic agent and those persons in positions of power, wealth, and authority in the larger social sphere. This understanding also sheds light on the logic behind the highly visible alliances between celebrities, musicians, artists, and others within the economic and cultural elite and the gurus and institutions of yoga—prominent examples being Krishnamacharya's relationship with Indra Devi, Iyengar's association with Yehudi Menuhin, and Pattabhi Jois's relationship through the *aṣṭāṅgayoga* methodology with celebrities and musicians such as Gwyneth Paltrow, Madonna, and Sting. Here we might also recall our earlier passage regarding Vyāsa's analysis of YS III.51, wherein the *yogin* or *yoginī* is approached by the "established ones," who offer all sorts of spiritual and material goods, as a cautionary tale of the "pitfalls" of yoga that are known all too well in contemporary yoga circles, such as the sexual indiscretions of gurus (comparable to psychoanalytic transference) and the disruptive power of wealth and prestige. Such a commentary on the dangers or perils of power may well have broader significance and relevance (in sports and politics, for example), but within the often charismatic domain of yoga it seems to be particularly relevant and timely to consider.

The Trajectories of Modern Yoga

It has been argued that modern yoga traditions and their contemporary descendents continue to embody the dynamic relationship between the numinous and the cessative that has been associated with yoga in its multiple stages of development and in its various philosophical, literary, and sectarian permutations. One of the underlying assumptions of discussions regarding the "authenticity" of yoga traditions in the contemporary context is that yoga is inherently cessative or liberatory in nature and that the idea of the practice of yoga as a source of power or personal gain is somehow a deviation from the "true" goal or nature of yoga. However, as has been discussed, the numinous component of yoga is a central component of conceptions of asceticism and contemplation in the Indian context. In addition, many, if not most, discussions of these issues in contemporary yoga do not factor in the composite nature of modern yoga and the historical and cultural processes at work behind its intersection with other bodily disciplines and cultures. There is no authentic yoga aside from the organic, living traditions that have been intimately intertwined with the "tradition texts" or dominant philosophical and other discursive and bodily paradigms that have been characteristic of their historical moments. The cessative model is emphasized, in part, owing to the fact that modern yoga is rooted in the Hindu Renaissance and its ethical and modernist visions of Hinduism as represented by figures such as Vivekananda and Sivananda. The emphasis on the cessative in yoga has also filtered through some of the most important academic scholarship on yoga over the last century, including that of Eliade, arguably in part through his affinity and association with S.N. Dasgupta.

The "inner workings" or "inner logic" of yoga—or phenomenologically speaking, the bodily disciplines and contemplative practices that constitute it—have a reflexive relationship with the world in terms of the social and cultural situation of its practice, with its political, economic, and other complexities. Its tremendous popularity and visibility as an international phenomenon has been fueled in part by the multiplicity of trajectories that are possible within yoga, given the range of applications into which it can be integrated. It is likely that what makes yoga so compelling to a modern or postmodern audience is not simply one factor but the concatenation of a number of factors. The traditions of yoga have had multiple "sites" of intersection with its modern and contemporary milieus. Part of its success has been its codification within a moment of transformation toward a global cosmopolitanism and thus the integration in its modern form of existing threads of Indian and European and—ultimately—American culture. At the same time, these transformations have been effected in a way that is coextensive with some of the most important underlying assumptions or principles that ground the way in which yoga operates and what it yields. These assumptions may not be explicit, and in fact they may be glossed over by other narrative structures that deemphasize certain aspects (such as the numinous, as has been described), but that does not inhibit their continued functioning or reemergence. The purpose of this chapter has been to make such underlying assumptions, functions, and principles explicit and, in the process, demonstrate that investigating the modern and contemporary forms of yoga in light of their historical predecessors has great potential for bringing clarity to the dynamics of these practices.

Notes

1 The distinction between "modern" and "contemporary" used throughout this chapter is primarily a genealogical one, with modern forms of yoga being understood to be the precursors conceptually, temporally (late nineteenth to mid-twentieth century), and geographically (India) to those of the current, and thus contemporary range of forms (early twenty-first century in an international sphere). The designation *modern* can also be said to suggest contextuality in terms of discourses of science, colonialism, and cosmopolitanism, among others, as has been discussed by Alter (2006) and De Michelis (2004), among others. Contemporary (current) practice in many traditions is rooted in, and often inseparable from, its modern precursors. As is argued, this has a number of implications with regard to the claims and questions of authority and authenticity of yoga traditions and their techniques.

2 This paradigm is a crucial one, in that it establishes a sense of ultimacy with respect to teleologies of liberation, characterized by a range of terminology, such as *mokṣa*, *mukti*, *nirvāṇa*, *kevala*, and *kaivalya*.

3 The eight-limbed system seems to have been codified as a standard in mainstream literature. However, this is only one possibility among others, one of the notable examples being *ṣaḍaṅga* systems found in the *Maitrī Upaniṣad* and in that of the *Kālacakratantra*. See Wallace (2001: 25–30) for a discussion of these two examples. On *duḥkha*, links can be made between the clear parity among representations of the nature of suffering represented in Buddhist Nikāya and Abhidharma literature and in the *Yogasūtra* (verse II.15), given the clear parity of defining *duḥkha* in terms of *pariṇāma*, *duḥkha/tāpa*, and *saṃskāra*.

4 YS II.30–1.

5 *Mahāvyutpatti* 996–1004.

6 In the context of Theravāda Buddhism, for example, even if one cannot secure liberation, following the precepts and conditioning the mind and body through practice will yield favorable rebirth, the ideal case being one that provides continuity to practice over the course of more than one lifetime, exemplified by the disciple that is a *sotāpanna*, a "stream enterer," who has not secured liberation but is on a course toward that destination over a series of lives (Harvey 2000: 39–40).

7 It might be pointed out, however, that both Iyengar and Jois at times appear to collapse the *aṣṭāṅgayoga* into the limb of *āsana* or portray *āsana* as the first limb to be mastered. For a discussion of this issue, see Bühnemann (2007: 22–4). This could be viewed as a negotiation of the degree of emphasis on the moral dimension of yoga, especially as presented to different audiences.

8 Urbanization also represents a distancing from the agricultural or pastoral setting and therefore renunciation that is a leaving of the urban for the rural (especially the forest), or the rural within the urban (the yoga studio) plays into this strongly.

9 An extensive discussion of possession in Indian literature and culture can be found in Smith (2006).

10 This is exemplified in Mahāyāna Buddhism by the attainment of *abhijñā* and *nirmāṇa*, the powers of knowledge and manifestation that are the basis for the compassionate activity of a *buddha* or *bodhisattva*.

11 See, for example, *Śvetāśvatara Upaniṣad* II.1–17.
12 See, for example, *Agni Purāṇa* XIII.1–23.
13 *Dharmasaṃgraha* 20; *Mahāvyutpatti* 201–9.
14 *Dīgha Nikāya* i.211ff.
15 *Cullavagga* V.8.2.
16 Literary accounts of the Kālāmukha and Kāpālika sects testify to this; see Briggs (1998: 223–7) for examples.
17 This might not be true of the postliberatory experience, however. See Whicher (1998: 275–300) for a discussion of this issue in the context of the YS.
18 One of the most prominent forms of women's asceticism in India, the *pativrata*, revolves around the connection between female *tapas* and a ritual or devotional relationship with particular deities, often for the purpose of a husband's or family's well-being. The logic of the toleration of hardship in exchange for a "reward" is clearly demonstrated in such domestic contexts and demonstrates the economy of ascetic practice in its logical mode operation.
19 On the dynamic between *vyutthāna* and *nirodha*, see Rukmani (1997).
20 Compare *Dhammapada* XXVI.35.
21 A systematic examination of motifs of the miraculous might provide some insight into contemporary narratives and their historical predecessors here. The rubric of "folk religion" might be particularly useful in understanding the role of narrative in contemporary yoga.
22 This may be tied into ideas of the charismatic king that embodied the powers of a god (*deva*) in the Vedic context and the idea of "worldly" *siddhi* that were possessed by the king. See Gonda (1969: 24–70) and the entry on *siddhi* in Rhys Davids and Stede (2003, 120–1).
23 On the historical and contemporary contexts of this, see Pintch (2006); Briggs (1998); McKean (1996); and van der Veer (1988); for a philosophical critique, see Gier (2000).
24 There are numerous possibilities for talking about this physiologically—including the metabolism of various substances in the body, such as stress hormones or the effect that body temperature has on circulation or nervous system functioning.
25 One might speculate here about important cultural, political, and religious figures in American and European culture that integrate physical fitness and exercise into their lives in a virtually "religious" manner.
26 A similar pattern with respect to revelation connects Krishnamacharya with Jois via the *Yoga Korunta*, a text described as an innovative *haṭha* discourse by Vamana Rishi, said to be originally found in the Calcutta Library but at some point lost (Jois 2007).
27 Comparison can be made with the statements of Krishnamacharya as quoted by Desikachar (1998: 89–90) and those of Jois (2002: 3-4). Iyengar refers to Pant as "the founder of the Surya Namaskar system" (Iyengar 1987: 25).
28 The latter being an ability for which Krishnamacharya was quite renowned (Iyengar 1987: 15–17; Desikachar 1998: 27–8). The "burial" demonstration has a considerable history, according to at least one account (Lanman 1917: 148–9).
29 These narratives are quite common in contemporary practice, one type revolving around stories of students of a particular teacher that "infiltrate" the ashram of a rival teacher and demonstrate their superior skills before being thrown out by the rival teacher. Another common narrative is of other teachers either having been a student of, or dependent for their technique on, one's guru.
30 A strong parallel that can be made is between contemporary yoga and contemporary manifestations of Chinese, Korean, and Japanese martial arts, which also demonstrate a curious admixture of physical discipline, spirituality, nationalism, aesthetics, and competition (both in terms of battles and in terms of "feats of strength" and so forth). It would not be surprising if there is in fact a historical link between the non-Indian martial arts systems and yoga and the Indian martial arts

such as Kalarippayatu (Zarrilli 1998). On the other hand, that bodily disciplines such as yoga and the martial arts more broadly defined would bear resemblance should not be surprising, given the similar time frames and contexts out of which they have emerged.

31 The pervasiveness of the numinous element is also demonstrated by the impact of charismatic guru figures that have established enduring institutions, such as Swami Satchidananda, Swami Muktananda, Maharishi Mahesh Yogi (the TM guru, known for "yogic flight" programs), Bhagwan Shree Rajneesh (currently known as Osho), and perhaps even latter-day gurus such as Deepak Chopra in part through the force of their charismatic presence. In the case of Satchidananda, chanting the mantra *oṃ* at the beginning of the Woodstock Music Festival in 1969 was a paradigmatic moment of charismatic authority, amply demonstrating the connection between antistructural ecstasy and countercultural forces in the United States. In virtually all of these cases (perhaps excluding Rajneesh), the initial ecstatic intensity of the community has shifted toward a more institutionalized mode of practice—analogous to Victor Turner's conceptions of liminal and liminoid communities—and have moved toward a more cessative mode of emphasis in their operation.

Bibliography

Alter, J. (1992) *The Wrestler's Body: Identity and Ideology in Northern India*, Berkeley: University of California Press.

—(2000) *Gandhi's Body: Sex, Diet, and the Politics of Nationalism*, Philadelphia: University of Philadelphia Press.

—(2006) *Yoga in Modern India: The Body Between Science and Philosophy*, Princeton: Princeton University Press.

Bailey, S.R. (1997) *Hatha Yoga as a Practice of Embodiment* [M.A. thesis], Los Angeles: University of California.

Bailey, G., and Mabbett, I. (2003) *The Sociology of Early Buddhism*, New York: Cambridge University Press

Briggs, G.W. (1998) *Gorakhnāth and the Kānphaṭa Yogīs*, Delhi: Motilal Banarsidass Publishers.

Brockington, J. (2003) Yoga in the *Mahābhārata*, in I. Whicher and D. Carpenter (eds) *Yoga: The Indian Tradition*, London: Routledge Curzon: 13–24.

Bronkhorst, J. (1993) *The Two Traditions of Meditation in Ancient India*, Delhi: Motilal Banarsidass Publishers.

—(1998) *The Two Sources of Indian Asceticism*, Delhi: Motilal Banarsidass Publishers.

Bühnemann, Gudrun (2000) The Six Rites of Magic, in D.G. White (ed.) *Tantra in Practice*, Princeton: Princeton University Press.

—(2007) *Eighty-four Āsanas in Yoga: A Survey of Traditions, With Illustrations*, New Delhi: D.K. Printworld.

Choudhury, Bikram (2007) *Bikram Yoga: The Guru Behind Hot Yoga Shows the Way to Radiant Health and Personal Fulfillment*, New York: Collins.

Davidson, R.M. (2004) *Indian Esoteric Buddhism: A Social History of the Tantric Movement*, Delhi: Motilal Banarsidass Publishers.

De Michelis, E. (2004) *A History of Modern Yoga: Patañjali and Western Esoterism*, London: Continuum.

Desikachar, T.K.V. (1998) *Health, Healing, and Beyond: Yoga and the Living Tradition of Krishnamacharya*, New York: Aperture.

Doniger, W. (1981) *Śiva: The Erotic Ascetic*, New York: Oxford University Press.

Dow, T. (1978) An Analysis of Weber's Work on Charisma, *British Journal of Sociology* 29 (1): 83–93.

Edgerton, F. (1972) *Buddhist Hybrid Sanskrit Grammar and Dictionary Volume 1*, Delhi: Motilal Banarsidass Publishers.

——(1972b) *Buddhist Hybrid Sanskrit Grammar and Dictionary Volume 2*, Delhi: Motilal Banarsidass Publishers.

Eliade, M. (1990) *Yoga: Immortality and Freedom*, Princeton: Bollingen.

Flood, G. (2004) *The Ascetic Self: Subjectivity, Memory, and Tradition*, Cambridge: Cambridge University Press.

Gier, N. (2000) *Spiritual Titanism: Indian, Chinese, and Western Perspectives*, Albany: State University of New York Press.

Gonda, J. (1969) *Ancient Kingship from the Religious Point of View*, Leiden: E.J. Brill.

Glucklich, A. (2001) *Sacred Pain: Hurting the Body for the Sake of the Soul*, New York: Oxford University Press.

Goldberg, E. (2006) Worshipping the Sun Indoors: Surya Namaskar Mixed Up with Muscle Cult and Hatha-Yoga Cult [unpublished manuscript].

Granoff, P. (1985) Scholars and Wonder-Workers: Some Remarks on the Role of the Supernatural in Philosophical Contests in Vedānta Hagiographies, *Journal of the American Oriental Society* 105 (3): 459–67.

Harvey, P. (2000) *An Introduction to Buddhist Ethics: Foundations, Values, and Issues*, New York: Cambridge University Press.

Iyengar, B.K.S. (1987) *Iyengar: His Life and Work*, Porthill, ID: Timeless Books.

——(1994) *Light on Yoga: Yoga Dipika*, New York: Schocken Books.

Jaini, P. (1990) *The Jaina Path of Purification*, Delhi: Motilal Banarsidass Publishers.

Jois, K.P. (2002) *Yoga Mala*, New York: North Point Press.

——(2007) *Method*, Mysore: Ashtanga Yoga Research Institute. Available HTTP: <http://www.ayri.org/method.html> (accessed July 12, 2007).

Lanman, C. (1917) Hindu Ascetics and Their Powers, *Transactions and Proceedings of the American Philological Association* 48: 133–51.

Lewis, I.M. (1989) *Ecstatic Religion: A Study of Shamanism and Spirit Possession*, New York: Routledge.

McKean, L. (1996) *Divine Enterprise: Gurus and the Hindu Nationalist Movement*, Chicago: University of Chicago Press.

Masson, J.M. (1980) *The Oceanic Feeling: The Origins of Religious Sentiment in Ancient India*, Boston: D. Reidel Publishing Company.

Nakamura, H. (2000) *Gotama Buddha: A Biography Based on the Most Reliable Texts*, Tokyo: Kosei Publishing Co.

Obeyesekere, G. (1990) *The Work of Culture: Symbolic Transformation in Psychoanalysis and Anthropology*, Chicago: University of Chicago Press.

Olivelle, P. (1992) *Saṃnyāsa Upaniṣads: Hindu Scriptures on Asceticism and Renunciation*, New York: Oxford University Press.

——(1998) *The Early Upaniṣads: Annotated Text and Translation*, New York: Oxford University Press.

Pintch, W. (2006) *Warrior Ascetics and Indian Empires*, New York: Cambridge University Press.

Radhakrishnan, S. (1999) *The Dhammapada: With Introductory Essays, Pāli Text, English Translation, and Notes*, New York: Oxford University Press.

Rhys Davids, T.W. and W. Stede (2003) *Pali-English Dictionary*, Delhi: Motilal Banarsidass Publishers.

Rukmani, T.S. (1997) The Tension Between Vyutthāna and Nirodha in the Yoga-Sūtras, *Journal of Indian Philosophy* 25 (6): 613–28.

Sarbacker, S. (2005) *Samādhi: The Numinous and Cessative in Indo-Tibetan Yoga*, Albany: State University of New York Press.

Shaw, S. (2006) *Buddhist Meditation: An Anthology of Texts from the Buddhist Canon*, London: Routledge.

Singleton, M. (2005) Salvation through Relaxation: Proprioceptive Therapy and its Relationship to Yoga, *Journal of Contemporary Religion* 20 (3): 289–304.

Sjoman, N.E. (1996) *The Yoga Tradition of the Mysore Palace*, New Delhi: Abhinav.

—(2004) *Yoga Touchstone*, Calgary: Black Lotus Books.

—(2007) *Dead Birds: The Commentary on Yoga Touchstone*, Calgary: Black Lotus Books.

Smith, B. (2004) Adjusting the Quotidian: Ashtanga Yoga as Everyday Practice [paper presented at Cultural Studies Association of Australasia (CSAA) Conference], Murdoch University, December 2004.

Smith F. (2006) *The Self Possessed: Deity and Spirit Possession in South Asian Literature and Civilization*, New York: Columbia University Press.

Strong, J. (2001) *The Buddha: A Short Biography*, Oxford: Oneworld.

van der Veer, P. (1988) *Gods on Earth: The Management of Religious Experience and Identity in a North Indian Pilgrimage Center*, Atlantic Highlands, NJ: Athlone Press.

Wallace, V. (2001) *The Inner Kālacakratantra: A Buddhist Tantric View of the Individual*, New York: Oxford University Press.

Whicher, I. (1998) *The Integrity of the Yoga Darśana: A Reconsideration of Classical Yoga*, Albany: State University of New York Press.

White, D.G. (2004) Tantra in Practice: Mapping a Tradition, in D.G. White (ed) *Tantra in Practice*, Princeton: Princeton University Press.

Zarrilli, P. (1998) *When the Body Becomes All Eyes: Paradigms, Discourses, and Practices of Power in Kalarippayattu, a South Indian Martial Art*, New Delhi: Oxford University Press.

9 From Fusion to Confusion

A Consideration of Sex and Sexuality in Traditional and Contemporary Yoga

Mikel Burley

> Wipe out the sexual Samskaras (impressions) and Vasanas (subtle desires). Annihilate lust from my mind. Make me a true ... Yogi (Swami Sivananda).[1]

> Yoga enables one to get into meaningful relationships and enjoy sex[2] (I Love India Web site).

Attitudes to sex and sexuality within the milieu of contemporary yoga are both confused and confusing. A twisted skein of opinions and imagery obtains, wherein we find, for example, idealizations of chastity and asceticism, often couched in neo-Puritanical terminology, competing with eroticized depictions of the yogic body and advertisements for yoga's capacity to enhance sexual performance and orgasmic ecstasy. The overall effect is a confusing melange of messages for the aspiring yoga student. In this chapter, I argue that this confusion is symptomatic of the blending of a rather superficial understanding of a diverse range of yogic traditions on the one hand, with certain cultural trends, such as commercialism, and the emphasis on desirable physicality, on the other. This blend constitutes the flavorful soup that is contemporary globalized yoga.

I begin by examining the gendered metaphysical representations that pervade traditional accounts of the purpose and methodology of spiritual liberation, first within the philosophically monovular schools of Classical Yoga and Sāṃkhya, and then within certain strands of Vedic cosmogony. Second, I consider how the imagery of erotic coitus and climax is utilized within traditional *haṭha* yoga and the extravagant tapestries of tantric symbology, and how the masculine spiritual ideal of virility and self-control is iconically depicted in the mythic figure of Śiva. I also give some attention to the overt application of physical intercourse adumbrated in the *Haṭhayogapradīpikā* and to the differing reactions to this adumbration evinced by several contemporary yogic commentators. Third, I look at some attitudes to chastity expressed by founders of influential contemporary yoga schools, highlighting certain variations within an overall emphasis on sexual restraint and contrasting this emphasis with the commercialization and eroticization of the yogic body in contemporary globalized cultural contexts. Finally, after drawing together the threads of the complicated, and necessarily selective, story of yoga's relation to sex and sexuality that is presented in this chapter, I propose that, despite the pervasiveness of confused depictions of yogic tradition, contemporary yoga nevertheless provides opportunities for a more discerning inquiry into yoga's intricate past.

Gendered Metaphysical and Cosmological Narratives in Yoga Traditions

The foundational text of Classical Yoga is commonly known as the *Yogasūtra* (YS) of Patañjali. No reliable historical evidence is available concerning its compiler or date, yet scholars generally situate it within the second or third century C.E. This text is frequently cited by contemporary yoga schools as being among the highest sources of instruction, including those schools that give primary emphasis to postural and breathing techniques, such as Iyengar Yoga and Pattabhi Jois's Ashtanga Yoga, and those that focus on sedentary meditative practice, such as the Self-Realization Fellowship and Maharishi Mahesh Yogi's Transcendental Meditation.[3] Though these schools less frequently make reference to the system of Indian philosophy known as *Sāṃkhya*, it is this latter system that can reasonably be regarded as providing the metaphysical backdrop to the contemplative methodology of Patañjali's Yoga.[4] The classical formulation of Sāṃkhya philosophy is expounded in the *Sāṃkhyakārikā* (SK) of Īśvarakṛṣṇa (*c.* fourth or fifth century C.E.), and it is in this text, along with its traditional commentaries, that we find the most elaborate expression of Sāṃkhya-Yoga's metaphysical vision.

At the heart of the vision is a fundamental binary opposition between two mutually irreducible principles, each of which is ascribed a variety of names and epithets. Discernible among these names and epithets is a theme of the complementarity between that which experiences or "sees" (*draṣṭṛ*) and that which is experienced or "seen" (*dṛśya*). It is the conjunction (*saṃyoga*) of these two contraries—the noumenal sources of subjectivity and objectivity respectively—that engenders the polymodal effusion constitutive of our everyday experiences, and it is the goal of life, as assessed by Sāṃkhya and Yoga, to annul this conjunction.

The YS, being the more condensed and imaginatively attenuated of the two texts, tends to be constrained to a higher degree than the SK with respect to gendered metaphors. The SK, meanwhile, openly portrays as masculine the subjective pole of the metaphysical duad, which it normally terms *puruṣa* ("self," "person"),[5] and as feminine the objective pole, which it normally terms *prakṛti*. This latter term has no precise semantic equivalent in English, although etymologically it is closely related to "procreatrix";[6] it is that which, though unmanifest in itself, constitutively produces the general features of possible experience. The gendered relation between these two principles is most vividly evinced in the following passage:

> Just as, having displayed herself before the gaze of the audience, the dancer desists from dancing, so *prakṛti* desists, having manifested herself to *puruṣa*. She, being endowed with qualities (*guṇas*), moves without any benefit [to herself] for the sake of *puṃs* [i.e., *puruṣa*], who, being without qualities, does not reciprocate. ... [T]here is no one more tender than *prakṛti*, who, saying "I have been seen," never again comes into *puruṣa*'s sight (SK 59–61; my trans.).

Here, the feminine is the one who reveals herself to the masculine onlooker. Empirical reality—the world of experience—is the dance of the dancer; though not quite the product of sexual union, it is certainly presented as a performance resonating with erotic undertones. The relationship between *prakṛti* and *puruṣa* is thoroughly asymmetric: *prakṛti* dances for the sake of *puruṣa*; *puruṣa* does nothing except observe.

Phrases such as "for the sake of *puruṣa*" (*puruṣa-artha*) have a twofold sense in Sāṃkhya and Yoga: the engagement between seer and seen is for the purpose of both experience, or "enjoyment" (*bhoga*), and "liberation" (*apavarga*) (*YS* 2.17–18; SK 21). *Puruṣa* is temporarily absorbed, seduced by *prakṛti*'s performance, and yet the ultimate purpose of the performance is for *puruṣa* to appreciate his nonidentity with both the performance and the performer herself, to awaken to his own "aloneness" (*kaivalya*).[7] The "union" sought through Classical Yoga and Sāṃkhya is, then, not a union of masculine seer and feminine seen; it is, rather, the union of the seer with himself. It is the seer's recognition that he is nothing other than himself, his true nature being the aloneness of consciousness, devoid of objectual content. *Prakṛti*'s role in the whole affair, as exposited in the SK, is purely subordinate: She is the objectual world (both external and intrapsychic) whose charms entice *puruṣa* away from his essence and then lead him back to the recovery of salvific completeness. Thus, though the most prevalent metaphor for the process of moving from ignorance to spiritual fulfillment is that of voyeuristic erotic encounter, the predominant metaphor for the fulfillment itself is that of ascetic isolation from worldly distractions. At the level of personal meditative practice, this is the withdrawal of attention from sensory stimuli and the identification of the self with the dimensionless point of transcendent subjectivity.

In comparison with many other strands of ancient Indian mythopoesis, the sexual imagery of Classical Yoga and Sāṃkhya is austere and restrained. In both pre- and post-classical sources, we encounter a far greater profusion of coital metaphors for the primordial act by means of which the world comes into appearance. An especially noteworthy early source of such imagery is the *Śatapathabrāhmaṇa* (ŚB) (*c.* 800 B.C.E.), wherein it is said of the masculine creator-god Prajāpati that he copulates with the goddess of the voice (*vāc*) to emit the auxiliary deities that give rise to the world (ŚB 6.1.2.6 ff.). Prajāpati is associated with preverbal mentation (*manasā*), whereas Vāc is the expression of that mentation through phonemic vibration or speech. Tracy Pintchman remarks of this relationship that it again represents the feminine participant as occupying a subordinate position:

> Mind is often considered to be more subtle and more fundamental than speech, which simply gives expression to the mind's contents. It is stated, for example, that mind supports speech, going before it and preparing it, and of the two, mind is better because speech only imitates mind (Pintchman 1994: 49).

As Pintchman also notes, however, there are passages wherein the importance of speech is emphasized, on the basis that it is only through the medium of speech that mind is "made known" (ibid.: 223). Speech manifests thought, thereby furnishing it with potency that it would otherwise lack.[8]

In a later passage of the ŚB, the performance of the creative sexual act is attributed to the masculine and feminine deities Indra and Indrāṇī and, in this instance, direct indications are given that the act occurs within the microcosmos of the human organism. Indra is said to be located in the right eye and Indrāṇī in the left. They "descend to the space in the heart" where their divine copulation engenders "the highest bliss" and produces "seed (*retas*) from which all this, whatever exists, springs" (ŚB 10.5.2.9–12, quoted in Pintchman 1994: 52). This passage is echoed in the *Bṛhadāraṇyaka Upaniṣad* (4.2.2–3), wherein Indra's consort is named Virāj.[9]

The association, in the ŚB, of Prajāpati with mentation and of Vāc with its vocal expression foreshadows the association, especially prevalent in tantric texts, of the masculine deity (Śiva in the Śaiva Tantras and Viṣṇu in the Vaiṣṇava Tantras) with pure consciousness and of the feminine deity (Pārvatī for Śaivas, Nārāyaṇī for Vaiṣṇavas) with the dynamic power (*śakti*) of life and sound.[10] However, there is a significant difference to be noted here. In the ŚB, the sexual union between the masculine and feminine principles is the act that brings the empirical world into being, just as, in Classical Yoga and Sāṃkhya, the conjunction of the masculine seer and the feminine seen is what engenders empirical involvement. Conversely, in much tantric literature, which is generally considered to postdate both the Vedic period and the flourishing of the classical period, sexual imagery is typically deployed to represent the culmination of sustained salvific endeavor. Thus, although the aim of both Classical Yoga and tantric *haṭha* yoga, which we look at below, is to bring about a final dissolution of worldly experience, in Classical Yoga the precipitator of this dissolution is depicted as the separation of masculine and feminine principles, whereas in tantra it is portrayed as their orgasmic fusion.

Physical and Symbolic Coitus in Tantric Yoga

Haṭha yoga is a form of soteriological discipline that is firmly rooted in the tantric tradition, and the primary textual sources of *haṭha* yoga can themselves be classed as tantric documents. What gets practiced today in most public yoga classes is often called "*hatha* yoga" (pronounced with a soft *th*, as in "theory," as opposed to the retroflexed aspirate of the original Sanskrit), but this form of practice tends to bear only a faint family resemblance to that which is expounded in the tantric sources.

From among the traditional *haṭha* texts, two stand out as being most accessible to modern readers. One is the *Haṭhayogapradīpikā* (HYP)—sometimes published under the shorter title *Haṭhapradīpikā*—which, within the text itself, is attributed to a sage named Svātmārāma and is standardly dated around the fourteenth or fifteenth century C.E. The other is the *Gheraṇḍasaṃhitā* (GhS) (*c.* late seventeenth century C.E.), whose title means simply "Gheraṇḍa's collection [of teachings]."[11] Of these two texts, it is the former that has been translated most often into European languages and has received the most attention from contemporary yoga schools, despite its being the GhS that offers a slightly more detailed body of practical instruction.

Though each of these texts (the HYP and GhS) presents a distinct system of practice, the two systems exhibit a number of common features. Both are designed to promote a set of three main processes whose interrelations, though not precisely defined, have a shared orientation. One of these processes is the progressive purification of the practitioner's energy-matrix, comprising the complex network of channels (*nāḍīs*) that might be interpreted either as conduits along which vital energy or "breath" (*prāṇa, vāyu*) flows or as the flows of energy themselves. A second process is the diminution and ultimate cessation of the downward movement of *bindu*. This is a vital fluid (literally "droplet") that is identified both with semen and with the essence of selfhood (Alter 1997). It is to be drawn upward and retained near the center of the brow rather than allowed to fall and be consumed in the solar fire of the navel region or ejaculated through uncontrolled orgasm.[12] The third process is the arousal and sedulous elevation of the "power" (*śakti*), which is depicted as a coiled snake (*kuṇḍalinī, kuṇḍalī, bhujaṅgī*) anatomically located in the perineum. When appropriately stimulated—by means of the internal heating effect of *prāṇāyāma* (the retention and concentration of vital energy)—the serpent stands erect and sequentially penetrates the "wheels" (*cakra*s) strung along the "gracious channel" (*suṣumnānāḍī*), the medial axis of the energy-body (HYP 3.104 ff.). Despite what might be construed as the phallic nature of the imagery surrounding this ophidian power, the serpent itself represents the *feminine* partner in the divine couple. She is referred to as, among other things, the "supreme goddess" (*parameśvarī*, HYP 3.106) and a "child-widow" (*bālaraṇḍa*, HYP 3.109–10), the latter epithet being due to her having "been born in separation from her husband Śiva," with whom she wishes to unite (Digambarji and Kokaje 1998: 118).

Though such concepts as *prāṇa*, *cakra*s, and *kuṇḍalinī* are often alluded to in contemporary *haṭha* yoga classes and manuals, these are usually abstracted from their tantric symbolic context. In particular, the theme of controlling seminal fluid and raising it to the level of the cranium is generally eschewed, probably owing to its incongruity with contemporary physiological opinion but also owing to the tenuity of its relevance to the predominantly female constituency for whom modern yoga caters.

For the most part, the processes that traditional *haṭha* yoga seeks to promote operate at the level of the lone practitioner, who is conceived as having an androgynous subphysical nature. As David White observes, "The subtle body is androgynous ... in that it contains both sperm (*bindu*) and blood (*śoṇita*), the bodily essences of Śiva and Śakti" (1984: 59).[13] The yogin's mind and body constitute the site for the transmutation of erotic desires, impulses, and energy (which would, ordinarily, be outwardly directed) into the inwardly channeled impulse for divine conjugation. Despite this overall intrapersonal emphasis, however, the HYP does contain instructions concerning a technique that appears to involve physical coitus between a male and a female practitioner.

The technique in question is designated *vajrolīmudrā* ("thunderbolt seal") and, in the HYP, is presented alongside two related practices, namely *amarolī* and *sahajolī* (HYP 3.82 ff.). The GhS also mentions a technique called *vajrolīmudrā*, which from the terse description seems to be some sort of hand-balance.[14] The description in the HYP, however, is of a method for manipulating the flow of sexual fluid through the urethra and within the body more generally. By means of muscular contractions in the pelvic area, it is declared, both men and women can induce sexual fluids upward (HYP 3.84). White offers the following description of the method as it applies to men:

> In technical terms, *vajrolī mudrā* is urethral suction or, more prosaically, the "fountain pen technique," by which the male practitioner, having ejaculated into his female partner, withdraws his own semen, now catalyzed through its interaction with her sexual essence or uterine blood, back into his own body. In so doing, he also draws back into himself, along with his own refined seed, a certain quantity of that female essence which may in turn serve to catalyze the yogic processes (the raising of the *kuṇḍalinī*, etc.) by which his semen becomes transmuted into nectar (White 1996: 199).

Sahajolī, meanwhile, is described as a postcoital practice. Having performed intercourse according to the *vajrolī* method, the male and female partners should then smear their bodies with a mixture of water and burnt cow dung ash (HYP 3.92–3). The third in this intriguing trio of practices, *amarolī*, consists in drinking one's own urine and also smearing it (mixed with ashes) on one's skin (3.96–8). Presumably, if one has been practicing *vajrolī* effectively, the urine is likely to be combined with the male and female sexual secretions that have been imbibed into one's bladder.

One of the remarkable features of these sexual practices is the way in which they appear to integrate an ostensibly procreative act with certain trappings of asceticism. In procreative intercourse, the intermingling of male and female fluids is often a precursor of reproduction—the conception of a new living being. In *vajrolīmudrā*, however, conception is obviated by the male partner's reclamation of his semen.[15] The besmearing of the skin with ash gives to it a ghoulish corpse-like semblance, which may be interpreted as an outward indication of the yogin's having "died to the world."[16] In ordinary sexual union between a man and a woman, the act is an expression of love and desire directed toward one's partner. If both partners are fertile and no contraceptive method is used, the act possesses a life-giving potential. In the case of the esoteric sexual practices intimated in the HYP, by contrast, the objective is quite different. It would appear that, if loving desire is present at all, it is merely accidental to the main purpose at hand, which is to generate an alchemical substance that will contribute toward the capacity of at least one of the participants not to *give* life, but to turn away from worldly life and to find absolution in pure consciousness.

If one is interested in the elements of *haṭha* yoga that involve physical sexual intercourse, one needs to be discerning about which editions of the HYP one reads. One of the most readily available editions is that published by Om Lotus on behalf of the Sivananda Yoga Vedanta organization, containing a translation attributed to Swami Vishnudevananda (1927–1993). The edition is, however, incomplete. When one turns to the section of the third chapter that I have been discussing, one encounters the following notice: "(84–103) [These verses have been omitted, as they describe Vajroli, Sahajoli, and Amaroli mudrās, practices which are not followed in sattvic sadhana]" (Vishnudevananda 1997: 138, square brackets original). A translation by Hans-Ulrich Rieker expurgates the same verses and declares that "In leaving out these passages, we merely bypass the description of a few obscure and repugnant practices that are followed by only those yogis who lack the will power to reach their goal otherwise" (Rieker 1989: 127).

The censorious approach taken by some translators of the HYP reflects a broader attitude of aversion and embarrassment concerning the tantric tradition. This attitude was present in the construction of "Tantrism" (by certain Western scholars and missionaries of the eighteenth and nineteenth centuries) as that aspect of Indian culture that is most vulgar and degenerate, and was taken up and emphasized by indigenous advocates of a particular conception of Hindu spirituality such as Swami Vivekananda (1863–1902) and Swami Sivananda of Rishikesh (1887–1963).[17] The widespread portrayal of tantra as transgressive and morally suspect has, however, been mitigated by rival characterizations that have highlighted the sophisticated philosophical and ideological components of tantric literature, this tendency being pioneered and typified by Sir John Woodroffe.[18]

The concept of tantra resembles, as Hugh Urban has noted, "a great tangled snarl of crisscrossing strands" (2003: 272), and hence a full discussion of its many competing interpretations in contemporary academic and nonacademic discourse lies far beyond the scope of the present chapter. However, with respect to the handling of controversial elements of *haṭha* yoga practice in particular, it is important to point up the contrast between the disapprobation exemplified by, on the one hand, the likes of Vishnudevananda and Rieker and on the other hand, the more nuanced and elucidatory approach adopted by certain other contemporary purveyors of yoga, notably the Bihar School of Yoga (founded by Swami Satyananda Saraswati in 1964).

Not only does the Bihar School's edition of the HYP retain the passages referring to *vajrolī*, *sahajolī*, and *amarolī*, but it includes a commentary by Swami Muktibodhananda on these practices to the length of forty-seven pages (1998: 370–416). Muktibodhananda maintains that there is no necessary incompatibility between "spiritual life" and "sexual life", and to distinguish three possible purposes of the latter she utilizes a traditional threefold schema of personality types: "For the tamasic person it is for progeny; for the rajasic person it is for pleasure; for the sattwic person it is for enlightenment" (1998: 371). These distinctions—articulated here in terms of the *Sāṃkhyan* concepts of *tamas* ("dullness"), *rajas* ("activity," "radiance"), and *sattva* ("lucidity," "pure being")—echo those found within certain treatises of Hindu tantra between grades of practitioner who possess one or other of three "natural dispositions" (*bhāvas*): the "animal" (*paśu*), the "heroic" (*vīra*), and the "divine" (*divya*; Avalon 1974: 53; Bharati 1992: 229).

Emblematic of the overcoming of "animal" inclinations is the primordial guru of tantric *haṭha* yoga, the "great lord" (*maheśvara*) Śiva. It will therefore be informative for our discussion of competing yogic conceptions of the relation between sexuality and spirituality if we briefly examine some aspects of the ritual symbolism and mythology associated with this archetypal figure.

As Stella Kramrisch observes, "the harnessing of the sexual urge and the mastery over its working have their image in Śiva, lord of yogis, with the *ūrdhvaliṅga* as his cognizance" (1981: 12). The *ūrdhvaliṅga* is the erect phallus, pointing straight upward and pressing against the abdomen. *Ūrdhva* means "upward," and a *liṅga* is, over and above the manifest phallus, a "sign" or "cipher" of something beyond (Wake 1870: 205). In the case of the deity Śiva, it is the sign of harnessed creative potency. Śiva's *liṅga* is a pervasive symbol employed as a ceremonial object of worship throughout the Hindu world. It is commonly represented by a dark stone column or bollard, domed and smooth like an egg. The approximately keyhole-shaped base out of which the *liṅga* rises is the *yoni*—the "vulva," "source," or "birthplace"— belonging to the Goddess. Thus, at the heart of Hindu religious culture, at least in its Śaiva forms, we find a sculptural depiction of genital intercourse, albeit somewhat abstract. To view the *yoniliṅga* in these terms might, however, be to oversimplify matters. To explain this point, I draw an analogy with a certain conception of religious love in Christianity.

It is the view of many Christian theologians that religious eros or love of God is not,

> sexual eros gone astray or rechanneled, and it isn't sexual eros (important as it is) that is basic or fundamental, with religious eros somehow derivative from it. The fact is things are just the other way around. It is *sexual* desire and longing that is a sign of something deeper: it is a sign of this longing, yearning for God that we human beings achieve when we are graciously enabled to reach a certain level of the Christian life. It is love for God that is fundamental or basic, and sexual eros that is the sign or symbol or pointer to something else and something deeper (Plantinga 2000: 316).

Picking up this proposal that interpersonal erotic love is symbolic of—or, perhaps better, homologous with—the love between a mortal person and the divine, something similar might be said of the relation between, on the one hand, interpersonal copulation and, on the other hand, the divine congress between Śiva and Śakti. It need not be the case that the *śivaliṅga* "represents"or "stands for" an erect human penis or that the *yoni* "represents" a human vulva; rather, the *liṅga* and *yoni* may be regarded as representing suprahuman—indeed, supracosmic—principles, whose coming together is homologically reflected at the human level in the act of heterosexual union.[19] Of course, a common psychological interpretation of Hindu erotic symbolism is likely to be that the notion of divine copulation is merely a projection from the human case. According to the alternative viewpoint that I have suggested here, however, the human sexual act may be conceived as made in the image of the *maithunā* (intercourse) of the God and Goddess.

In the mythology of the Śaiva Purāṇas, a central motif is the conflict between Śiva and Kāma, this latter figure being the personification of desire, especially carnal desire. In several tales, Kāma surreptitiously enters Śiva's heart and disturbs his lofty contemplations with lustful thoughts of the goddess Pārvatī. Śiva succeeds in ejecting Kāma by means of intensified meditation, but Kāma continues to pester him with arrows aimed at his heart. In a fit of rage, Śiva incinerates Kāma with a heat ray discharged from the third eye in the centre of his brow.[20] This incident is normally taken to represent the overcoming of distracting desires through focused spiritual fervor. However, according to some accounts, Śiva subsequently revives Kāma—albeit in a purely mental rather than bodily form—at Pārvatī's request (O'Flaherty 1981: 156 ff.). Pārvatī is depicted as both spiritual devotee, performing austerities (*tapas*) to propitiate Śiva, and voluptuous seductress, whose charms Śiva strives earnestly to resist (ibid.: 154). In one place, Śiva grants Pārvatī her wish of begetting a son by his seed and declares that he, unlike ordinary men, is able to do this without the aid of sexual desire. In an apparently contradictory move, however, he then proceeds to give "Kāma [i.e. desire] a place in his own heart." At this, Pārvatī rejoices, "and Śiva [makes] love to her for a thousand years" (*Kathāsaritsāgara*, quoted in O'Flaherty 1981: 163).

Even without attempting any sophisticated exegesis of these convoluted mythic themes, we can see that Śiva's sexuality is far from straightforward. What at first appears to be an overarching narrative of the expurgation of erotic conation by the iconic exemplar of yogic self-mastery turns out, on closer inspection, to involve twists and nuances that complicate the role of desire in the soteriological quest. With these complications in mind, we now turn to consider the sex-related directives of some prominent yoga gurus, whose influence on contemporary postural yoga has been prodigious, though by no means univocal.

The Ideal of *Brahmacarya* and the Erotization of Contemporary Yoga

We saw earlier, in the discussion of physical sexual practices in traditional *haṭha* yoga, that there are diverse attitudes to these practices and to the relation between sex and spirituality more broadly, expressed by eminent figures associated with contemporary yoga institutions. It is the view of the Bihar School of Yoga that the *sāttvika* person is capable of engaging in sexual practices such as *vajrolīmudrā* as a means to enlightenment, whereas Vishnudevananda implies that a "sattvic" regimen (*sāttvika sādhana*) excludes such practices. Interestingly, both Satyananda and Vishnudevananda were disciples of the same guru, namely Swami Sivananda of Rishikesh, who himself founded the Divine Life Society in 1936 (Strauss 2005: 40; cf. Strauss 2002).

Sivananda was a prolific author and was unflinchingly outspoken in his views on sexual morality. From the evidence of his books and pamphlets and reports of oral instructions from his disciples, it would appear that Sivananda's stance on sexual matters was much closer to Vishnudevananda's than to that of Satyananda and the Bihar School. A prime document illustrative of this point is Sivananda's book *Practice of Brahmacharya* (first published in 1934), *brahmacarya* being the principle of moral and religious purity, which, though literally meaning "moving (*carya*) in or towards *brahman* (the supreme spiritual being)," is used in most contexts as a euphemism for chastity, principally *male* chastity. As Alter notes, "Above all else, brahmacharya means total control over the flow of one's semen. Without question it signifies an immunity from sexual desire," though it also "evokes a much broader range of meanings" (1997: 282).

Sivananda takes a particularly hard line on *brahmacarya*, and his pontifications on this topic are couched in a style and vocabulary that is undoubtedly influenced by his contact with certain strands of puritanical Christianity.[21] The following excerpts are illustrative of his general approach:

> The gratification of every worldly desire is sinful ... Man was created for a life of spiritual communion with God, but he yielded to the seduction of evil demons ... Moral goodness ... consists in renouncing all sensuous pleasures, in separating from the world through discrimination and dispassion, in living solely after the spirit, in imitating the perfection and purity of God. Sensuality is inconsistent with wisdom and holiness. The great business of life is to avoid impurity. ... (Sivananda 1988: 3).

> Complete celibacy is the master-key to open the realms of Elysian bliss. The avenue to the abode of supreme peace begins from Brahmacharya or purity (ibid.: 24).

The first statement in the above passages—"The gratification of every worldly desire is sinful"—is ambiguous. It could mean either that (1) it is sinful to gratify *all* of one's worldly desires (but gratifying just *some* of them might be acceptable), or (2) it is sinful to gratify *any* of one's worldly desires. In view of the remainder of the passage, and the remainder of the book, I take it that (2) is what Sivananda means, though given how extreme such a viewpoint would be, it is tempting to suppose that he must be expressing himself in these terms merely for rhetorical effect. It is perhaps passages such as those quoted above that led at least one fellow swami and scholar to dub Sivananda (with comparably hyperbolic invective) "the most grotesque product of the Hindu Renaissance" (Bharati 1976: 74).

One of the major difficulties associated with interpreting traditional Indian attitudes toward the place of "worldly desire" in the spiritual life is that of determining the relation between *absence of attachment to* and *elimination of* those desires. Sivananda speaks as though spiritual progress requires a systematic suppression and ultimate extinguishing of every desire that has as its aim the gratification of some sensual urge. This severe stipulation is consistent with a strict reading of the concept of *vairāgya*, which is one-half of the twofold methodology of Classical Yoga outlined at YS 1.12–16. *Vairāgya* consists in the diminution of *rāga*, which is the "coloring" of one's mind by affective or conative factors.[22] Common translations of *vairāgya* thus include "dispassion" and "nonattachment." The latter expression can be interpreted in at least two ways. On the one hand, it could mean nonattachment to worldly phenomena and, taken in this sense, the nonattachment would presumably result in a reduction of affective experience on the part of the practitioner: One would become increasingly emotionally sterile. On the other hand, it could denote a higher-order nonattachment involving the progressive loosening of attachments to one's own affective and conative states while nevertheless continuing to undergo those states.

Phenomenologically, it is difficult to see how these two kinds of nonattachment could be kept apart: if one attenuates the attachment to one's own affective and conative states—if, that is, one dis-identifies with, or dissociates oneself from, those states—it would seem inevitable that the states themselves will tend to diminish in qualitative strength and potency. However, there remains a conceptual difference that is worth maintaining.

In Classical Yoga and Sāṃkhya, it is evident that nonattachment to worldly phenomena goes hand in hand with nonattachment to one's own affective-conative responses to those phenomena. The goal of Classical Yoga, notwithstanding some controversial but implausible modern interpretations, is presented not as a mere "purification" of one's experience of the world such that one's embodied life becomes altogether more comfortable and pleasant; it is, over and above this purification, the cessation of one's encounter with the world and the dissolution of experience.[23] For modern, largely secular scholars of this material, it is hard to conceive of how an escape from worldly existence could be beneficial or desirable, and it is even harder to conceive of what could possibly replace it that would amount to anything other than oblivion. Classical Yoga and Sāṃkhya, however, conceive of the cessation of *prakṛti*'s display—the cessation of objectual experience—as immediately precipitating *puruṣa*'s isolation, the aloneness of the pure subject. We may be incapable of giving phenomenological meaning to this account of Yoga's soterial destination; but a balking of the phenomenological imagination on our part is no reason for distorting the statements of the classical texts to make them conform to our preferred models of spiritual awakening.

With specific regard to sexual detachment, Agehananda Bharati has contended that the sort of "moralistic interpretation" of *brahmacarya* typified by Sivananda (and also by M.K. Gandhi) is an innovation of the "Hindu Renaissance" and that the traditional emphasis on sexual purity has more to do with the retention of the magical power that semen instantiates than with the putatively intrinsic virtuousness of chastity (Bharati 1976: 230). However, though Bharati is right to distinguish magical or esoteric motivations from more overtly ethical ones, it seems to me that the distinction between these two motivations is not as sharp as he suggests and that the ethical stance, which he takes to be a relatively recent development, has its origins in ancient Brahmanical religious culture. Indeed, the prohibitive position adopted by Sivananda and other neo-Hindu moralists appears to be foreshadowed in many places throughout Indian textual history, wherein we find injunctions to refrain not only from overt sexual activity but from amorous mentation as well. Typifying this anti-erotic bent is a passage from the *Agnipurāṇa* (*c.* ninth century C.E.), which stipulates that *brahmacarya* entails one's renouncing eight modes of libidinous activity, namely: *smartana* (thinking [about sex]); *kīrtana* (praising sexual conduct or attributing sexual attractiveness to persons); *keli* (flirtation or sex-play); *prekṣaṇa* (gazing at someone with amorous intent); *guhyabhāṣaṇa* ("secret" sex-talk); *saṃkalpa* (fantasizing); *adhyavasāya* (resolving to engage in erotic acts); and *kriyānivṛtti* (actually having sex; *Agnipurāṇa* 372.9). As Feuerstein points out, other texts (such as the *Liṅgapurāṇa* 1.8.17 [*c.* 600–1000 C.E.]) specify that, though this narrow definition applies to avowed renunciants and widowers, a married male householder is permitted to have sex with his wife (Feuerstein 1990: 63), though it is not clear whether this is for reproductive purposes only or for sensual enjoyment as well.

Among the leading proponents of contemporary postural yoga, B.K S. Iyengar (b. 1918) ranks as a staunch advocate of the looser construal of *brahmacarya*, according to which it can encompass both a monogamous marital status and strict celibacy. In support of his position, he provides a somewhat partial account of Indian religious history, maintaining that:

> Almost all the yogis and sages of old in India were married men with families of their own. They did not shirk their social or moral responsibilities. Marriage and parenthood are no bar to the knowledge of divine love, happiness and union with the Supreme Soul (Iyengar 1991: 35).

The insinuation that those who have renounced social and familial ties are "shirk[ing] their ... responsibilities" is striking, given the tenacity and prevalence of the anchoritic tradition in India.[24]

On the face of it, the viewpoint of K.P. Jois (b. 1915), another key figure in contemporary postural yoga, appears to be at odds with the more householder-friendly stance of Iyengar. "This, of course, is true," writes Jois:

> householders lose *brahmacharya* owing to seminal loss. With the loss, they lose the strength of their bodies, minds, and sense organs; in addition, *moksha* [spiritual liberation] and the capacity to perceive the soul or realize the true Self become impossible. In the absence of the knowledge of one's own Self, one remains in the cycle of birth and death, and thus must continue to suffer in this sapless and despicable world (Jois 1999: 20; square brackets original).

In a later passage of the same work, however, Jois opines that it is "*Too much* sex" that "leads the body, sense organs, and mind to become weak" (ibid.: 37; my emphasis), thereby implying that *some* sex may be permissible. In view of the fact that Jois himself was married to his wife Savitramma for sixty years prior to her death in 1997, it is understandable that he should refrain from extolling the spiritual merit of celibacy to the complete exclusion of wedded domesticity. However, regardless of whether marriage and parenthood are tacitly endorsed (as in the case of Jois) or more actively validated (as in the case of Iyengar), there remains among Indian gurus of contemporary postural yoga a general emphasis on continence and on the enervating consequences of seminal loss, which is part of a broader religious and medical ideology that regards semen as the biological instantiation of spiritual vitality and truth (cf. Alter 1997).[25] This ideology constitutes a common stream running through all the various channels of yoga's convoluted history that have been discussed in this chapter and oozes into the contemporary and transnational yoga milieu in intriguing and problematic ways. One of these ways, on which I focus in this latter part of the chapter, is the contemporary promotion of yoga's efficacy for molding desirable bodies.

Probably the most remarkable feature of contemporary forms of *haṭha* yoga is the heavy stress that they place on the attainment of physical fitness by means of the regular performance of postural sequences. This emphasis receives traditional sanction from texts such as the HYP, wherein several postures are described and physical vitality, especially the luster of skin and eyes, is invoked as indicative of soteriological progress (see HYP 2.78). The extent of the sanction relies, however, on selective reading, because at other places the *haṭha* texts make it clear that the cleansing and strengthening of the body is merely the necessary prelude to the eruptive upthrust of *kuṇḍalinīśakti*, which inaugurates a state wherein the mind is perfectly stable and the body is left rigid like a wooden plank (HYP 4.106). Death is transcended, not because one has acquired a body of perpetual youthfulness but rather because one has achieved a level of consciousness from whose perspective embodiment is no longer required—the body remains corpse-like (*mṛtavat*), its role as temporary tabernacle fulfilled.

In contemporary postural yoga, by contrast, physical fitness appears to have been elevated to the status of supreme eschaton. It is this aspect that has been most forcefully accentuated by schools such as Iyengar Yoga and Jois's Ashtanga Yoga, the latter school in particular being largely responsible for the steady gymnasticization of *haṭha* yoga throughout many economically developed countries since the late 1980s (and especially since the dawning of Ashtanga's offshoot "Power Yoga" in the mid-1990s).[26] Though it is likely that the gymnastic element in some forms of *haṭha* yoga practice antedates the twentieth century (Sjoman 1996), it is undoubtedly the case that this element was cultivated and embellished with great entrepreneurial flair by Jois's guru (who also happened to be the brother-in-law of B.K S. Iyengar), namely Sri Tirumalai Krishnamacharya, from the 1930s onward (Srivatsan 1997: 49–58; De Michelis 2005: 196–7).

Since the prodigious expansion of the export market in gymnastic and other styles of postural yoga in the late twentieth century, these styles have undergone substantial assimilation into the transnational cultural domain inhabited by the likes of "aerobics, jogging, tai chi, or organized sports" (Strauss 2005: 11). Yoga has been marketed as an integral component of a healthy lifestyle in the fast-paced and urbanized world of late capitalism, and this marketing strategy has been especially attractive to a constituency of largely middle-class women. Beneath the proliferating mass of glossy magazines, videos, and DVDs featuring glamorous models wearing trendy figure-hugging outfits and immaculate smiles, the traditional emphasis on the controlled diminution of conative impulses, especially those with lascivious content, has been largely submerged and forgotten. Indeed, what we see instead in some quarters is a blending of gymnastic yoga with a romanticized conception of "tantric sex" to form the burgeoning commercial category of sex-enhancing yoga.[27]

Rather than yoga classes being loci of male and female segregation, as has typically been the case in India, the contemporary yoga class has become a locus of potential romantic encounter. Though single-sex classes in the West are not uncommon, this is normally not due to any deliberate policy to reduce libidinal distractions but merely because no men have chosen to attend. In a few instances, the yoga class is explicitly advertised as a site of erotic experience, such as in the case of Aaron Star's "Hot Nude Yoga" classes for gay men in New York (see Star 2007), and the unabashed confluence of yoga and eroticism is actively disseminated in an expanding range of books and digital media.[28] In many of these contemporary appropriations of *haṭha* yoga, there is not only a promotion of forms of sexual expression that would have scandalized the likes of Swami Sivananda; there is also an abandoning of the traditional emphasis on sublimating sexual energy, and this is something that even ostensibly nonmoralizing swamis such as Agehananda Bharati would have regarded with profound indignation.

Conclusion: Fusion, Confusion, and Innovation

In this chapter, I have canvassed a range of phenomena within yoga's long history that bear on attitudes to sex and sexuality. Rather than trying to trace a lineage of causal connections, my purpose has been to call attention to some of the key factors that filter through into the variegated pottage of contemporary yoga and to expose some continuities and contrasts between this contemporary environment and the ancient tradition that stands behind it. We have seen that the erotic tension between masculine and feminine principles is a prevalent motif in the symbolic frameworks of both Classical and non-Classical Yoga. Vedic cosmogony, wherein the cosmos is begotten through the fusion of gendered deities, prefigures the metaphysical dualism of Classical Yoga and Sāṃkhya, according to which it is the coming together of the masculinized seer and the feminized seen that provides the conditions for the efflorescence of worldly experience. In the tantric imagery surrounding the discipline of traditional *haṭha* yoga, the gendered principles are again in evidence, and yet the fusion of these principles on the microcosmic level is here represented as the mechanism for instigating the spiritual orgasm that signifies not the fructification of worldly experience but its dissolution into pure consciousness.

The tantric homological associations between bodily fluids and spiritual principles—and especially the association between semen and authentic selfhood—constitute the imaginative theoretical background that motivates the use of physical sex for ostensibly soteriological purposes. We have seen, further, how the ideal of mastery over sexual potency has been represented, albeit not unambiguously, in the mythic figure of Śiva and also how the explicitly sexual *haṭha* practice of *vajrolīmudrā* has had a problematic reception in the modern commentarial context. It is evident that the antagonistic attitude of some modern gurus to sexual practices is linked to a more general perceived dichotomy between sex on the one hand and spiritual and moral purity on the other. In some instances, as we have seen in the case of Sivananda, the articulation of moral vexation takes on forms reminiscent of, and almost certainly influenced by, puritanical strands of Christianity.

Though not universally shared by contemporary Indic yoga schools, the paragon of the celibate male, radiating spiritual potency, remains a pervasive idea among recent and contemporary yogic doctrinaires. We have seen how this idea contrasts starkly with some prevalent tendencies in globalized yoga, wherein tantric sexual practices are romanticized and the postural techniques of *haṭha* yoga are frequently touted as methods for molding a desirable body and improving sexual performance.

In the light of yoga's complex history and of the mixed messages that are imparted by purveyors of yogic practices and products, it is little surprise that there should be a considerable amount of confusion about sex and sexuality in the contemporary yoga arena. Though it is clear that the yoga tradition itself has not been uniformly averse to sexual activity, it is also clear that, where intercourse has been openly endorsed, this has typically been in the context of stipulated ritualized constraints. In short, when physical coitus has been deployed at all, this has been done for strategic soteriological purposes. In the contemporary transnational milieu, meanwhile, this approach has, in many instances, been turned on its head: Traditional soteriological techniques have been appropriated to serve mundane and sensual ends; a traditionally austere vision of intrapersonal spiritual liberation has been reimagined as part of a movement towards social and sexual liberation.

Though this reimagining is indeed confused with respect to its multiple misunderstandings of the traditions from which it draws, it is also dynamic and innovative. Globalized contemporary yoga offers a farrago of teachings and practices for the many kinds of modern seeker. For those who prefer their yoga to remain strictly an accoutrement to a generally unquestioned lifestyle, it offers opportunities for fitness training, stress management, and perhaps enhancement of sexual enjoyment, whereas for those who wish to look beyond the commercial varnish, it offers opportunities to investigate the fascinating world of yoga's convoluted, and sexually complex, heritage.

Acknowledgments

I am grateful to Jean Byrne and Mark Singleton for helpful comments on earlier drafts of this chapter.

Notes

1 From a "Prayer for Purity" in Sivananda 1988: vii.
2 *I Love India* (n.d.) "Yoga and Sex," <http://yoga.iloveindia.com/yoga-benefits/yoga-and-sex.html> (accessed May 2006).
3 Iyengar asserts that "Like pearls on a thread, the Yoga*sūtras* form a precious necklace, a diadem of illuminative wisdom" (1993: 1). The name of Jois's Ashtanga Yoga derives from the eight (*aṣṭa*) components or "limbs" (*aṅgas*) of Patañjali's system, which are listed at YS 2.29. Paramahansa Yogananda, who founded the Self-Realization Fellowship in 1920, praises the YS in chapter 24 of his autobiography (Yogananda 1979); and, in Transcendental Meditation, the "TM-Sidhi Program" (*sic*) is advertised as "the revival of the theoretical and practical knowledge of Yoga *(Patanjali's Yoga Sutras)* after thousands of years" (AllTM.org 2007).
4 One renegade voice on this matter is Georg Feuerstein, who maintains that the "conceptual and doctrinal divergencies" between Sāṃkhya and Yoga amount to a "chasm" (Feuerstein 1996: 116). I have argued elsewhere that this reading is unwarranted (see Burley 2007: ch. 2; cf. e.g., Zimmer 1953: 280; Chakravarti 1975: 65).
5 *Puruṣa* can also, in certain contexts, be translated as "a man, male, human being" (Monier-Williams 1963: 637).
6 It is noteworthy that the term *procreatrix* has, on occasions, been used to define feminine deities from Vedic mythology with a cosmogonic status comparable to that of the *Sāṃkhyan prakṛti* (see e.g., Long 1977: 33).
7 SK 68; YS 2.25, 3.50, 3.55, 4.26, 4.34.
8 This attribution of potency to the feminine consort anticipates the tantric dictum that "Śiva without Śakti is a corpse (*śava*)." Cf. Bharati 1992: 202; Feuerstein 1998: 68.

9 *Virāj*—literally, "shining about" or "wide-ruling" (Coomaraswamy 1945: 395n.)—can denote a male or a female ruler. In its feminine form, it can also designate the *quality* of being regal, and hence might be translated as "majesty," "dignity," or "sovereignty." Cf. Monier-Williams 1963: 982.

10 The gender roles are, roughly, reversed in Tantric Buddhism. Cf. Vaudeville 1962: 32; Bharati 1992: 200–1.

11 A third text, the *Śivasaṃhitā* (*c.* seventeenth or eighteenth century C.E.), is also often mentioned among the core texts of *haṭha* yoga. Though fairly accessible, it lacks the degree of systematic coherence exhibited by the HYP and GhS.

12 *Haṭha* texts are far from consistent in their descriptions of *bindu*. I here follow Digambarji and Kokaje (1998: 90) in assuming that Brahmānanda's commentary on HYP 3.49 uses *soma* as a synonym for *bindu* when it states that "*soma* is located to the left of the mid-brow" (my trans.).

13 Cf. Eliade (2006: 165): "... all of Indian erotic mysticism is expressly aimed at perfecting man by identifying him with a 'divine pair,' that is, by way of androgyny."

14 The relevant verse is 3.39 in the Digambarji and Gharote edition, and 3.45 in the Vasu edition.

15 HYP 3.99 states that female practitioners can also perform *vajrolī*—by drawing up the man's semen. It is difficult, however, to see how this would differ from the result of ordinary penetrative sex.

16 The practice evokes the iconographic image of Śiva as a supine corpse: "depicted with a massive erection, yet with a body besmeared from toe to crown with ashes, clearly suggesting that he is indifferent to his sexual arousal and the world at large" (Feuerstein 1998: 80).

17 For detailed discussion of the influence of Orientalist scholarship in the construction of "Tantrism" as a religiocultural category, see Urban 1999. For discussion of Vivekananda, see Urban 2003: 147–63. Sivananda will receive further attention below.

18 For an overview of Woodroffe's glorificatory treatment of tantra, see e.g., Urban 2003: 134–47.

19 Here I am using "homological" to denote a relation of structural (or formal) correspondence. I take this usage to be consistent with that of the likes of Eliade (e.g. 1969: 108) and White (e.g. 1996: 12 et passim); cf. Kaelber 1981 and Taylor (2002: 4).

20 See e.g., *Matsya-purāṇa* 154.235–48 and *Skanda-purāṇa* 5.2.13.27–35, both of which passages are quoted in O'Flaherty (1981: 149).

21 As a relatively Westernized brahman who trained as a medical doctor, Sivananda was certainly familiar with Christian teachings and those of other religions. He stresses similarities between his views on celibacy and those of Christianity, especially in its monastic forms, at 1988: 31 and 107.

22 Cf. Monier-Williams (1963: 1025): "Vairāgya ... change or loss of colour, growing pale ... ; freedom from all worldly desires ... ."

23 For what I am calling here a "merely purificatory" reading of Yoga's goal, see e.g., Whicher 1998. I argue against this reading at Burley 2004: 231–2 and 2007: 138–41. For a more circumspect approach to the issue, see Sarbacker 2005.

24 It is also perhaps worth mentioning here that Iyengar's son and daughter, Prashant and Gita (well-known yoga teachers in their own right), have both remained unmarried.

25 We should also be wary of drawing firm conclusions about the opinions of contemporary gurus from written sources alone. Practitioners of Ashtanga Yoga, who have visited Jois's Ashtanga Yoga Research Institute in Mysore, can vouch for the fact that both Jois and his grandson Sharath (b. 1971) view positively the desirability of marriage and parenthood (Jean Byrne, personal correspondence, July 2007).

26 Birch's 1995 book has been especially significant for the rapid growth of interest in "Power Yoga" since the mid-1990s. Purveyors of this style, including Birch herself, typically view it as being continuous with Jois's Ashtanga Yoga, though Jois has tended to distance himself from it.

27 An especially poignant illustration of the eroticization of yoga is the "Topless Yoga Week" feature run by the British newspaper *The Sun* (July 2007), which, under the guise of promoting yoga, presents photographs of bare-breasted "Page 3 Girls" in titillating poses.

28 Examples include Barrett 2004; Greaux et al. 2007; and Star 2005.

Bibliography

Primary sources

Agnipurāṇa

Upādhyāya, Ā.B. (ed.) (1966) *Agnipurāṇa of Maharṣi Vedavyāsa*, Kashi Sanskrit Series No. 174, Varanasi: Chowkhamba.

Gheraṇḍasaṃhitā

Digambarji, S., and M. L. Gharote (eds and trans) (1997) *Gheraṇḍa Saṁhitā*, 2nd edn, Lonavla: Kaivalyadhama.

Vasu Ś.C. (trans) (1976) *The Gheraṇḍa Saṁhitā: A Treatise on Haṭha Yoga*, 3rd edn, London: Theosophical Publishing House.

Haṭhayogapradīpikā

Iyangar, S. (trans) (1972) *Haṭhayogapradīpikā' of Svātmārāma, with the Commentary "Jyotsnā" of Brahmānanda*, Adyar: Adyar Library and Research Centre.

Digambarji, S. and R.S. Kokaje (eds and trans) (1998) *Haṭhapradīpikā of Svātmārāma*, 2nd ed, Lonavla: Kaivalyadhama.

Muktibodhananda, S. (trans) (1998) *Hatha Yoga Pradipika*, 2nd edn, Munger: Bihar School of Yoga.

Vishnudevananda, S. (trans) (1997) *Hatha Yoga Pradipika*, New York: Om Lotus.

Śatapathabrāhmaṇa

Eggling, J. (trans) (1882–1900) *The* Śataphata *Brāhmaṇa according to the Mādhyandina School*, Sacred Books of the East, vols 12, 26, 41, 43, 44, Delhi: Motilal Banarsidass, 1963 [reprint].

Sāṃkhyakārikā

Burley, M. (trans) The Text of the *Sāṃkhyakārikā*, in Burley 2007, App. A.

Śivasaṃhitā

Vasu, R.B.S.C. (trans) (1996) *The Siva Samhita*, New Delhi: Munshiram Manoharlal.

Yogasūtra

Feuerstein, G. (trans) (1989) *The Yogasūtra of Patañjali: A New Translation and Commentary*, Rochester, VT: Inner Traditions India.

Secondary sources

AllTM.org (2007) Maharishi's Achievements: A Glimpse of Forty Years Around the World, 1970–1979, Available HTTP: <http://www.alltm.org/Maharishi/Maharishi_year2.html> (accessed July 2007).

Alter, J. (1997) Seminal Truth: A Modern Science of Male Celibacy in North India, *Medical Anthropology Quarterly*, new series, 11 (3): 275–98.

Avalon, A. (John Woodroffe) (1974) [1919] *The Serpent Power: The Secrets of Tantric and Yoga*, New York: Dover [reprint].

Barrett, E. (2004) *Sexy Yoga: 40 Poses for Mindblowing Sex and Greater Intimacy*, Berkeley, CA: Amorata Press.

Bharati, A. (1976) *The Light at the Center: Context and Pretext of Modern Mysticism*, Santa Barbara, CA: Ross-Erikson.

—(1992) [1965] *The Tantric Tradition*, London: Rider.

Birch, B.B. (1995) *Power Yoga: The Total Strength and Flexibility Workout*, New York: Simon & Schuster.

Burley, M. (2004) "Aloneness" and the Problem of Realism in Classical Sāṃkhya and Yoga, *Asian Philosophy*, 14 (3), 223–38.

—(2007) *Classical Sāṃkhya and Yoga: An Indian Metaphysics of Experience*, London: Routledge.

Chakravarti, Pulinbihari (1975) *Origin and Development of the Sāṃkhya System of Thought*, 2nd edn, New Delhi: Oriental Books Reprint Corporation.

Coomaraswamy, Ananda K. (1945) On the Loathly Bride, *Speculum: A Journal of Medieval Studies*, 20 (4): 391–404.

De Michelis, E. (2005) *A History of Modern Yoga*, London: Continuum.

Eliade, M. (1969) *Yoga: Immortality and Freedom*, Princeton: Princeton University Press.

—(2006) *Coincidentia Oppositorum*—the Mythical Pattern [1949], in B. Rennie (ed) *Mircea Eliade: A Critical Reader*, London: Equinox, 162–8.

Feuerstein, G. (1990) *Encyclopedic Dictionary of Yoga*, London: Unwin.

—(1996) [1980] *The Philosophy of Classical Yoga*, Rochester, VT: Inner Traditions.

—(1998) *Tantra: The Path of Ecstasy*, Boston: Shambhala.

Greaux, J. N., J. Langheld, and G. Rich (2007) *Better sex Through Yoga: Easy Routines to Boost Your Sex Drive, Enhance Physical Pleasure, and Spice Up Your Bedroom Life*, New York: Broadway.

I Love India (n.d.) Yoga and Sex, Available HTTP: <http://yoga.iloveindia.com/yoga-benefits/yoga-and-sex.html> (accessed May 2006).

Iyengar, B.K S. (1991) [1966] *Light on Yoga*, London: Aquarian Press.

—(trans) (1993) *Light on the Yoga Sūtras of Patañjali*, London: Thorsons.

Jois, K. Pattabhi (1999) *Yoga Mala*, New York: Stern.

Kaelber, W.O. (1981) The *Brahmacārin*: Homology and Continuity in Brāhmaṇic Religion, *History of Religions*, 21 (1): 77–99.

Kramrisch, S. (1981) *The Presence of Śiva*, Princeton: Princeton University Press.

Long, J.B. (1977) Dakṣa: Divine Embodiment of Creative Skill, *History of Religions*, 17 (1): 29–60.

Monier-Williams, M. (1963) [1899] *A Sanskrit-English Dictionary*, Delhi: Motilal Banarsidass [reprint].

O'Flaherty, W.D. (1981) *Śiva: The Erotic Ascetic*, Oxford: Oxford University Press.

Pintchman, T. (1994) *The Rise of the Goddess in the Hindu Tradition*, Albany: State University of New York Press.

Plantinga, A. (2000) *Warranted Christian Belief*, New York: Oxford University Press.

Rieker, H.U. (1989) *The Yoga of Light: Hatha Yoga Pradipika*, trans E. Becherer, London: Unwin.

Sarbacker, S.R. (2005) *Samādhi: The Numinous and Cessative in Indo-Tibetan* Yoga, Albany: State University of New York Press.

Sivananda, S. (1988) [1934] *Practice of Brahmacharya*, Shivanandanagar: Divine Life Society.

Sjoman, N.E. (1996) *The Yoga Tradition of the Mysore Palace*, New Delhi: Abhinav.

Srivatsan, M. (ed.) (1997) *Śrī Krishnamacharya the Pūrnācārya: A 108th Jayanti Offering*, Chennai: Krishnamacharya Yoga Mandiram.

Star, A. (2005) *Hot Nude Yoga Box Set: Virgin, Strength, Partner, Tantra* [DVD], New York: Hot Nude Yoga.

—(2007) *Aaron Star's Hot Nude Yoga*, Available HTTP: <http://hotnudeyoga.com> (accessed July 2007).

Strauss, S. (2002) "Adapt, Adjust, Accommodate": The Production of Yoga in a Transnational World, *History and Anthropology*, 13 (3): 231–51.

—(2005) *Positioning Yoga: Balancing Acts Across Cultures*, Oxford: Berg.

Taylor, M. (2002) At the Crossroads of Religion and Medical Anthropology [paper delivered at the Conference of the Nordic Society of Medical Anthropologists], University of Helsinki, Finland. Available HTTP: <http://medanthro.kaapeli.fi/nordic2002/papers/plenary/taylor.pdf> (accessed June 2007).

Urban, H.B. (1999) The Extreme Orient: The Construction of "Tantrism" as a Category in the Orientalist Imagination, *Religion*, 29 (2): 123–46.

—(2003) *Tantra: Sex, Secrecy, Politics, and Power in the Study of Religion*, Berkeley, CA: University of California Press.

Vaudeville, C. (1962) Evolution of Love-Symbolism in Bhagavatism, *Journal of the American Oriental Society*, 82 (1)31–40.

Wake, C.S. (1870) The Influence of the Phallic Idea in the Religions of Antiquity, *Journal of Anthropology*, 1 (2): 199–227.

Whicher, I. (1998) *The Integrity of the Yoga Darśana*, Albany: State University of New York Press.

White, D.G. (1984) Why Gurus are Heavy, *Numen*, 31 (1): 40–73.

—(1996) *The Alchemical Body: Siddha Traditions in Medieval India*, Chicago: University of Chicago Press.

Yogananda, P. (1979) [1946] *Autobiography of a Yogi*, Los Angeles: Self-Realization Fellowship.

Zimmer, H.R. (1953) *Philosophies of India*, Campbell, J (ed), Princeton: Princeton University Press.

Index

Lightning Source UK Ltd.
Milton Keynes UK
UKOW06f1150040915

258006UK00005B/121/P

9 780415 570862